A FALCON GUIDE®

Hiking Southern California

A Guide to Southern California's Greatest Hiking Adventures

Ron Adkison

FALCON®

GUILFORD, CONNECTICUT
HELENA, MONTANA
AN IMPRINT OF THE GLOBE PEQUOT PRESS

A **FALCON** GUIDE®

ISSN 1545-6382
ISBN 0-7627-1124-8

Manufactured in the United States of America
First Edition/First Printing

Acknowledgments

This book is the culmination of more than thirty-five years of exploration in the diverse and beautiful part of the state where I was raised. But I didn't explore and discover its secrets alone. I had the privilege of being accompanied by many longtime friends. Without the companionship, encouragement, suggestions, and photography of Rick Marvin, John Reilly, Ken Kukulka, Randy Judge, Crawford Judge, John Rihs, Greg Rebitz, and Kevin Duck, this book would never have been written.

One person above all others deserves the most credit. Scott Adams, of The Globe Pequot Press, steadfastly supported me and this project from the beginning. Without him, this book would not have been published. Thanks, Scott, I couldn't have done this without you.

Help Us Keep This Guide Up to Date

Every effort has been made by the author and editors to make this guide as accurate and useful as possible. However, many things can change after a guide is published—trails are rerouted, regulations change, techniques evolve, facilities come under new management, etc.

We would love to hear from you concerning your experiences with this guide and how you feel it could be improved and kept up to date. While we may not be able to respond to all comments and suggestions, we'll take them to heart and we'll also make certain to share them with the authors. Please send your comments and suggestions to the following address:

The Globe Pequot Press
Reader Response/Editorial Department
P.O. Box 480
Guilford, CT 06437

Or you may e-mail us at:

editorial@globepequot.com

Thanks for your input, and happy travels!

Contents

The Hikes

Death Valley National Park

Mojave National Preserve

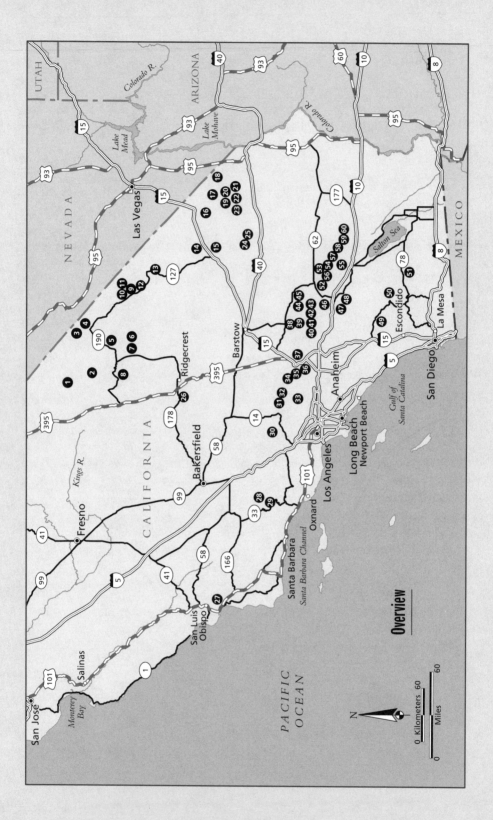

Overview

The Mountainous Backbone of Southern California 125

Joshua Tree National Park 225

Map Legend

═══〈30〉═══	Interstate
═══〈70〉═══	U.S. highway
──〈7〉──	State highway
────────	Paved road
════════	Gravel road
= = = = =	Unimproved road
▬▬▬▬▬▬	Featured trail
- - - - - - - - -	Other trail
··············	Fence
– – – – –	Ski lift/aerial tramway
≍	Bridge
▲	Campground
○	City
)(	Gap/saddle
•–•	Gate
▣	Overlook/viewpoint
▲	Peak/elevation
⊞	Picnic area
■	Point of interest/other trailhead
⬧	Ranger Station
⚲	Spring
⚲	Dry spring
START 🥾	Trailhead
ℹ	Visitor center
∥	Waterfall
∥	Dry waterfall

Introduction

Southern California is world renowned as the land of sun, sand, and surf. Yet the most outstanding feature of the Southland is its mountains. Coastal, inland, and desert mountains dominate the landscape. It is in these diverse mountains, and many neighboring desert valleys, that you will find the best hiking in southern California. A dozen national forest wilderness areas, plus an additional sixty-nine Bureau of Land Management (BLM) and National Park Service wildernesses protect more than five million acres, nearly half of all federally designated wilderness in California.

Hikes ranging from short strolls to multiday backpacks can be enjoyed year-round in southern California. From chaparral-clad slopes to alpine heights, desert sand dunes to cool canyon waterfalls, and rocky peaks, grassy ridges, and cool conifer forests, the hikes in this book sample the spectrum of landscapes here. Hikers can find refuge from oppressive summer heat in the high mountains; from spring through autumn, trails beckon in the mountains' foothills and in the Mojave and Colorado Deserts.

This book includes hikes in the heart of southern California, including the traditional hiking areas in the San Gabriel, San Bernardino, and San Jacinto Mountains. Also included are areas on the fringes of the Southland, including trails in the extreme southern Sierra Nevada, the South Coast Ranges, and Death Valley. Of course, no single guidebook could possibly log every potential hike in a region as vast and diverse as southern California. Each hike described here is itself an introduction to innumerable hiking opportunities nearby—explorations that could encompass many lifetimes of adventure.

Using This Book

For the most part, hike descriptions are self-explanatory. A few points, however, require some discussion to help you get the most from each hiking trip.

The **General location** indicates geographical location, wilderness area (if any), and mileage in a straight line and direction from major towns and cities.

Distance notes the total distance of a hike and the type of hike. Four basic types of hikes are described in this guide: *round-trips,* where you hike to a particular destination then retrace your route to the trailhead; *loops,* where you hike in on one trail and hike out to the same trailhead via a different route, perhaps retracing as much as 1.0 mile of trail; *semiloops,* where you negotiate a small loop but retrace a portion of your route; and *point-to-point* or *shuttle trips,* where you begin at one trailhead and hike out to another. This fourth type requires that you hitchhike back to your car, leave another car at the opposite trailhead, have someone pick you up, or divide your group—hiking from opposite trailheads and exchanging car keys in the backcountry.

Hikes classified as strictly day hikes are too short for backpacking or do not have adequate water or campsites available. Classification of hikes as suitable for either day or backpack hikes indicates that they can be completed in one strenuous day or can be taken at a slower pace, allowing for nights spent camping in the backcountry.

Occasionally, a hike is listed as suitable for backpacking if water is carried along. Packing water, however, is usually practical only for one-night campers or if snow patches are available from which you can melt the water you need. If lugging pounds of water for miles doesn't sound appealing, remember this: Dry camps are usually insect free and tend to be more remote and less used than campsites near water. For many solitude-seeking hikers, the advantages of dry camps far outweigh any inconvenience of packing in water. (One gallon of water per person for each night at a dry camp is usually adequate.)

Hikes listed as cross-country or part cross-country should be attempted only by those experienced in off-trail hiking and routefinding. Many of these hikes are straightforward, but some require skills that novice hikers may not have developed. A few cross-country hikes include routes classified as Class 2 or Class 3. Class 2 routes are essentially scrambles over rough terrain, often involving boulder-hopping or scrambling along steep and occasionally unstable slopes—you must sometimes use your hands to maintain balance or latch onto a hold. Most hikers with some cross-country experience should have no trouble on Class 2 routes, but lug-soled boots are recommended.

Class 3 routes entail basic rock climbing skills, where hand- and footholds come into play. These routes are often quite exposed, and the unsteady or novice climber may need to be roped up on Class 3 routes. No hike described in this guide involves Class 3 climbing, but nearby peaks suggested for side trips often do.

Occasionally the text refers to a mountain peak or lake as "Peak 11071" or "Lake 6730." This refers to unnamed peaks or lakes and indicates their elevation of such a feature.

The **Difficulty** rating is based on the "average" hiker's ability and may vary depending on your physical condition, weather conditions, and trail or route conditions.

Best season listings indicate the optimum season in which to take a given hike. Since conditions vary on a yearly basis, these listings are certainly not decisive. For high-country hikes, the season indicated is the most snow- and storm-free period of the year; for low-elevation or desert hikes, the ideal season is the coolest time of year. For some hikes the season indicated is year-round; during the "storm season" (November through March), you should stay updated on weather forecasts and avoid stormy periods.

Knowing the **water availability** is crucial for a safe and enjoyable hike in the backcountry. Reliable water sources are listed for the benefit of backpackers taking extended hikes. Day hikers are advised to bring their own water, since few day hikers carry water filters to purify backcountry water sources. Day hikers should always carry *at least* one quart of water per person.

Maps

Three types of maps are commonly listed in *Hiking Southern California:* United States Geological Survey (USGS) topographic quadrangles, national forest maps, and wilderness maps.

Each national forest is covered by its individual map, which is most useful for locating the general area of a given hike and can be invaluable in trailhead location. The cost of these maps is modest, and they are available at all Forest Service stations.

USGS topographic quadrangles are preferred by most hikers. These maps have contour lines that help hikers visualize the landscape and identify landmarks and such landscape features as lakes, streams, and peaks.

California is now covered by 7.5-minute quadrangles, which usually have contour intervals of 40 feet, cover an area of approximately 9 miles by 7 miles, and are on a scale of 1:24,000 (1 inch on the map is equivalent to 24,000 inches on the ground).

Most trails and roads are depicted accurately on these topographic quadrangles. Maps used in *Hiking Southern California* show the correct location and configuration of trails and roads and are designed to complement the listed quadrangles.

Topographic maps are available at most backpacking and sporting goods stores and at some national forest and most national park visitor centers, or they can be ordered directly from the USGS. Standard topographic quadrangles are currently $6.00 each when ordered from the USGS, with a $5.00 handling charge per order. To order, simply list the name of the maps needed in alphabetical order, indicate how many of each you want, indicate the product ID number, for which state (all USGS maps for this guide are California quadrangles unless otherwise indicated), the scale desired, and the price. Send orders to U.S. Geological Survey Information Services, Box 25286, Denver, CO 80225. Or fax your order to (303) 202–4693. Or, on the Web, go to mapping.usgs.gov. (Request a Map Index Kit for California from the USGS prior to mailing orders. The kit includes a map index for the state, order forms, and a list of map dealers.)

Some wilderness areas in southern California are covered by topographic wilderness maps produced by the USDA Forest Service. In addition to showing trails and trailheads, these excellent maps provide useful information about each wilderness and tips on zero-impact practices and wilderness regulations. These maps are available by mail or in person at district ranger offices.

Bureau of Land Management (BLM) maps are listed for some desert areas covered in this book. These maps are on a scale of 1:2,500,000 and cover an area approximately 50 miles by 30 miles. They are invaluable for finding your way on remote desert roads in eastern California and are available at all eastern California BLM offices.

Wilderness Permits

The wilderness permit system in southern California's wild areas has been greatly simplified since the 1980s, and today few wilderness areas have permit requirements. The **Permit** listing tells you which areas require permits. A California Campfire Permit is *required* for the use of open fires and backpack stoves outside developed campgrounds anywhere in California. These permits are free of charge and are good for one year. They can be obtained at any national forest office in the state.

Trailheads listed in this guide under **Finding the trailhead** vary—some are located alongside major state highways; others are found in remote backcountry locations. Consistent with highway signs, state highways in this book are referred to as California Highway 38, California Highway 2, etc. Forest roads (abbreviated FR) are labeled on forest maps, if not on the site, with a multiple number-letter designation (e.g., FR 14N11).

To locate the hikes in this book, use the general location maps in this guide in tandem with a good California road map and Forest Service or Park Service maps.

Trail Markers

Backcountry hikers occasionally encounter ducks or blazes, and these trail markers are often referred to in this book. Ducks—small stacks of rocks—are most common in timberline or alpine areas and mark obscure or cross-country routes. Avoid building ducks when traveling cross-country. Other hikers can find their own way, and you do no one a favor marring the wilderness with unnecessary ducks. Hikers who need ducks to lead the way shouldn't be traveling cross-country in the first place.

Blazes—usually the figure "i" carved into the bark of trees—are found along most wilderness trails. Often blazes are the only clues to the location of an obscure or abandoned trail, and they become invaluable when the trail is buried in snow. Individuals should never blaze trees in the backcountry. And keep in mind that most trail signs are semipermanent fixtures at best and may be unreliable. The detailed hike descriptions in this guide, on the other hand, will get you where you want to go, trail signs or not.

National Forest Adventure Pass

In all southern California national forests (Los Padres, Angeles, San Bernardino, and Cleveland), visitors must purchase and display on their vehicle a National Forest Adventure Pass while engaging in recreational activities (picnicking, hiking, fishing, etc.) on national forest lands. The Adventure Pass is widely available in gateway communities near the national forests and are also available at all Forest Service offices. A single-day pass is $5.00; an annual pass is $30.00. Eighty percent of fees collected from the sale of National Forest Adventure Passes is returned to the local national forest and used to fund maintenance and improvements to recreation sites and facilities.

Elevation Profiles

Each hike description includes an elevation profile. These charts are not meant to be a detailed foot-by-foot account of the route but serve as a general picture of the overall elevation gain/loss a hike entails.

You don't need to hike each described route in its entirety or in the described direction to enjoy a particular hiking area. Simply choose an area that appeals to you, and let your ability and desire dictate how far to go or which trail to take. After all, enjoyment is what hiking is all about.

Backcountry Rules and Wilderness Regulations

All users of backcountry lands in southern California have a responsibility to become familiar with and abide by the rules and regulations governing use of those lands. Many backcountry areas have specific restrictions regarding the use of campsites, open fires, etc., for reasons as diverse as preserving solitude for visitors, protecting delicate environments such as riparian zones and alpine areas, and allowing damaged campsites to recover from overuse. Specific regulations attached to wilderness permits are in addition to the regulations listed below. Visitors should become familiar with all regulations, including those in The Art of Hiking section of this guide, before venturing into California's wilderness backcountry. There is no better way to ensure a safe, enjoyable trip while minimizing disturbance of the land and other visitors.

I. In state park, national park, and national monument backcountry:

- Firearms, loaded or unloaded, are prohibited.
- Pets are prohibited on backcountry trails. Dogs are permitted in national forest wilderness but are not encouraged. They can pollute water sources, harass wildlife and other hikers, and endanger their owners by leading an angry bear back to camp. If you must bring your dog into national forest wilderness, please keep it under restraint as much as possible, particularly on trails and near other hikers and campers.
- Collection of natural features, such as wildflowers, antlers, and rocks, is prohibited. Fishing is allowed under California state fishing regulations, but hunting, shooting, molesting, or disturbing with intent to harm wildlife is prohibited.
- Backcountry permits are required for all overnight use of backcountry areas.

II. In national forest wilderness only:

- Discharging of firearms is permitted in national forest wilderness areas only for emergencies and taking of wildlife as permitted by California game laws. However, some wilderness areas are also game refuges where firearms are prohibited.
- Using a trail, campsite, or other area in any wilderness by a group larger than twenty-five persons is prohibited.

III. In both national forest and national park backcountry:

- Where terrain permits, locate campsites at least 100 feet from trails, streams, lake shores, meadows, and other campers. (Damaged lakeshore and streamside vegetation may take generations to recover.) Campsites located away from water are comparatively insect free and are often considerably warmer. Carry a supply of water to your camp for drinking, cooking, and washing to avoid continually trampling delicate vegetation.

- Shortcutting switchbacks and walking off established trails is prohibited. Shortcutting causes erosion, which contributes to the deterioration of the existing trail. You'll save little, if any, time by shortcutting trails, and the additional energy required to negotiate rugged country makes this practice unproductive.

- Any destruction, defacement, or removal of natural features is prohibited. Avoid disturbing wildflowers, trees, shrubs, grasses, and the like, which are important segments of the ecological community. Don't chop, drive nails or carve initials into, cut boughs from, or otherwise damage live trees or standing snags. Damaged trees are vulnerable to insects and disease.

- Pack out all unburnable refuse. Aluminum foil and plastics do not burn and must be packed out along with cans, bottles, and leftover food scraps—not buried. Many foods carried by backpackers are packaged in airtight foil-lined containers that will not burn—pack them out. And even if buried, leftover food scraps will attract animals. As wild animals become accustomed to eating human food, their natural foraging habits are disrupted, creating problems for future campers at the site.

- Do not litter the trail. Put all trash such as cigarette butts, gum, orange peels, and candy wrappers in your pocket or pack while traveling.

- Stop to smoke. Smoking while traveling is not only hazardous, it is also against the law. Locate a safe spot in a cleared or barren area free of flammable material, such as a large rock or a sandy area. Never crush out a cigarette on a log or stump. Be sure all matches, ashes, and burning tobacco are dead out before leaving the area.

- Protect water quality. Bury body waste in a shallow hole, 5 to 8 inches deep, in the biologically active layer where bacteria and fungi will help decompose waste fairly rapidly. (This is a good reason to carry a small, lightweight garden trowel.) Locate a spot at least 200 feet from campsites, trails, and existing or potential watercourses so that rain and snow runoff will not carry pollutants to lakes and streams. Fish entrails should be burned whenever possible and should never be thrown into water sources.

- Keep all wash water at least 100 feet from water sources. Do not use any type of soap or detergent in or near water sources or potential watercourses. Even "biodegradable" soaps contain ingredients that can pollute water. Usually, sand or gravel can clean pots effectively.

- A California fishing license is required by anyone over sixteen years of age who plans to fish. California fishing regulations apply in wilderness areas.

- All mechanized and motorized equipment, including bicycles, motorcycles, chainsaws, and snowmobiles, are prohibited in wilderness areas. Some roadless areas not officially designated as wilderness may also have restrictions regarding the use of motorized equipment. Some state parks do allow bicycles on trails, but they are prohibited in other backcountry areas.

- Yield the right-of-way to pack and saddle stock on trails. Stand well off the trail until the animals have passed. Simple-minded pack animals are easily spooked by sudden noises and movements, so talk to the packer in a normal tone of voice to let the animals know you are there.

- Collecting plant and animal life, minerals, or other natural and historical objects is permitted for scientific study only. Special written authorization is required and must be obtained in advance from either a park superintendent or a forest supervisor. These permits are not issued for personal collections. Please do not pick wildflowers; leave them for others to enjoy.

- Constructing rock walls, large fireplaces, fire rings, benches, tables, shelters, bough beds, rock or wood bridges, trenches, or other similar structures alters the natural character of the land and is not permitted. Make an effort to leave the least possible trace of your passing.

- Wilderness Visitor Permits are required year-round for entry into some national forest areas in California. A permit is free to anyone who agrees to abide by the regulations listed above and any special restrictions applying to a travel area. Permits are issued at the ranger station nearest the point of entry and must be obtained in person.

  The permit system allows the issuing agency to obtain information on where, when, and how much use a particular area receives—valuable information that enables the agency to make important management decisions, such as whether to limit use to preserve wilderness qualities of a particular area. Information recorded on wilderness permits may also aid in locating lost or injured hikers.

  In most southern California wilderness areas, the maximum group size is twenty-five persons, but that number is lower in some areas. If you plan on hiking with a large group, be sure to check with the ranger station nearest your trailhead about group size limits.

  A quota system has been implemented at many of the most heavily used wilderness trailheads, particularly in the San Gorgonio and San Jacinto Wildernesses. This system allows the managing agency to limit the number of backpackers entering the wilderness on a daily basis to protect qualities of solitude and prevent continued degradation of campsites and trails.

A wilderness permit also allows the building of campfires where permitted. If you plan to build a campfire or use a backpack stove outside wilderness areas, you must obtain a California Campfire Permit. A Special Campfire Permit is required for the Los Padres National Forest. This permit is available at Forest Service stations in person only and requires that applicants have at least a small shovel available for use at the campfire site.

If the above list of wilderness rules and regulations seems confusing, or overwhelmingly restrictive, it shouldn't. In most cases, these regulations simply embody common sense. They represent choices between degradation or preservation of California's vanishing wilderness resource.

The National Wilderness Preservation Act of September 3, 1964, defines wilderness as "an area of undeveloped federal land retaining its primeval character and influence without permanent improvements or human habitation . . . where the earth and its community of life are untrammeled by man . . . where man is a visitor who does not remain . . . and is protected and managed so as to preserve its natural condition. . . . " The USDA Forest Service, Bureau of Land Management, and National Park Service manage wilderness areas in accordance with the Wilderness Act, striving to maintain their primitive character by protecting native plants and animals and preserving healthy watersheds, while at the same time providing the public an opportunity to use the wilderness and benefit from the wilderness experience.

With increasingly heavy use in California's roadless areas, such wilderness qualities and experiences are becoming more problematic. The regulations applied in California's wilderness areas simply attempt to maintain those qualities that we, as backcountry visitors, seek.

Backcountry Hazards

There are as many reasons for seeking wild places as there are hikers. One thing that hikers have in common is the desire for a safe and enjoyable outdoor experience.

A long weekend in the wilderness may be the focus of anticipation all year for some city dwellers. But in their haste to escape the rat race, some hikers forget the potential hazards that exist in wild areas.

Refer to The Art of Hiking section at the back of this book for details of typical backcountry hazards. The following information addresses the kinds of hazards peculiar to southern California. No matter what the situation, though, good judgment—an awareness of potential hazards and how to deal with them—is your best insurance.

Flash Floods and Fast Water

In the desert, where summer thunderstorms are more common, avoid hiking—and never make camp—in a wash or canyon bottom. It doesn't have to be raining where you are for a flash flood to occur. One can emanate from heavy rainfall several miles away.

Some of the most frequently encountered hazards in the backcountry are swiftly running streams or rivers. Although many large backcountry streams in California are bridged, those that are not require special precautions, especially during spring snowmelt or after heavy rains. The power of a swiftly running mountain stream is as easy to underestimate as it is impressive. Take no chances; search upstream or downstream for a crossing via logs or boulders—but remember, these can be very slippery. If you can't find a crossing, your only choice is to ford the stream. During spring runoff, creeks will be at their lowest in the early-morning hours before the sun again begins melting the snowpack.

Before entering the water, plan exactly what you will do. Never ford a stream above a cascade or waterfall. Look for a level stretch of water, perhaps where the stream has divided into numerous channels. Choose a spot where you and/or your gear will wash onto a sandbar or shallow area in the event you lose your footing.

Try to cross at a 45-degree angle downstream. Some hikers use a pole or stout staff on their upstream side to aid in crossing swift waters. Remove your pants (bare legs create less friction) and your socks, but put your boots back on for better footing on the slippery stream bottom. Unhitch the waist strap on your pack so that you can dump it if you lose your footing.

Insects

Don't let insects bug you. They are unavoidable—but not unbeatable—in the backcountry, especially in June and July at higher elevations. The most common nuisance to hikers is the persistent mosquito. Your best line of defense is to carry a good insect repellent. Consider using a natural insect repellent; products containing citronella are quite effective.

Ticks are fairly common throughout wooded, brushy, and grassy areas of southern California and are most active from March until early summer. All ticks are potential carriers of Rocky Mountain spotted fever, Colorado tick fever, and tularemia (rabbit fever). The western black-legged tick, only ⅛ inch long, is responsible for transmitting Lyme disease, a bacterial infection named for the Connecticut town where it was first recognized. The majority of Lyme disease infections have occurred in the coastal counties of Marin, Sonoma, Mendocino, and Humboldt, all north of San Francisco.

Read The Art of Hiking for ways to protect yourself against ticks and the diseases they carry.

Rattlesnakes

Rattlesnakes are an important segment of the ecosystem. Given a chance, a rattler sunning itself on the trail will usually attempt to escape. But be wary; rattlers won't always give warning before striking. The most abundant California rattler, the western diamondback, can deliver a painful and dangerous bite that's rarely fatal to healthy individuals.

Rattlers are common near water sources below 6,000 feet elevation, and sometimes range as high as 8,000 feet. Watch where you put your hands and feet in snake country, especially when stepping over logs or climbing in rocky areas, and wear good boots. (The majority of snake bites occur on the lower limbs.) Always carry a snakebite kit and familiarize yourself with its use.

Poison Oak

Poison oak is quite common in most areas of California (except the desert) below 5,000 feet elevation. The green leaves of poison oak are divided into three leaflets, which are lobed and shiny. The plant has a white or greenish-white berry and grows as a shrub or vine. The leaves turn bright red in summer and fall, dropping off the plant in winter.

Avoid contact with any part of the poison oak plant, which can produce an irritating rash. Also avoid touching clothes, pets, or equipment that has come into contact with poison oak. If you do come into contact with poison oak, wash the area with soap and water as soon as possible and apply an itch-relieving ointment (a wise addition to any first-aid kit). Also wash clothing that has come into contact with the plant. Squaw bush, which does not cause a rash, is nearly identical to poison oak and the two are often confused. Play it safe and beware of any plant you suspect might be poison oak.

Bears

Black bears inhabit most mountainous regions of California. Although seldom seen in more wild areas, they have become a problem in places where they have grown accustomed to easily attainable food.

If you suspect there are bears in your travel area, take steps to keep your food supply from becoming the main course for a hungry bear. Keep your camp clean of food scraps, and keep food odors away from gear. Never leave dirty dishes or cooking utensils lying around camp overnight.

In all national parks and in some national forest areas, the law requires that you store your food properly. The counterbalance method of suspending food from a tree is one method of protecting your food supply. Put all food, and any other items having an odor that might attract bears (such as toothpaste, soap, or trash), into two evenly weighted stuff sacks and hang them from a sturdy tree limb at least 15 feet above ground and 10 feet from the tree trunk. Food should hang about 5 feet below the tree limb. Leave nonfood packs on the ground with all flaps and zippers opened so that a curious bear won't damage them while nosing around.

The most effective way to protect food from bears is a bear-resistant food storage canister. These virtually indestructible canisters are lightweight and store about one week's supply of food for one person. Although the canisters are expensive, they will pay for themselves over the course of a few backcountry trips by keeping your food safe. In some backcountry areas, you are required to use these canisters if food-storage boxes are unavailable in the backcountry.

Keep your distance from all bears, especially bear cubs. Don't even consider trying to recover food from a bear—just chalk the loss up to experience.

Note: Not all black bears are black, but you can be sure there are no grizzly bears left in California. The last grizzly sighting in the state occurred in 1924 in Sequoia National Park.

Fires

Exercise extreme caution when using any form of fire. California has dense blankets of chaparral and forests that are tinder dry in summer and fall. You are responsible for keeping your fire under control at all times and will be held accountable for the costs of fighting any fire and for any damage resulting from your carelessness. Those costs are enormous, not to mention the destruction to vegetation, wildlife habitat, and human life and property.

California typically has long, hot, very dry summers, when the fire danger is acute. Open fires are prohibited in many areas during this period. Some national forest areas of California, primarily low elevation areas with an abundance of brush, are closed to entry during the fire season, usually from about July 1 until the first substantial fall rains. Other areas may also be closed periodically due to high or extreme fire danger. Fire restrictions and periods of closure vary on a yearly basis, so check with the appropriate agency in advance of your trip.

If you plan on building a campfire, or if you use a backpack stove, you must obtain a California Campfire Permit (see Backcountry Rules and Wilderness Regulations). If you must have a campfire, it is crucial that you keep it small, build it on bare mineral soil, never leave it unattended, and drown—don't bury— it before you leave, making sure it is cold and completely extinguished.

Driving to the Trailheads

Driving to southern California trailheads often involves negotiating rough, dirt-surfaced mountain roads that require the use of caution and common sense. When driving to any trailhead via long, winding, and often narrow dirt or paved roads, stay on your side of the road; watch for cattle, logging trucks, and other vehicles. Mishaps can be avoided by driving with care and attention.

When driving in remote locations, either in the desert or the mountains, always be sure your vehicle is in good condition. Check your brakes, make sure you have plenty of fuel, and carry basic emergency equipment. A shovel, ax, saw, at least five gallons of water, and extra food and clothing should help you deal with a variety of unforeseen problems and may indeed be your only hope in some remote areas. If you have a cellular phone, bring it with you. Most high points anywhere in the state offer the possibility of obtaining a signal. And be sure to check ahead with the appropriate agency on road conditions before setting out for the trailhead.

Before You Head Out

- Know the limitations of your body, your equipment, and the members of your group. Don't exceed those limits.

- Choose a hike within the capability of the members of your group, and stay together on the trail, particularly toward nightfall.

- If a storm develops or darkness is descending, make camp as soon as possible. Never hike at night. Keep in mind that darkness comes quickly to the mountains and desert.

- It is never wise to hike alone. Solo cross-country hiking is especially dangerous.

- Don't take unnecessary chances. Don't hesitate to turn back or end your trip if someone in your group becomes ill, if swollen streams or snow block your route, or if inclement weather sets in. The wilderness will always be there—make sure you are able to return and enjoy it.

- If you think you are lost—or you are injured—stop traveling at once; stay calm and decide on a course of action. Study maps and try to locate landmarks that will help orient you. Do not continue until you know where you are. If you left a travel plan with a responsible person, and if you followed that plan, a search party should have no trouble finding you.

    In some areas, following a creek downstream will lead out of the mountains. But in larger wilderness areas, this practice may lead further into the wilderness and compound the problem.

- A series of three signals—such as whistles, shouts, or light flashes—is universally recognized as a distress signal. Only contemplate starting a signal fire in emergencies, and even then make sure it can be done safely. Rescuers will be directed to you by smoke, not flames.

Death Valley National Park

In the minds of many people, Death Valley National Park is a stark, dry, hot-as-an-oven landscape of desert valleys and mountains best suited for a road trip during cooler months, rather than a hiking destination. Yet Death Valley provides some of the finest hiking in the California desert, ranging from short nature trails to the most demanding and challenging desert hiking imaginable.

Diversity best describes the landscapes of Death Valley National Park. Five major Great Basin valleys lie within the park's boundaries: the Saline, Eureka, northern Panamint, and Greenwater Valleys and most of the 156-mile-long trough of Death Valley itself. Separating these valleys are five nearly barren mountain ranges, where colorful rocks expose 1.8 billion years of Earth history. The Panamint Range features 11,331 feet of relief (the greatest relief of any mountain range in the lower forty-eight states) between Badwater Basin on the valley floor and 11,049-foot Telescope Peak, the Panamint's highest summit. Death Valley also contains five large sand dune systems representing all types of dune structures.

Although wildlife is rarely observed in great numbers here, the park supports 51 species of native mammals, 307 species of birds, 36 species of reptiles, 3 species of amphibians, and 5 species of native fishes. Due to Death Valley's location in the northern Mojave Desert, in a zone of overlap between the Great Basin Desert to the north and the Sonoran (Colorado) Desert to the south, the park hosts vegetation ranging from the lower Sonoran to the Arctic/Alpine life zones.

Death Valley National Park, our nation's largest, comprises 3,396,192 acres. Ninety-five percent (3,158,033 acres) is forever protected behind the boundaries of federally designated wilderness. Most of the hikes in this chapter penetrate only the fringes of that wilderness; many are located in frontcountry nonwilderness areas. The trips in this section sample the spectrum of park landscapes, ranging from windswept piñon-juniper woodlands atop the Panamint Range to barren badlands lying below sea level. Hiking routes also vary, including trail-less routes in canyon bottoms to long-closed 4WD roads and constructed trails.

Death Valley is the location of the world's second-highest recorded temperature (134 degrees Fahrenheit), and from May through September daily high temperatures exceeding 100 degrees Fahrenheit are routine. However, late autumn (November) through early spring (March) afford comfortable temperatures that make hiking in the park a joy. Rain seldom falls in the valley, though the highest elevations, particularly in the Panamint Range, receive modest precipitation and usually enough snow to close the Telescope Peak and Wildrose Peak Trails from December or January through April.

Even cooler weather in the dry climate of the park can cause significant dehydration. Hikers following any trip in this chapter are strongly advised to carry ample water (at least two quarts per person for longer hikes), sunscreen, and a wide-brimmed hat. Hikers should avoid going solo in Death Valley's remote backcountry, and every hiker should leave an itinerary with a friend or family member. The park's landscapes can be harsh and unforgiving to hikers who go unprepared or take unnecessary chances.

Whether you follow a few short nature trails or tackle some of Death Valley's lofty peaks or precipitous canyons, you will surely return again and again to experience panoramas of great mountain ranges, sprawling desert valleys, and shadowed canyons and revel in the stark vastness of the park's dramatic landscapes.

1 Eureka Dunes

This remote hike visits the tallest sand dunes in the California desert, in the far north-west corner of Death Valley National Park.

Start: The cross-country route begins at the southeast edge of the picnic site.
General location: Death Valley National Park, 20 miles east of Big Pine
Distance: Variable; up to 2.6-mile round-trip or loop day hike; no trail
Approximate hiking time: 1–1.5 hours
Difficulty: Moderate
Trailhead elevation: 2,870 feet
High point: 3,497 feet
Land status: National park
Best season: October through May

Water availability: None available; bring your own
Maps: USGS Last Chance Range SW; Death Valley National Park visitor map; USGS Death Valley National Monument and Vicinity, CA/NV (1:250,000 scale)
Fees and permits: No fees or permits required
Trail contact: Death Valley National Park, P.O. Box 579, Death Valley, CA 92328; (760) 786-2331; www.nps.gov/deva

Finding the trailhead: From U.S. Highway 395 at the north end of Big Pine, turn east onto California Highway 168, signed ANCIENT BRISTLECONE PINE FOREST, WESTGARD PASS, DEEP SPRINGS, AND HIGHWAY 95 JUNCTION. Be sure to top off your gas tank in Big Pine, and carry ample water and other supplies; the desert ahead is remote and assistance is far away.

After 1.5 miles the highway bridges the Owens River. A short distance ahead, 2.4 miles from US 395, reach the right-branching, eastbound Death Valley Road, signed SALINE VALLEY, EUREKA VALLEY, AND SCOTTY'S CASTLE. Turn right onto this two-lane, paved road, which ascends steadily, winding up the western slopes of the Inyo Mountains via Waucoba Canyon. After 10 miles, the center-line stripe ends and the pavement narrows and becomes rougher.

Pass the junction with Saline Valley Road near the crest of the Inyos after 13.2 miles, then follow the long descent into Eureka Valley. The pavement ends in Eureka Valley at the boundary of Death Valley National Park, 32 miles from US 395. At 38.6 miles, ignore northbound North Eureka Valley Road where it branches left. After 39.1 miles the pavement resumes; a short distance ahead, the road forks. Follow the right fork, signed EUREKA DUNES. This sometimes rough-graded road crosses gravel and sand for 9.4 miles to a junction with a left-branching 4WD road that curves around the dunes and ascends to Silver Pass en route to Saline Valley. Bear right at the junction and drive another 0.4 mile to a picnic site at the base of the dunes. The hike begins here.

Note: The last mile of the road to the dunes crosses the sump of Eureka Valley just above a dry lake. Following periods of heavy rain and flooding, this section of the road may become impassable. Contact Death Valley National Park for updated information on road conditions.

Eureka Dunes, the tallest sand dunes in the California desert, punctuate Eureka Valley in the northwest corner of Death Valley National Park.

The Hike

Punctuating the south end of the remote desert basin of Eureka Valley is a grand pile of dune sand, the largest of three prominent dune fields in this northwest corner of Death Valley National Park. From top to bottom, the Eureka Dunes rise 650 feet, rivaling some of North America's great sand piles, including Colorado's Great Sand Dunes National Monument.

With a backdrop of some of the most colorful mountains in the Great Basin (the Last Chance Range), no developed trails nor any particular destination, and the freedom and quiet solitude of the dunes' remote location, few hikers can resist the attraction of a day's outing at this incredible place. Eureka Dunes are possibly the most remote in North America. The dunes are predominately white, featuring wind-sculpted swirls of black and tan sand—an ever-changing and dynamic landscape. Try to plan your trip for spring or fall, following rainfall that makes the sand firm and easier to negotiate.

As you spend a day exploring the Eureka Dunes, keep in mind that two plant species here occur nowhere else: Eureka Dunes evening primrose (a spreading,

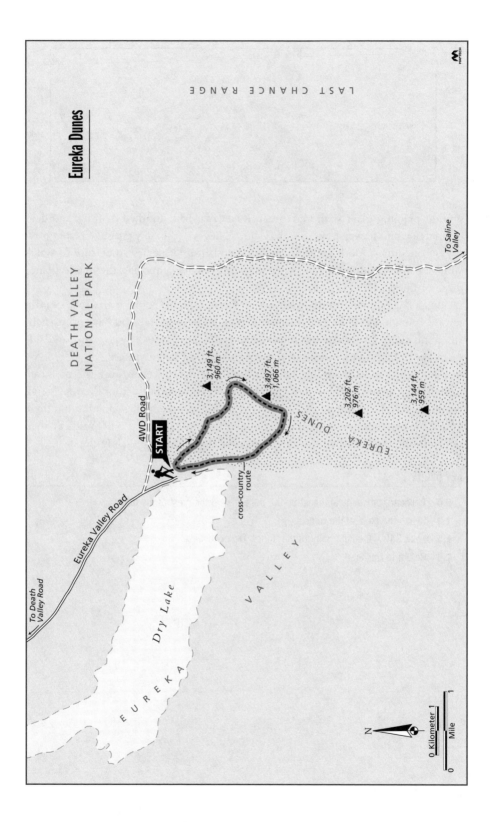

Eureka Dunes

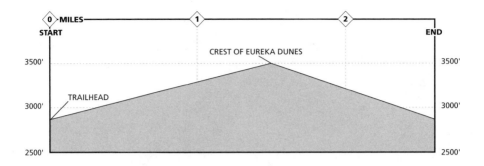

ground-hugging plant with gray-green leaves that have toothed margins and delicate, large white flowers), and Eureka Valley dunegrass (the only grasslike plant growing on the dunes). Both are federally listed endangered species, so be sure to watch your step and avoid trampling fragile vegetation while exploring the magical landscape of Eureka Dunes.

In such a remote and dramatic desert setting, simply being at the road's end is reward enough. Those with a yearning to wander beyond the road have no particular destination other than the dunes, and being surrounded by a giant sand pile rekindles childhood memories in the imaginations of many visitors.

One of the most rewarding hikes at Eureka Dunes is a loop from the trailhead, including an ascent to the dunes' high point. Ascend southeast from the road's end, gaining 650 feet in 1.0 mile to the crest of the dunes at the highest point. From there follow the crest southwest 0.5 mile, climbing up and over Point 3497 midway, then return to the trailhead by glissading northwest down the steep sandy slopes.

Key points

0.0   Trailhead; proceed southeast up the ridge toward the crest of the dunes.

1.0   Reach the crest of the dunes.

1.5   Point 3497, the high point of the dunes. Descend west.

2.6   Return to trailhead.

2 The Racetrack to Ubehebe Peak

This rigorous but rewarding day hike traces the route of an old mining trail to a remote desert peak in the northern reaches of Death Valley National Park.

Start: The trail begins at the west edge of the parking area.
General location: Death Valley National Park; 25 miles northwest of Stovepipe Wells
Distance: 4.0-mile round-trip day hike
Approximate hiking time: 2–2.5 hours
Difficulty: Strenuous
Trailhead elevation: 3,710 feet
High point: Ubehebe Peak, 5,678 feet
Land status: National park
Best season: October through May (expect occasional light snow during winter)

Water availability: None available; bring your own
Maps: USGS Ubehebe Peak; Death Valley National Park visitor map; USGS Death Valley National Monument and Vicinity, CA/NV (1:250,000 scale)
Fees and permits: No fees or permits required
Trail contact: Death Valley National Park, P.O. Box 579, Death Valley, CA 92328; (760) 786–2331; www.nps.gov/deva

Finding the trailhead: Follow California Highway 190 to the Furnace Creek visitor complex on the floor of Death Valley, 120 miles northwest of Baker, 110 miles northeast of Ridgecrest, and about 90 miles east of Olancha and Lone Pine. The visitor center and Death Valley Museum are located here; books, maps, drinking water, and information are available.

Proceed northwest along the paved highway, following signs that indicate Scotty's Castle and Ubehebe Crater. An entry fee is collected at the Grapevine Entrance Station, 48 miles northwest of Furnace Creek. Proceed 0.1 mile beyond the entrance station, then turn left where a sign points to Ubehebe Crater. The right-forking road leads to Scotty's Castle and eventually joins U.S. Highway 95 in Nevada in 28 miles.

The paved road heads northwest across upper Death Valley. Avoid the signed dirt road branching right (northwest) to Big Pine (75 miles) in 2.7 miles. In another 2.8 miles, turn right onto a dirt road signed RACETRACK. On your return, the left-branching loop road will take you south to the rim of immense Ubehebe Crater (500 feet deep and nearly 0.5 mile across) and a pair of short trails. One trail leads into the crater; the other climbs 0.5 mile above to Little Hebe Crater. Both are worthwhile excursions if you have the time and energy.

The road ahead climbs 2,500 feet in 11 miles upon a broad alluvial surface between the Cottonwood and Last Chance Ranges. The road typically has a rough washboard surface and occasional deep gravel. Passenger cars occasionally make the trip, but a high-clearance vehicle is recommended. After the road tops out on a Joshua tree–clad saddle, it descends gradually for 8 miles to Teakettle Junction, where you bear right. In another 5.7 miles reach a turnout on the right (west) side of the road opposite an interpretive sign on the edge of the Racetrack playa. The hike begins here.

The Hike

Ubehebe Peak, rising to a modest 5,678 feet at the southern end of the remote Last Chance Range, is an obscure summit that escapes the notice of many visitors traveling to this isolated corner of the park, most of whom make the long, rough journey to contemplate the mysterious trails left behind by the sliding rocks of the Racetrack.

At 3,700 feet, the Racetrack is one of the highest elevation dry lakes in the park. Its shimmering white surface is highlighted at its northern end by the Grandstand, a cluster of gray boulders buried deeply in lakebed sediments. But despite the interpretive sign opposite the Grandstand, this is not the best spot on the playa to see evidence of the "racing" rocks. After climbing Ubehebe Peak, consider driving 2 miles south to the southern end of the playa and walking eastward toward the foot of prominent Peak 4560. Rocks eroded from this steep mountain, including some large boulders, have left many noticeable tracks on the playa surface. The phenomenon is not fully understood, but apparently the rocks move when the lakebed is slickened by abundant rainfall and swept by very strong winds.

Hikers on the summit of Ubehebe Peak are treated to an aerial-like view of the Racetrack and panoramic vistas ranging from lofty Sierra Nevada peaks to sunken desert flats. Spring wildflowers and shrubs from two distinct life zones are well represented along the old mining trail that climbs to the crest of the range. To attain the summit of Ubehebe Peak, a brief Class 2 to Class 3 scramble is necessary, but hikers who choose to forgo the scramble will still enjoy broad vistas from the open crest.

The trail begins west of the parking area. Faint at first, it soon becomes obvious as its rock-lined course leads west, climbing gently up the alluvial fan at the foot of Ubehebe Peak. The prominent knob rises nearly 2,000 feet above and less than 1 mile distant. The fan is clothed in creosote bush, and in spring the intriguing desert trumpet briefly decorates trailside slopes before the trail jogs northwest.

The trail climbs steadily beneath the broken desert-varnished cliffs of imposing Peak 5519. Broken rock along the trail attests to the natural gray color of the rocks in this portion of the Last Chance Range.

Above the fan, seemingly endless switchbacks lead you up the rocky slope on a moderately steep grade. Creosote bush dominates here, but buckwheat, bunchgrasses, and the showy yellow spring blooms of Death Valley goldeneye are also common.

Finally you negotiate two final switchbacks while passing through a band of limestone where colorful malachite, a blue-green copper ore, is exposed in a shallow

◄ *Hikers en route to Ubehebe Peak will enjoy crag-framed views of the Racetrack playa, home to the mysterious sliding rocks.*

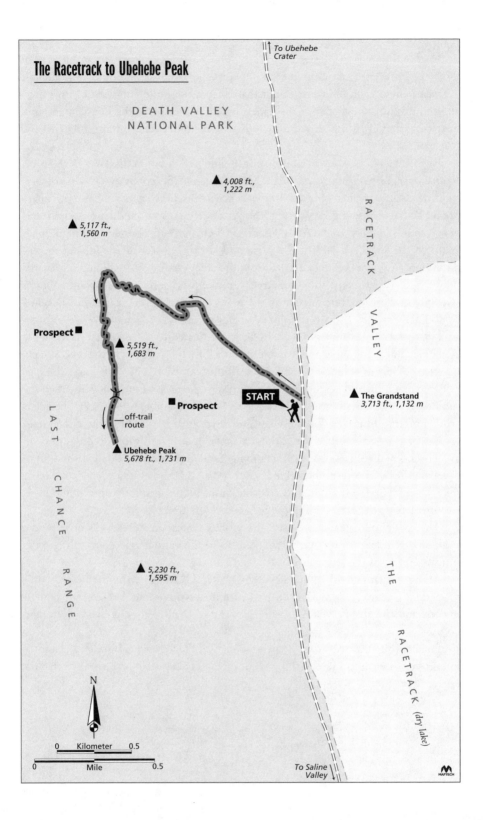

The Racetrack to Ubehebe Peak

To Ubehebe
Crater

DEATH VALLEY
NATIONAL PARK

▲ 4,008 ft.,
1,222 m

▲ 5,117 ft.,
1,560 m

R
A
C
E
T
R
A
C
K

Prospect ■

▲ 5,519 ft.,
1,683 m

V
A
L
L
E
Y

L
A
S
T

■ Prospect

START

▲ The Grandstand
3,713 ft., 1,132 m

off-trail
route

C
H
A
N
C
E

▲ Ubehebe Peak
5,678 ft., 1,731 m

R
A
N
G
E

▲ 5,230 ft.,
1,595 m

T
H
E

N

R
A
C
E
T
R
A
C
K
(dry lake)

0   Kilometer   0.5

0   Mile   0.5

To Saline
Valley

MAPTECH

prospect pit. After hiking 1.5 miles, surmount the crest of the Last Chance Range at 4,950 feet, where you can pause and enjoy well-earned panoramas of deserts and distant mountains. Peaks to the north are inviting and easily climbed, but the best views are those captured from Ubehebe Peak, only 0.5 mile south.

From the saddle, the trail is less well defined as it climbs steadily southward very near the crest of the range. As you gain elevation, creosote bush is left behind and the vegetation is dominated by horsebrush and boxthorn. The latter is a rigid spiny shrub with small, succulent gray-green leaves. Its spine-tipped branches are an adaptation typical of succulent (and some nonsucculent) desert plants to protect their moist foliage from hungry and thirsty wildlife. These two shrubs are indicators of the Shadscale Scrub plant community of the northern Mojave Desert, generally found between 3,000 and 6,000 feet elevation.

The trail switchbacks a few times above another prospect pit, its blue-green copper ore contrasting with the surrounding desert varnish–stained slopes and dull green shrubs. The trail soon climbs to a rocky shoulder just short of Peak 5519, a short easy scramble to your left. Here the trail fades into obscurity and hikers must choose their own route. The logical course follows a short scrambling traverse to a rocky knoll atop the crest. Eastward, broken cliffs plummet nearly 2,000 feet into the broad expanse of the Racetrack.

The knob of Ubehebe Peak lies a short distance south along the crest. But to reach it you must first carefully follow this narrow rocky ridge as it descends 200 feet into a saddle, then negotiate the Class 2–3 ridge, quickly gaining 470 feet. The small summit area, composed of quartz-poor granitic rock, offers an unobstructed and particularly striking eagle's-eye panorama.

The Last Chance Range is a subrange of the more extensive Panamint Range, and its steep flanks, typical of Great Basin ranges, rise steeply and abruptly on either side to a narrow crest. The deep trough of Saline Valley lies 4,500 feet below to the west; beyond it soars the 10,000-foot eastern wall of the Inyo Mountains, punctuated by a crest of lofty, pointed summits. This range is one of only four California mountain ranges featuring more than 10,000 feet of vertical relief. Still farther west are a few snowy peaks of the Sierra.

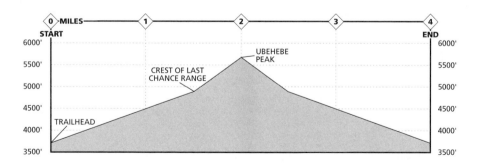

Eastward, beyond the Racetrack and its namesake valley, the colorfully banded barren wall of the Cottonwood Mountains rears abruptly skyward to a crest of 7,000- to 8,000-foot desert peaks. The view southeastward includes the extensive wooded plateau of 7,454-foot Hunter Mountain. From the peak, return the way you came.

Key points

0.0 Trailhead.

1.5 Reach crest of Last Chance Range; turn left (south).

2.0 Ubehebe Peak.

3 Fall Canyon

This memorable day hike ascends a narrow, colorful canyon into the rugged interior of the Grapevine Mountains above the eastern margin of Death Valley.

Start: The trail begins immediately north of the vault toilet.
General location: Death Valley National Park; 22 miles west-southwest of Beatty, Nevada, and 14 miles north of Stovepipe Wells
Distance: 6.6-mile round-trip day hike
Approximate hiking time: 3 hours
Difficulty: Moderate
Trailhead elevation: 960 feet
High point: 2,360 feet
Land status: National park
Best season: October through May

Water availability: None available; bring your own
Maps: USGS Fall Canyon; Death Valley National Park visitor map; USGS Death Valley National Monument and Vicinity, CA/NV (1:250,000 scale)
Fees and permits: No fees or permits required
Trail contact: Death Valley National Park, P.O. Box 579, Death Valley, CA 92328; (760) 786-2331; www.nps.gov/deva

Finding the trailhead: From the junction of California Highway 190 and northwestbound Death Valley Road (leading to Scotty's Castle), 7.2 miles east of Stovepipe Wells and 17.4 miles northwest of Furnace Creek, follow Death Valley Road northwest for 14.9 miles. Where a sign points to Titus Canyon, turn north off the pavement and follow the graded but rough and rocky dirt road up the alluvial fan for 2.7 miles to the parking area at the mouth of Titus Canyon. Ample parking is available here; the unsigned trail begins immediately north of the vault toilet.

The Hike

Fall Canyon, a precipitous gorge cleaving the west slopes of the Grapevine Mountains, is one of many profound yet uncelebrated canyons that bound the eastern flanks of Death Valley. This memorable trip, passable to hikers of every ability, follows a boot-worn trail into Fall Canyon's wash, then ascends the wash through colorful, ancient rocks, finally ending at an impassable dry waterfall deep inside the Grapevine Mountains.

From the parking area at the mouth of Titus Canyon follow the well-worn, unsigned trail generally northward. The path is gravelly and sometimes rocky as it undulates into minor gullies and over low ridges; only a sparse scattering of creosote bush and desert holly stud the rocky slopes of the alluvial fan. Fine vistas reach west

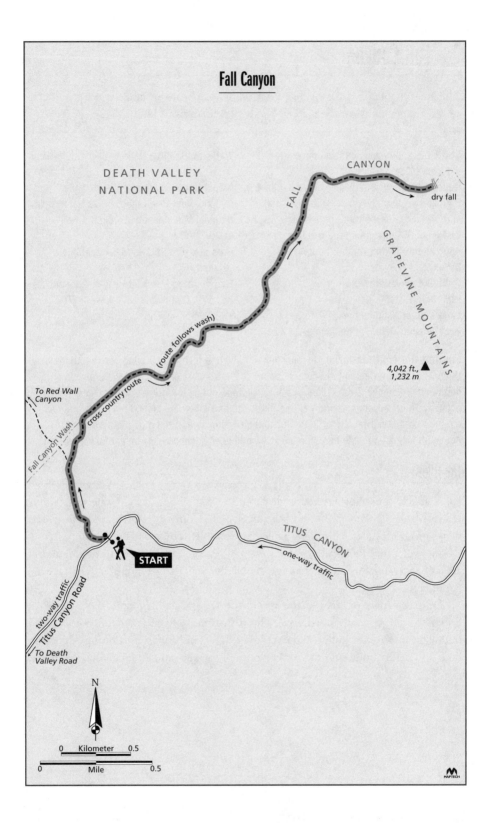

Fall Canyon

CANYON

DEATH VALLEY
NATIONAL PARK

FALL

dry fall

GRAPEVINE MOUNTAINS

4,042 ft.,
1,232 m

(route follows wash)

To Red Wall
Canyon

cross-country route

Fall Canyon Wash

TITUS CANYON

one-way traffic

START

two-way traffic

Titus Canyon Road

To Death
Valley Road

N

0   Kilometer   0.5
0   Mile   0.5

MAPTECH

across Death Valley to the stark east wall of the Cottonwood Mountains and southwest to the bulk of Tucki Mountain and the Panamint Range.

After 0.4 mile you drop into a prominent wash, where the trail forks. The left fork ultimately leads to Red Wall Canyon, a major canyon about 2.5 miles northwest. Take the right-branching trail at this junction and soon enter the broad mouth of Fall Canyon wash. Head northeast up the wash and soon reach the canyon's portal at 0.7 mile, where broken limestone cliffs jut skyward.

As the serpentine canyon winds its way deeper into the Grapevine Mountains, it gradually but steadily becomes a more confined hallway, with the space between canyon walls ranging from as much as 50 yards to as little as 15 to 20 feet. You certainly don't want to be in this gorge when thunderstorms or heavy rains are in the forecast.

Vegetation in the confines of the canyon is sparse, limited to occasional mounds of brittlebush, cheesebush, goldenbush, brickellbush, and various other coarse shrubs. The tread in the wash is often loose and soft gravel and sand, occasionally slowing steady progress, yet the majesty of the canyon constantly distracts you from your labors.

After 2.0 miles the first tributary canyon enters on your left (northwest). Continue north (right) up the main channel of Fall Canyon. Ahead the gray and tan sedimentary rock layers of the Grapevine Mountains dominate the view—a wall of ancient rock soaring more than 4,000 feet over the canyon's floor.

During the final mile of the hike, the canyon briefly widens, and then narrows to a slot barely 10 feet wide. The canyon then opens up and shortly thereafter heads into a 20-foot dry fall, a waterworn cliff, at 3.3 miles.

Only skilled desert canyoneers should consider going any farther. The rest of us will be content with our upcanyon journey, and we'll all enjoy the memorable views as we return to the trailhead.

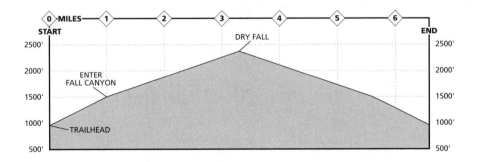

Key points

0.0 Titus Canyon trailhead; head north from parking area on the well-worn but unsigned trail.

0.4 Reach a junction with northwestbound path leading to Red Wall Canyon; bear right (north).

0.7 Enter Fall Canyon wash and turn right (northeast), heading upcanyon.

2.0 Prominent side canyon opens up on the left (northwest).

2.8 Enter short section of narrows.

3.3 Reach dry fall.

◀ *The precipitous gorge of Fall Canyon cleaves the west face of the Grapevine Mountains.*

4 Hells Gate to Death Valley Buttes

This rewarding cross-country day hike, recommended for experienced hikers, leads to a panoramic vista point along the eastern edge of central Death Valley.

Start: The cross-country route begins opposite (southwest of) the Hells Gate picnic site/parking area.
General location: Death Valley National Park; 17 miles southwest of Beatty, Nevada, and 11 miles northeast of Stovepipe Wells
Distance: 3.2 to 4.0 miles, round-trip or loop day hike, cross-country
Approximate hiking time: 1.5–2 hours
Difficulty: Moderate
Trailhead elevation: 2,260 feet
High point: 3,017 feet
Land status: National park

Best season: October through April
Water availability: None available; bring your own
Maps: USGS Stovepipe Wells NE, Chloride City; Death Valley National Park visitor map; USGS Death Valley National Monument and Vicinity, CA/NV (1:250,000 scale)
Fees and permits: No fees or permits required
Trail contact: Death Valley National Park, P.O. Box 579, Death Valley, CA 92328; (760) 786-2331; www.nps.gov/deva

Finding the trailhead: This hike begins at Hells Gate, a Y road junction and rest stop partway between Death Valley and Beatty, Nevada. Follow California Highway 190 east from Stovepipe Wells for 8.7 miles to the junction with the northbound road to Scotty's Castle; turn left (northwest), proceeding 0.7 mile to another junction. A sign here points to Beatty; turn right (northeast), following the paved road through Mud Canyon's badlands hills for 6.5 miles to the large parking area and road junction at Hells Gate. Picnic tables and Death Valley information are available here.

From the east, Nevada Highway 374 leaves U.S. Highway 95 in Beatty, leading 19 miles to the trailhead via Daylight Pass.

From the Furnace Creek Visitor Center, follow CA 190 northwest for 11 miles to the Beatty cutoff; turn right and reach the trailhead in 10 miles.

The Hike

Hikers with a desire to gain broad vistas of Death Valley must usually commit themselves to one or more strenuous days of trail-less desert walking to reach the distant peaks of the surrounding mountains. But the short scramble to Death Valley Buttes, three prominent hills at the foot of the Grapevine Mountains, should appeal to hikers without the time or energy required for more-demanding treks. For a modicum of effort, this short hike provides the feeling of accomplishment gained by forging your own route across a trail-less desert ridge, where the sweeping panoramas of central Death Valley and the tall mountains nearby are ample reward.

Each year with the onset of spring, a profusion of tiny yellow flowers decorates the creosote bush—California's most ubiquitous desert shrub.

The buttes are eroded remnants of the Grapevine Mountains, buried by detritus derived from that range by erosion. In a region as arid as Death Valley (Furnace Creek averages a scant 1.65 inches of moisture annually), little vegetation exists to control erosion. Over time fans of alluvium coalesce to form a continuous apron of debris at the foot of mountains, known to geologists as bahadas. As the mountains continue to erode, lower ridges are eventually buried in alluvium, until only isolated hills rise above this "sea" of sand, gravel, and boulders. In this phase, the alluvial surface is termed a pediment. Death Valley Buttes are surrounded by such a pediment, a vast sloping surface that stretches for miles along the foot of the Grapevine and Funeral Mountains. Other examples of a pediment and remnant mountains can be seen west of Ubehebe Crater on the flanks of the Last Chance Range.

The route to the buttes is straightforward and easy to follow, but the narrow rocky ridge that must be climbed is recommended only for experienced hikers. The hike can be taken as a round-trip or done as a loop. The area can be quite cool in winter and very hot at times during spring and fall. Hikers are likely to become

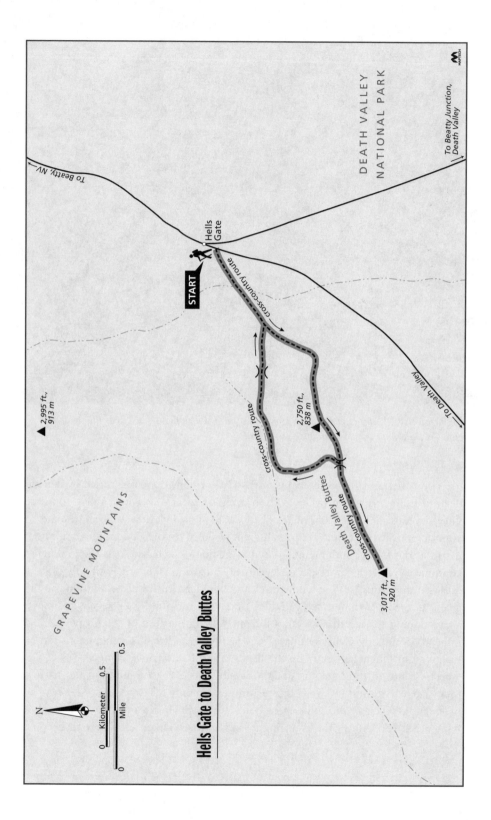

Hells Gate to Death Valley Buttes

GRAPEVINE MOUNTAINS

DEATH VALLEY NATIONAL PARK

To Beatty, NV

To Beatty Junction, Death Valley

To Death Valley

Hells Gate

START

cross-country route

cross-country route

Death Valley Buttes

cross-country route

▲ 2,995 ft., 913 m

▲ 2,750 ft., 838 m

▲ 3,017 ft., 920 m

N

Kilometer 0.5

0

Mile 0.5

0

dehydrated in the dry desert air, even on such a short hike as this, so carry plenty of water.

From Hells Gate proceed cross-country toward the buttes in a southwesterly direction. Quite soon you are likely to encounter remnants of the old phone line that connected the mining boomtowns of Rhyolite (near Beatty, Nevada) and Skidoo, high in the Panamint Mountains to the southwest, around the turn of the twentieth century.

A 0.6-mile jaunt across the cobble-strewn pediment allows hikers to become familiar with shrubs typical of the creosote bush scrub plant community, the most ubiquitous assemblage of shrubs in the California desert below 5,000 feet. Perpetually green creosote bush dominates and is especially attractive when covered with yellow blooms in early spring. Also common are bursage, desert holly saltbush, and beavertail cactus, which brightens the landscape with its delicate rose-colored springtime blooms. As you rise toward the buttes, desert trumpet, with their unusual bulbous stems, make an interesting addition to the scattered groundcover.

Soon leave the gentle terrain and scramble southward to the prominent ridgeline emanating from the easternmost butte. Upon attaining the crest, follow it westward over a few minor summits. The loose and broken rock makes for poor footing.

You may notice that creosote bush has been left behind, but desert holly saltbush persists on the dry and rocky ridge. This plant prefers dry, alkaline slopes and washes and is quite common below 3,000 feet in the Death Valley region. Brittlebush decorates the slopes of the buttes with its large yellow blooms in early spring.

Approaching the easternmost butte, following a semblance of a climber's trail helps you avoid more rugged sections of the narrow crest. Soon you reach the 2,725-foot summit, 1.0 mile from Hells Gate. Vistas are breathtaking, surveying a vast sweep of desert and mountain scenery. The apex of the buttes, Peak 3017, blocks much of the westward view, but in other directions there are no obstructions.

From here hikers have the option of backtracking to the trailhead or continuing on to the next, and highest, summit. To proceed, carefully descend the steep ridge west to a saddle at 2,450 feet. Ahead the narrow ridge ascends 500 feet in 0.6 mile to Peak 3017.

From the high point you will be rewarded for your efforts as you gaze out on the immense landscape of Death Valley. From the northwest to northeast, the Grapevine Mountains reach skyward, exceeding 6,000 feet. This range receives so little precipitation that not a single juniper can be seen in the highest reaches. The prominent, colorful peak to the north-northeast is Corkscrew Peak, about 6,000 feet. This mountain would make a fine destination for a strenuous day hike or overnighter. The route is plainly visible from this vantage point, following the broad alluvial fan northward from Hells Gate.

The equally barren Funeral Mountains stretch far into the southeastern distance. The extensive playa on the valley floor, glistening white with salt and alkali, reaches

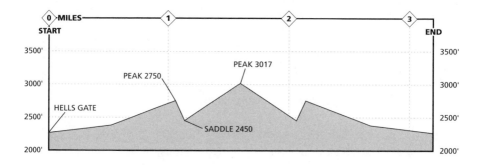

southeastward toward Badwater, which at -282 feet, is the lowest point on the continent. The impossibly high barrier of the Panamint Mountains rises above the valley in stark relief. The high point of the range, 11,049-foot Telescope Peak, may be sparkling with residual spring snow while the valley is baking in 100-degree heat.

The road leading to the valley from Hells Gate points westward toward massive Tucki Mountain, and north of there lie the sprawling sand dunes of Mesquite Flat. The Cottonwood Mountains form the western horizon—an immense, barren wall rising more than 8,000 feet from the valley floor.

At this point hikers can either return the same way to the trailhead or leave the crest at the above-mentioned 2,450-foot saddle. From there a possible route descends north to the valley below the buttes and then leads eastward north of the buttes and back to the trailhead. En route, hikers who keep their eyes peeled may find several sleeping circles, presumably used by native peoples during their hunting-gathering-trading forays through the valley.

Key points

0.0   Trailhead at Hells Gate.

1.0   Top out on Death Valley Buttes at Peak 2750.

1.6   Peak 3017.

5 Mosaic Canyon

This round-trip day hike follows a narrow, highly scenic canyon on the north slopes of Tucki Mountain, just south of Stovepipe Wells in Death Valley.

Start: The cross-country route begins at the south end of the road's end, immediately above Mosaic Canyon wash.
General location: Death Valley National Park; 30 miles southwest of Beatty, Nevada, and 2 miles south of Stovepipe Wells
Distance: 3.5-mile round-trip day hike
Approximate hiking time: 1.5–2 hours
Difficulty: Moderate
Trailhead elevation: 950 feet
High point: 2,000 feet
Land status: National park

Best season: October through April
Water availability: None available; bring your own
Maps: USGS Stovepipe Wells; Death Valley National Park visitor map; USGS Death Valley National Monument and Vicinity, CA/NV (1:250,000 scale)
Fees and permits: No fees or permits required
Trail contact: Death Valley National Park, P.O. Box 579, Death Valley, CA 92328; (760) 786-2331; www.nps.gov/deva

Finding the trailhead: From Stovepipe Wells Village on California Highway 190, 76 miles east of Olancha and U.S. Highway 395 and 24.8 miles northwest of Furnace Creek, proceed west along the highway to the MOSAIC CANYON sign and turn south. This dirt road is passable to passenger cars, but it is quite rough as it steadily ascends a broad, creosote bush–clad alluvial fan for 2.3 miles to the trailhead at the mouth of the canyon.

The Hike

The myriad canyons in the mountains of Death Valley National Park offer endless opportunities for both day hiking and venturing deep into mountain ranges on extended backpacks. Erosion in the often narrow canyons has exposed the rock strata in intricate detail, particularly in Mosaic Canyon, one of the most easily accessible canyons in Death Valley.

This canyon is a moderately popular day hiking area, owing to its proximity to the Stovepipe Wells tourist complex and its easy access. There is no trail in Mosaic Canyon; hikers simply follow the wash as far as their desire and ability will allow.

Keep an eye out for sidewinder rattlesnakes, the only poisonous snake in the park. Although they aren't as common here as in some other canyons, be alert when scrambling over and around dry falls in the upper reaches of the canyon. If rain—particularly thunderstorms—threatens, flash floods are a possibility and the hike should be avoided. As always, carry plenty of water on this or any desert hike.

From the trailhead, quickly drop into the canyon and follow the gravel bed of the wash upstream. Tucki Mountain's broken cliffs soar nearly a mile above. The wash

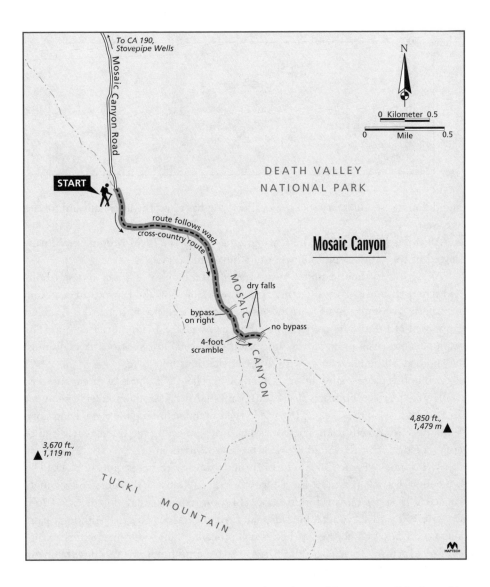

To CA 190,
Stovepipe Wells

N

0 Kilometer 0.5

0 Mile 0.5

DEATH VALLEY
NATIONAL PARK

Mosaic Canyon Road

START

route follows wash

cross-country route

dry falls

bypass
on right

no bypass

4-foot
scramble

Mosaic Canyon

MOSAIC

CANYON

4,850 ft.,
1,479 m

3,670 ft.,
1,119 m

TUCKI

MOUNTAIN

quickly leads hikers into a narrow chasm where beautiful stream-polished marble and mosaic breccia are well exposed. Much of the breccia (a formation composed of angular rock fragments recemented into stone) contains stream-polished marble set in a mosaic pattern.

After 0.3 mile the canyon bends east and widens a bit. Notice the stratified (layered) nature of the marble here. It is rock formed by the metamorphism of limestone

Many deep canyons afford easy access into the rugged mountains that surround Death Valley. Here hikers enjoy a leisurely stroll in colorful Mosaic Canyon, a popular day hike near Stovepipe Wells.

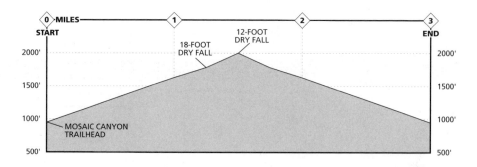

and dolomite (sedimentary rocks). Local faulting has tilted the layers upward toward the west.

All through the canyon, the soaring, broken cliffs of Tucki Mountain, virtually devoid of vegetation, are reminiscent of a lunar landscape.

Along this eastbound stretch, a use trail shortcuts the wash, where desert holly and desert trumpet make a fleeting appearance. But soon the canyon turns toward the south, becoming quite narrow once again. At one point, numerous boulders composed of breccia are wedged into the narrow gorge, forcing brief detours. The wash becomes even more narrow up ahead, and several low slickrock dry falls must be climbed. Some hikers may wish to terminate their hike here.

Along this narrow stint, hikers will enjoy excellent exposures of mosaic breccia, while gray marble dominates the wash up ahead. After 1.25 miles hikers encounter an 18-foot dry fall that is easily bypassed via a use trail climbing the right-hand slope about 50 yards downstream. There may be cairns indicating the route, which climbs above a ledge of marble amid creosote bush and Mormon tea.

At 1.5 miles Mosaic Canyon forks abruptly southward but is quickly blocked by a 12-foot dry fall (passable via a Class 3 ledge). Above, it becomes increasingly rugged. The larger canyon forking eastward soon requires a scramble over a 4-foot dry fall; 150 yards beyond, a high dry fall further impedes progress. Although passable via a Class 4 climb, average hikers will probably want to terminate their excursion here, pausing to soak up the barren yet majestic beauty of this desert canyon before backtracking to the trailhead.

Key points

0.0 Mosaic Canyon trailhead.

1.25 Reach 18-foot dry fall; bypass via path on the right (south) side.

1.5 Reach 12-foot dry fall.

6 Wildrose Peak

This fine round-trip day hike leads to a lofty Panamint Range summit, from which hikers can see the highest and lowest points of land in the contiguous United States.

Start: The trail begins immediately northwest of the charcoal kilns.
General location: Death Valley National Park; 23 miles south of Stovepipe Wells and 52 miles southeast of Lone Pine
Distance: 8.4-mile round-trip day hike
Approximate hiking time: 4–5 hours
Difficulty: Strenuous
Trailhead elevation: 6,870 feet
High point: Wildrose Peak, 9,064 feet
Land status: National park
Best season: Mid-April through November

Water availability: None available; bring your own
Maps: USGS Telescope Peak, Wildrose Peak; Death Valley National Park visitor map; USGS Death Valley National Monument and Vicinity, CA/NV (1:250,000 scale)
Fees and permits: No fees or permits required
Trail contact: Death Valley National Park, P.O. Box 579, Death Valley, CA 92328; (760) 786-2331; www.nps.gov/deva

Finding the trailhead: Proceed to the Wildrose Ranger Station in Wildrose Canyon, located in the west-central reaches of the park. To get there, follow California Highway 178 east from Ridgecrest, then north past Trona and into the Panamint Valley. After driving 52.6 miles, bear right onto the paved Trona-Wildrose Road. You'll reach the junction with the northbound Emigrant Canyon Road after another 9.7 miles.

Alternately, from California Highway 190, 9.3 miles southwest of Stovepipe Wells Village in Death Valley, follow the southbound Emigrant Canyon Road through the Panamints for 21 miles to the aforementioned junction. A sign at the junction indicates that Wildrose Campground (open year-round, with water and thirty campsites at 4,100 feet) is 0.25 mile and the charcoal kilns are 6 miles east (up the canyon).

Proceed generally eastward from that junction; drive past the campground and ranger station and follow the narrow paved road as it climbs into the broad valley of Wildrose Canyon. The pavement ends after 5 miles; the wide but rough dirt road leads another 2 miles to a wide turnout opposite the charcoal kilns. Park here.

The Hike

Of the few established trails that exist in the vast reaches of Death Valley National Park, most are very short nature trails that barely scratch the surface of the Death Valley hiking experience. Most Death Valley hikes are desert hikes, and caching water is a necessity for extended treks. By contrast, the two moderately long maintained trails to Telescope and Wildrose Peaks offer a mountain hiking experience.

The lofty Panamint Range stands high enough to bear the distinction of being the wettest area in the park. This island of high country hosts vast stands of piñon-juniper woodland and, atop 11,049-foot Telescope Peak, a forest of bristlecone pine.

These beehive-shaped charcoal kilns, located at the Wildrose Peak trailhead, offer hikers a glimpse into the colorful history of the region before they start on their climb to the panoramic viewpoint in the Panamint Range.

Aside from the sweeping vistas enjoyed from Wildrose Peak, the most notable features of this hike are the ten charcoal kilns at the trailhead. Constructed in 1876, the kilns supplied charcoal from the piñon-juniper woodlands of Wildrose Canyon to the Modoc Mine in the Argus Range, 20 miles distant across the Panamint Valley. The charcoal was necessary to process lead and silver ore. A pamphlet available at the trailhead describes the history of the kilns in detail.

This hike begins at the kilns and climbs through woodlands among scattered stumps dating back to the mining days to the crest of the Panamints and ultimately to Wildrose Peak, where an awe-inspiring panorama of desert and mountains unfolds. The popular trail to Telescope Peak, beginning a rough 2 miles up the road from the charcoal kilns, often remains closed by snow until mid to late May in most years. The trail to Wildrose Peak, even though it climbs above 9,000 feet, opens much earlier due to its southern exposure, and the vistas enjoyed from its summit rival those obtained from nearby Telescope. Even during summer, when Death Valley is sizzling in 120-degree-plus heat, Wildrose Peak remains relatively cool and is a pleasant jaunt until the snow flies.

Regardless of the temperature or season, be sure to carry an adequate water supply. And note that flies and gnats can be bothersome during summer.

The trail begins just northwest of the kilns, indicated by a small sign. An easy traverse ensues, passing above Wildrose Canyon amid a woodland of Utah juniper and singleleaf piñon, where sagebrush and Mormon tea form a scattered understory. From the start, views are magnificent. Westward lies the rugged High Sierra, from Mount Whitney southward beyond solitary Olancha Peak, framed by the broad foreground valley of Wildrose Canyon. That formidable alpine barrier, capped by giant granite crags and perpetually white with snow, is especially attractive on a hot summer day. Beyond the trough of the Panamint Valley to the west lies the Argus Range, former site of the Modoc and other rich mines, which blocks the remainder of the southern Sierra from view. Numerous trailside junipers are host to the parasitic juniper mistletoe, which may eventually kill some of these gnarled high-desert trees.

Proceeding into a shallow wooded canyon, the trail—actually an old doubletrack—descends slightly to reach the canyon bottom where, after 0.9 mile, it joins another old doubletrack (closed) southwestbound down the canyon. Bearing right, the grade becomes moderate as you ascend northeastward. Scattered stumps upslope to the south may be remnants of the trees cut during the heyday of the charcoal kilns, still well preserved in the dry climate of the Panamints.

After 1.2 miles, the trail passes a USGS water level recording device. A pause here reveals a fine view southward to the north slopes of lofty Rogers Peak, named for a member of the ill-fated party of settlers who became stranded in Death Valley in 1850. That peak's slopes, scarred by a road serving a transmitting facility, hosts snowfields that last through May in most years.

Beyond, cliffrose makes its debut among the understory, and in May penstemon decorates trailside slopes. The route soon narrows to a trail and rises steeply under the partial shade of the thick piñon-juniper woodland. Presently, old man prickly pear, bearing an armor of formidable spines, and buckwheat further diversify the understory.

After 1.8 miles the trail attains the crest of the Panamints at a 7,750-foot saddle, then begins a traverse upon the east-facing slopes, where hikers capture vignettes of the vast white playa on Death Valley's floor, lying 8,000 feet below. The Spring Mountains in southwestern Nevada, crowned by 11,918-foot Charleston Peak, form the distant eastern horizon when not obscured by clouds or late spring and summer heat haze.

At first the trail gives away a little elevation, but it soon begins climbing once again upon crunchy metamorphic rocks. The woodland briefly thins out, soon dominated by compact, conical piñons, offering even better views into the valley and the desert ranges beyond.

The grade soon eases as you regain the crest at 8,000 feet, where your destination, the broad dome of Wildrose Peak, looms closely ahead. The trail now climbs

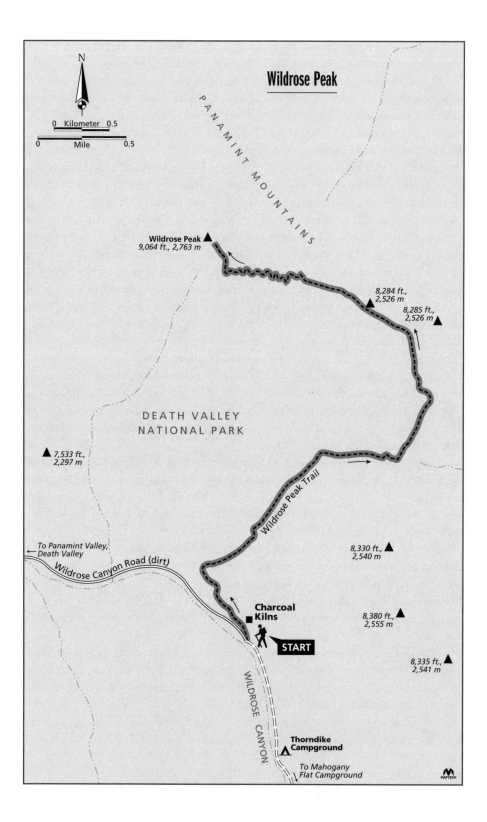

upon wooded south-facing slopes, where views of Rogers Peak and forested Telescope Peak are enjoyed. Dropping slightly into a wide saddle, hikers gear up for the final 900-foot ascent.

The trail then climbs steeply on or just north of the crest, where a few switchbacks help ease the grade. Prickly pear, sagebrush, buckwheat, lupine, and some penstemon grow on the rocky slopes amid scattered piñons. Junipers, preferring lower and drier elevations, are absent at this point.

Soon the trail begins ascending in earnest via switchbacks, elevating hikers beyond the last wind-flattened piñons and onto a false summit. Proceeding gently along the open, rocky crest, you reach the peak in another 0.2 mile.

From the small but flat summit area where sagebrush, Mormon tea, and prickly pear thrive, an unobstructed 360-degree panorama unfolds—more than ample reward for your efforts. Nearly the full length of Death Valley spreads out at your feet, stretching 90 miles from northwest to southeast. Beyond it rises the barren Amargosa Range, separated by fault zones into three distinct subranges. Beyond it are other desert ranges—the Nopah, Kingston, Resting Spring, and others—fading into the distant heat haze of the California and Nevada desert. The tree-clad oasis of Furnace Creek stands out on the searing flats of Death Valley below to the northeast.

Directly below to the northeast, exceedingly steep slopes, briefly clad in piñon-juniper woodland, fall away into the South Fork of Trail Canyon, where a few old mine buildings reflect the desert sun nearly 5,000 feet below. Beyond Trail Canyon, the layered east slopes of the Panamints dip steeply toward the east, indicating that portion of this fault-laced range is being downdropped along its eastern side. Just west of those layered slopes, the dirt road ending at Aguerreberry Point is visible. Hikers who so desire can continue beyond the peak, following the crest of the range to that road, but a car shuttle is necessary.

Northwest, the Panamints merge with the massive Cottonwood Mountains, plunging more than 1.5 vertical miles into Death Valley. Farther still are the White Mountains, crowned by 14,246-foot White Mountain Peak.

Barely a sliver of the Panamint Valley is visible to the west, above which rises the Argus Range and Inyo Mountains. On the western horizon is perhaps the most

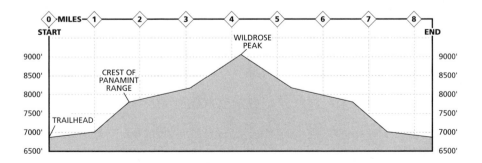

inspiring vista of all—the jagged summits of the Sierra Nevada, stretching from the Palisades in the northwest to Owens Peak in the southwest and including the incomparable heights of Mount Whitney. Far to the south, past the eroded ranges of the Mojave Desert, are the San Gabriel Mountains.

From the peak simply retrace your steps to the trailhead.

Key points

0.0 Charcoal kilns, Wildrose Peak trailhead.

0.9 Junction with southwestbound doubletrack in Wildrose Canyon; stay right (northeast).

1.8 Crest of Panamint Range at 7,750-foot saddle.

4.2 Summit of Wildrose Peak.

7 Nemo Canyon to Mud Spring

This trail-less hike follows the broad wash of Nemo Canyon between fluted canyon walls, ending at a rare desert oasis.

Start: The cross-country route begins at the mouth of Nemo Canyon wash.
General location: Death Valley National Park; 24 miles south-southwest of Stovepipe Wells and 47 miles southeast of Lone Pine
Distance: 4.0-mile round-trip day hike
Approximate hiking time: 2 hours
Difficulty: Moderate
Trailhead elevation: 3,200 feet
High point: 4,000 feet
Land status: National park
Best season: October through April

Water availability: None available; bring your own
Maps: USGS Maturango Peak NE, Jail Canyon, Emigrant Pass; Death Valley National Park visitor map; USGS Death Valley National Monument and Vicinity, CA/NV (1:250,000 scale)
Fees and permits: No fees or permits required
Trail contact: Death Valley National Park, P.O. Box 579, Death Valley, CA 92328; (760) 786-2331; www.nps.gov/deva

Finding the trailhead: From Ridgecrest, follow California Highway 178 east then north past Trona and into the Panamint Valley. After driving 56 miles, bear right onto the paved Trona-Wildrose Road. You'll reach the signed park boundary after another 3.2 miles and pass a water tank (for radiator water) at 5.9 miles. Nemo Canyon (unsigned) opens up on the left (north), 7.2 miles from the junction in Panamint Valley. (If you reach a picnic site in Wildrose Canyon, you've driven 0.9 mile too far.) There are a few wide shoulders on the east side of the road on which to park.

Alternately, from California Highway 190, 9.3 miles southwest of Stovepipe Wells Village in Death Valley, follow the southbound Emigrant Canyon Road through the Panamint Range for 21 miles to the junction with Trona-Wildrose Road, branching left (east) to the charcoal kilns and west to Panamint Valley. Turn right (west) at the junction and follow the winding, steeply descending road for another 2.5 miles to the mouth of Nemo Canyon.

The Hike

Nemo Canyon claims only modest beginnings on the west slope of the Panamint Range, about halfway between Emigrant Pass and Wildrose Peak. Starting as a minor drainage across a moderately high alluvial fan, Nemo Canyon trends west, then turns abruptly southwest and carves into a landscape composed of breccia (ancient angular rock fragments cemented into stone), where you find dramatic cliffs sculpted into fluted buttresses by ages of erosion. Halfway through this dramatic canyon is the seep of Mud Spring, a rare and precious source of water for a variety of wildlife, including bighorn sheep and many other mammals, birds, and reptiles. Respect this source of water as the lifeblood of native wildlife, and linger here only briefly.

Fluted cliffs embrace Nemo Canyon in the western reaches of Death Valley National Park.

From Trona–Wildrose Road, head north into the broad flood-scoured mouth of Nemo Canyon. The rabbitbrush-fringed wash is strewn with gravel that affords a moderately firm tread, not too soft to impede steady progress. Although you gain elevation steadily, you will best appreciate the moderate gradient of the wash on your return trip downcanyon.

Near the canyon's mouth the intricately carved buff-toned cliffs rise 400 to 500 feet above, displaying great columns and fluted chimneys. After about 1.0 mile, the cliffs begin to fade in the distance behind you and the canyon becomes flanked by badlands slopes colored in shades of gray, red, yellow, and brown.

After walking upcanyon for about an hour and 2.0 miles from the trailhead, begin looking for a series of three shallow draws that open up on the left (north) side of the canyon, each fringed with thorny mesquite at its confluence with Nemo Canyon. The first (westernmost) draw contains Mud Spring. Follow the narrow wash of this first draw northward for about 150 yards where, behind a pair of exotic tamarisk trees, you'll find the aptly named muddy seep of Mud Spring. Immediately

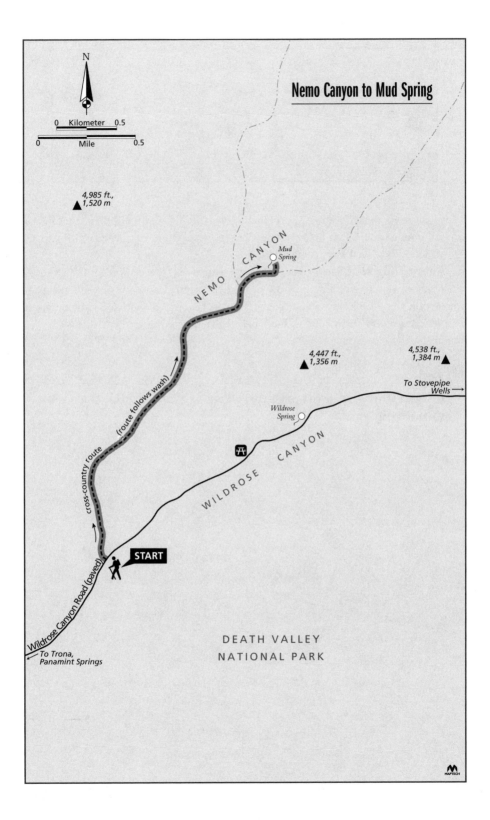

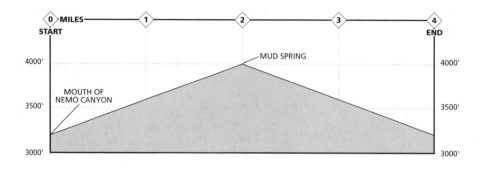

above the seep, tucked away in perpetual shade, you'll find a small tinaja, or tank—a small pool of water that helps sustain the tenacious wildlife that make this part of Death Valley National Park their home.

After visiting Mud Spring, you may have gained an appreciation for the tenuous existence of desert wildlife and how critical these rare oases are to their survival. Please don't stay too long at Mud Spring. Instead, find a place with a good view back in Nemo Canyon for a lunch break before backtracking to the Trona-Wildrose Road.

Key points

0.0 Mouth of Nemo Canyon on Wildrose Canyon Road.

2.0 Mud Spring.

8 Darwin Falls

This short hike follows one of only four perennial streams in Death Valley National Park, leading through areas of riparian vegetation en route to a spectacular and rare desert waterfall.

Start: The trail begins at the south edge of the parking area, behind the interpretive sign.
General location: Death Valley National Park; 30 miles southwest of Stovepipe Wells and 32 miles southeast of Lone Pine
Distance: 2.0-mile round-trip day hike
Approximate hiking time: 1 hour
Difficulty: Easy
Trailhead elevation: 2,490 feet
High point: 2,770 feet
Land status: National park
Best season: October through May

Water availability: Perennial water in Darwin Wash; treat before drinking or bring your own
Maps: USGS Darwin; Death Valley National Park visitor map; USGS Death Valley National Monument and Vicinity, CA/NV (1:250,000 scale)
Fees and permits: No fees or permits required
Trail contact: Death Valley National Park, P.O. Box 579, Death Valley, CA 92328; (760) 786-2331; www.nps.gov/deva

Finding the trailhead: From U.S. Highway 395 in Ridgecrest, follow California Highway 178 east then north past Trona and into the Panamint Valley. After driving 56 miles, turn left onto the Panamint Valley Road where it branches northwest from Trona-Wildrose Road. Follow this road for another 14 miles to the junction with California Highway 190, then turn left (west). Drive through Panamint Springs 2.6 miles west of the junction; 1 mile beyond the small resort, turn left (west) onto a dirt road signed DARWIN FALLS.

This graded dirt road is often rough and rocky, but it is usually passable to cars. After 2.4 miles a 4WD road branches left, leading to old mines in the Argus Range. Stay right at that junction and proceed 100 feet to the parking area at the Darwin Falls trailhead.

The Hike

Darwin Falls is perhaps the most uncharacteristic locale in Death Valley National Park, its setting beyond the scope of most people's perceptions of the quintessential desert landscape. Darwin Creek is one of the four perennial streams in the park's more than three-million-acre expanse of desert valleys and mountains. Darwin Wash drains the westernmost reaches of the park, flowing from the volcanic tableland of Darwin Bench between the Inyo Mountains to the north and the Argus Range to the south. With its ribbon of riparian greenery and echoes of cascading water in a land that sees little rain, a walk through the shadowed hallway of Darwin Wash may be the most unique short day hike in the park.

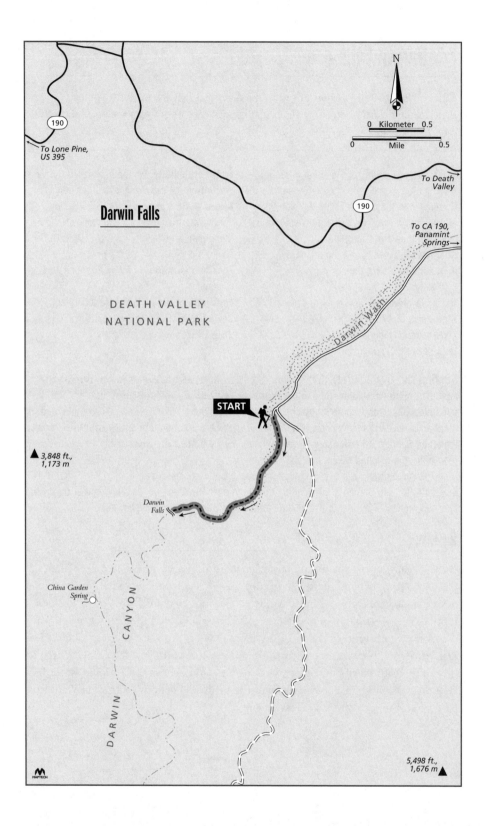

Darwin Falls

N

0   Kilometer   0.5

0   Mile   0.5

190

To Lone Pine,
US 395

190

To Death
Valley

To CA 190,
Panamint
Springs→

DEATH VALLEY
NATIONAL PARK

Darwin Wash

START

▲ 3,848 ft.,
1,173 m

Darwin
Falls

China Garden
Spring

CANYON

DARWIN

5,498 ft.,
1,676 m ▲

MAPTECH

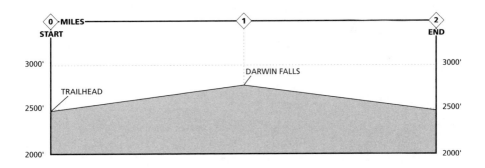

The trail begins as a long-closed doubletrack leading south (upcanyon) from the barricade at the trailhead. Follow the wash for several hundred yards to another barricade that spans the width of the canyon. Flowing water usually appears in the wash shortly beyond the barricade. Rabbitbrush fringes the wash, while a scattering of creosote bush and other coarse shrubs stud the broken limestone cliffs that flank the canyon.

In 0.5 mile the canyon begins to bend west and cleaves the volcanic landscape of Darwin Plateau. Here riparian vegetation begins to crowd the wash bottom, dominated by cattail and seep willow. The old doubletrack ends at the bend of the canyon; continue upcanyon on the singletrack of foot trail. Ahead the trail will lead you back and forth across the small stream, sometimes over slippery rocks, past a stream-gaging station, and finally to a lovely pool at the foot of the boisterous 20-foot cascade of Darwin Falls. This is a delightful grotto, where the music of the falls, rich hanging fern gardens, canopy of spreading willows, and cool, shady confines of the canyon combine to create a magical retreat, especially on a hot desert afternoon.

Key points

0.0 Darwin Falls trailhead.

1.0 Darwin Falls.

9 Coffin Peak

This view-filled hike, recommended for hikers with routefinding experience, leads to a mile-high summit in the Black Mountains near Dante's View.

Start: The cross-country route begins at the east edge of the picnic site parking area, east of Dante's View.
General location: Death Valley National Park; 20 miles southeast of Furnace Creek Visitor Center
Distance: 2.5-mile round-trip day hike
Approximate hiking time: 1–1.5 hours
Difficulty: Moderate
Trailhead elevation: 5,200 feet
High point: Coffin Peak, 5,503 feet
Land status: National park

Best season: October through May
Water availability: None available; bring your own
Maps: USGS Dante's View; Death Valley National Park visitor map; USGS Death Valley National Monument and Vicinity, CA/NV (1:250,000 scale)
Fees and permits: No fees or permits required
Trail contact: Death Valley National Park, P.O. Box 579, Death Valley, CA 92328; (760) 786-2331; www.nps.gov/deva

Finding the trailhead: From the junction of California Highway 190 and Badwater Road just south of Furnace Creek Visitor Center in Death Valley, proceed eastward via CA 190 past the Furnace Creek Inn, following Furnace Creek Wash southeastward. After 3.5 miles the short spur road to Zabriskie Point (see Hike 10) forks right. Continue on the highway to the signed junction with the road to Dante's View, 10.8 miles from Badwater Road. Drivers approaching from the east will find this turnoff immediately below and west of the 2000 FEET elevation sign, 16.2 miles northwest of Death Valley Junction on California Highway 127. Turning south here, follow a canyon east of the Black Mountains, ignoring a left-forking road leading to Ryan and the Butte Mine en route. Beyond the junction with Greenwater Road (dirt) leading to Shoshone, your road climbs a broad alluvial surface, ascending steadily into the Black Mountains. After 12.7 miles from CA 190, a sign indicates NO TRAILERS BEYOND THIS POINT. Turn left (south) here and park in the wide turnout, featuring pit toilets and a picnic table. Dante's View lies 0.6 mile up the road—a viewpoint famous for its tremendous vistas of Death Valley and the surrounding countryside.

The Hike

Experienced hikers driving to Dante's View are urged to take the easy cross-country jaunt to Coffin Peak, where equally unforgettable vistas can be enjoyed in solitude from this fine vantage point atop the Black Mountains. This seldom-trod route is not particularly notable for wildflowers, but some desert trumpet and Indian paintbrush adorn the trail.

This hike may entice you to return for extended treks in the Black Mountains. Water sources are virtually nonexistent, and it is necessary to cache water along the crestline route. A southbound trek along the Black Mountains' crest offers endless

Tall barrel cactus is a common denizen of the hot deserts of southern California.

panoramas, a true desert wilderness experience, and access to old mine ruins, including the mining-boom camp of Furnace. The Greenwater Road offers easy access to hikers establishing water caches.

The hike begins at the picnic site perched atop the crest of the range. Proceed over a minor hill, paralleling Dante's View Road just north of east. A few creosote bushes persist here in the upper limits of their range, but vegetation on the hike is dominated by members of the Shadscale Scrub plant community. At this point Mormon tea, shadscale, and spiny menodora—typical rigid, spiny desert shrubs—dominate the arid upper reaches of the range along with abundant grasses.

Soon the ridgecrest jogs southeast and you climb the first major rocky hill; note the debut of horsebrush and boxthorn among the previously cited shrubs. Topping out on this 5,360-foothill, proceed east along the broad crest amid desert-varnished boulders, enjoying views into Death Valley and the Panamint Mountains to one side and the prominent peaks of the southern Funeral Mountains on the other. Once over the next hill, your route descends 50 feet northeastward to a saddle along the narrow crest, only to climb once again to Hill 5484, not as rocky as the last hill.

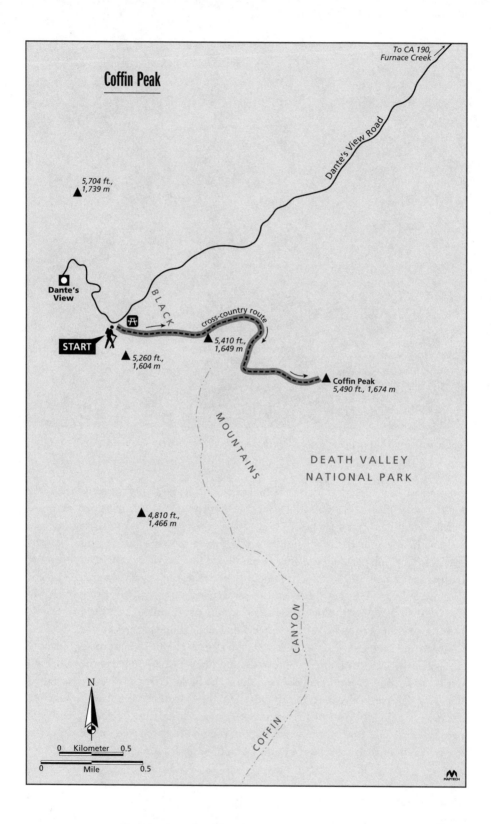

Coffin Peak

To CA 190,
Furnace Creek

Dante's View Road

▲ 5,704 ft.,
1,739 m

Dante's
View

cross-country route

START

▲ 5,260 ft.,
1,604 m

▲ 5,410 ft.,
1,649 m

▲ Coffin Peak
5,490 ft., 1,674 m

B L A C K

M O U N T A I N S

DEATH VALLEY

NATIONAL PARK

▲ 4,810 ft.,
1,466 m

C A N Y O N

C O F F I N

N

0   Kilometer   0.5

0   0.5
Mile

MAPTECH

Past this broad summit the crestline route jogs south then east as hikers enjoy increasingly expansive views. The conical summit to the southeast is Coffin Peak, today's goal. Bending eastward, a faint path can be used to avoid the rockiest section of the ridge as it drops to another saddle. A final ascent gaining 150 feet brings you to the commanding viewpoint of Coffin Peak.

The vista includes the dark peaks of the Black Mountains marching off toward the south and southeast, beckoning the adventurous to explore their seldom-visited environs. The broad expanse of the Greenwater Valley, clad in a perpetually green blanket of creosote bush, spreads out below to the east, and rising beyond are the eroded slopes of its namesake range. To the northeast, the prominent, colorfully layered southeastern peaks of the Funeral Mountains, featuring aptly named Pyramid Peak, lie in the foreground of the distant Amargosa Desert. Charleston Peak and the lofty Spring Mountains rise to form the eastern skyline 70 miles away in Nevada. Toward the southeast, prominent desert mountains include the Nopah and Kingston Ranges.

South slopes drop abruptly from the peak into the gaping maw of Coffin Canyon, its broad wash disappearing below into a narrow gorge flanked by the contorted red and black strata of the Copper Canyon conglomerate, a rock formation approximately ten million years old. Beyond those colorful foothills, Mormon Point juts out into the valley floor to the south; at the southern end of the valley are the Owlshead Mountains.

The broad alluvial fans draping the foot of the Panamint Mountains to the west are some of the most extensive such fans in the park. Those mountains, tilted eastward along an active fault zone, boast the greatest precipitation in the park. That moisture has washed a great deal of debris that has eroded from the mountains and subsequently deposited it at the eastern foot of the range. As floodwaters lose velocity, they dump first boulders, then gravel, and finally sand that over time forms the fans.

Death Valley is also being tilted toward the east and is actively sinking in relation to the surrounding ranges. This tilting has pushed the salt pan, or playa, toward the foot of the Black Mountains. The small fans at the foot of this range can be in part

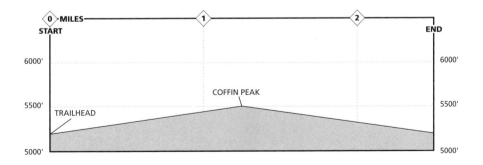

attributed to the relative youth of this fault block range; the fans here have not had as much time to develop as have those in the Panamints.

The great relief of the eastern wall of the Panamints, rising 11,331 feet in 15 lateral miles, is exceeded in only three other locations in North America. But the relief of the nearby Inyo Mountains and Sierra Nevada rivals that of the Panamints, with each range rising more than 10,000 feet above neighboring valleys. This is representative of the Great Basin landscape, where actively rising ranges abut actively sinking basins and valleys.

The sinking block of Death Valley, termed a graben by geologists, is the sump for the Amargosa River drainage, which arises northwest of Las Vegas in the Charleston Mountains of southwestern Nevada. In the past, when the climate was wetter, 600-foot-deep Lake Manly occupied Death Valley, fed not only by the waters of the Amargosa but also by the Owens and Mojave Rivers.

Closer at hand, shadscale and grasses clothe the summit, while a few formidable barrel cacti, and some boxthorn grow nearby. On the northwestern skyline, Dante's View and its usual crowds of sight-seers is in view but seemingly a world away. After enjoying this isolated yet easily accessible locale, hikers usually backtrack to the trailhead.

Key points

0.0 Trailhead at picnic site below Dante's View.
1.25 Coffin Peak.

10 Golden Canyon to Zabriskie Point

This memorable hike tours the starkly beautiful badlands landscape that central Death Valley is famous for.

Start: The trail begins at the mouth of Golden Canyon, behind the trail sign.
General location: Death Valley National Park; 4 miles southeast of Furnace Creek Visitor Center
Distance: 6.0-mile round-trip day hike
Approximate hiking time: 2.5–3 hours
Difficulty: Moderate
Trailhead elevation: 160 feet below sea level
High point: Zabriskie Point, 710 feet
Land status: National park
Best season: November through April

Water availability: None available; bring your own
Maps: USGS Furnace Creek; Death Valley National Park visitor map; USGS Death Valley National Monument and Vicinity, CA/NV (1:250,000 scale)
Fees and permits: No fees or permits required
Trail contact: Death Valley National Park, P.O. Box 579, Death Valley, CA 92328; (760) 786–2331; www.nps.gov/deva

Finding the trailhead: From the Furnace Creek Visitor Center on California Highway 190 in Death Valley, follow the highway south then east for 1.2 miles to a paved southbound road (California Highway 178) signed BADWATER. Proceed south on this road for 2 miles to a sign indicating Golden Canyon; turn left, reaching the parking area within 100 yards.

Hikers approaching the park from the south should take the Baker exit off Interstate 15 and follow California Highway 127 north for 56 miles to the small town of Shoshone. Slightly less than 2 miles north of town, turn left (west) onto CA 178. Follow this road for 68.8 miles to the Golden Canyon trailhead.

To shuttle a car to Zabriskie Point, or to begin the hike there, stay left on CA 190 at the junction with Badwater Road (1.2 from the Furnace Creek Visitor Center), and drive 3.5 miles to the signed Zabriskie Point parking area.

The Hike

This spectacular low-elevation hike tours the finest badlands scenery in the park and makes a fine winter jaunt when many other hiking areas are buried in snow. But beyond incredible scenery, the badlands of Golden Canyon offer insights into one of the more recent episodes of geologic history in the park, a region that is rich in fully exposed rock strata representing millions of years of earth history.

The initial 1.1 miles of the hike along the wash in Golden Canyon are a self-guiding nature trail. The guide available at the trailhead is keyed to numbered posts in the canyon, describing features along the way.

This canyon bottom segment is an easy jaunt for most any hiker, but the badlands can intensify the searing desert heat and should be avoided from midspring

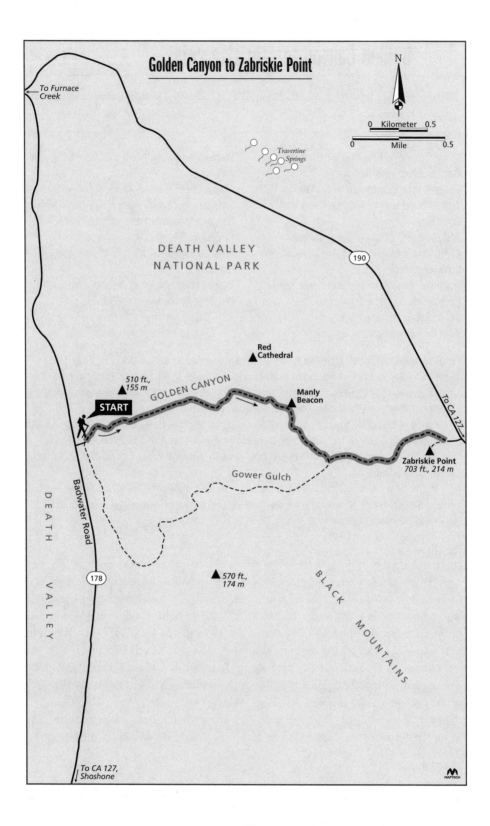

through midautumn. The segment from the canyon to Zabriskie Point is more demanding, with moderate climbing and no shade. Even during the cooler months, hikers should wear a hat and carry plenty of water.

Your trip to Zabriskie Point begins at the mouth of Golden Canyon, where bright red rocks quickly give way to dark brown conglomerate and layers of green mudstone. Remnants of the old oiled road that once enabled visitors to drive through the canyon persist only along the initial 0.1 mile, the remainder having been washed away by infrequent but often torrential flash floods.

The likelihood of being rained on in the canyon is indeed remote—the weather station at Furnace Creek records an average of only 1.65 inches of moisture annually. Entire years have passed without any significant moisture, giving Death Valley the distinction of being one of the driest regions in North America.

Shortly, yellow siltstones and mudstones dominate in the canyon. These soft rocks and those at the canyon's mouth are part of the Furnace Creek Formation, deposited in desert lakebeds three to eight million years ago. These sediments contain evaporites, or salt deposits, which are formed as saline water evaporates. Borax is one of the evaporites present in these sediments, and the twenty-mule-team wagons that hauled borax out of the valley are a famous part of the region's history.

The canyon remains quite narrow throughout its length, wedged between broken cliffs and badlands slopes. It is seemingly lifeless, save for the buzzing of a few insects and ravens soaring and croaking among the hills and cliffs.

As you proceed, the fluted cliffs of Red Cathedral, at the head of the canyon, loom even closer. Sighting a striking yellow pinnacle rising skyward to the east (Manly Beacon), you soon reach Post 10 at the end of the self-guiding nature trail, 1.1 miles from the trailhead. At this point, hikers can either return to the trailhead, continue up the canyon for 0.4 mile to the foot of Red Cathedral, or turn right onto the trail bound for Zabriskie Point.

Hikers turning right follow the trail into the heart of the badlands via a narrow gully. Ignore the numerous use trails climbing nearby slopes. Soon the trail climbs steeply to a sidehill ascent beneath the face of Manly Beacon, topping out on a 480-foot saddle at 1.6 miles. Superb views, framed by the badlands of Golden Canyon, extend westward to the mesquite-fringed salt pan of Death Valley and to the Panamint Range beyond. The upthrust strata flanking Golden Canyon are seen in raw detail—truly a landscape standing on edge. Southward, the colorful Black Mountains rise abruptly above the extensive badlands, which stretch eastward toward your goal, Zabriskie Point.

Amid a confusion of use trails, an arrow sign in the gully below to the south indicates the correct route. Descending at first, the trail then undulates through the badlands to a wash feeding Gower Gulch at 1.9 miles. This area is fun to explore (on a cool day), and hikers reaching Gower Gulch may notice evidence that the canyon is occasionally swept by an unusually large amount of runoff for a canyon with such a

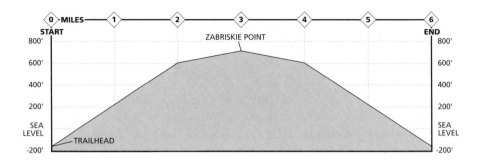

small drainage area. The reason is that the Park Service has diverted Furnace Creek Wash into the gulch just south of Zabriskie Point to protect the developments at Furnace Creek from destructive flash floods.

An alternative route to retracing your steps to the trailhead follows Gower Gulch generally southwest from this point for 1.4 miles to the mouth of the gulch. There you can bypass a high dry fall on the right (north), then follow a boot-worn path along the foot of the badlands. You return to the trailhead after 2.1 miles, completing a grand 4.0-mile loop through Death Valley's most colorful badlands.

To reach Zabriskie Point, watch for arrow signs that help guide you over hills and across gullies to the trail's terminus at the point after hiking 3.0 miles, 50 yards west of the parking area. From the point, the eroded badlands are seen in their entirety—the foreground for distant views of Death Valley and the immense bulk of the Panamint Range.

Hikers who haven't arranged a car shuttle to Zabriskie Point must retrace the route to the Golden Canyon trailhead or loop back via Gower Gulch.

Key points

0.0 Golden Canyon trailhead.

1.1 Post 10, end of nature trail. Backtrack to trailhead, continue 0.3 mile upcanyon to Red Cathedral, or turn right (east), heading for Zabriskie Point.

1.6 Top out on 480-foot saddle.

1.9 Junction with southwestbound route leading down Gower Gulch; bear left to reach Zabriskie Point.

3.0 Zabriskie Point.

11 Desolation Canyon

This lightly used route follows a narrow, serpentine canyon through a landscape of colorful badlands. The hike is an excellent alternative to often-busy Golden Canyon (Hike 10).

Start: The trail begins along the east edge of the road's end.
General location: Death Valley National Park; 6 miles southeast of Furnace Creek Visitor Center
Distance: 3.0-mile round-trip day hike
Approximate hiking time: 1–1.5 hours
Difficulty: Moderate
Trailhead elevation: 40 feet
High point: 600 feet
Land status: National park
Best season: November through April

Water availability: None available; bring your own
Maps: USGS Furnace Creek; Death Valley National Park visitor map; USGS Death Valley National Monument and Vicinity, CA/NV (1:250,000 scale)
Fees and permits: No fees or permits required
Trail contact: Death Valley National Park, P.O. Box 579, Death Valley, CA 92328; (760) 786–2331; www.nps.gov/deva

Finding the trailhead: Follow driving directions for Hike 10 to reach the junction of California Highway 190 and Badwater Road, and turn south onto Badwater Road. Pass the Golden Canyon trailhead after 2.0 miles, and continue south for another 1.7 miles to an eastbound dirt road, signed NO CAMPING. Turn left (east) onto this graded dirt road; after 0.5 mile stay left at a Y-junction. The road ends 0.9 mile from Badwater Road, at the foot of the badlands just southwest of Desolation Canyon wash.

The Hike

This fine short hike, an uncrowded alternative to nearby Golden Canyon, surveys the dramatic badlands landscape eroded from the Furnace Creek Formation at the foot of the Black Mountains along the eastern edge of Death Valley. The trail-less hike actually follows an unnamed canyon (the east fork of Desolation Canyon), a longer and deeper gorge than Desolation Canyon proper.

From the trailhead follow a boot-worn path generally east across badlands slopes for a few hundred yards to the east fork's wash, where you turn right (southeast) and proceed upcanyon. Unlike typical desert washes, the floor of this one is hardpacked and the walking is easy. Badlands slopes, barren of vegetation, flank the canyon, colored in pastel shades of red, green, yellow, and tan. Vegetation in the canyon is limited to widely scattered low gray desert holly bushes.

After a few minutes of walking, the canyon suddenly becomes a shady, narrow corridor through the badlands, where only 10 to 15 feet of space separate the canyon walls. After 0.5 mile you reach a point where rock stair-steps up to an 8-foot

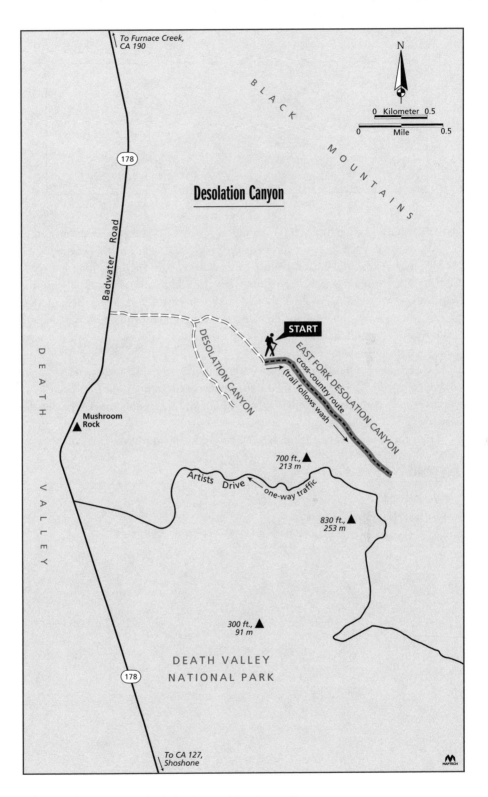

Desolation Canyon

To Furnace Creek,
CA 190

B L A C K

M O U N T A I N S

N

0 Kilometer 0.5

0 Mile 0.5

178

Badwater Road

DESOLATION CANYON

START

EAST FORK DESOLATION CANYON

cross-country route

(trail follows wash

D E A T H

Mushroom
Rock

700 ft.,
213 m

Artists   Drive

one-way traffic

830 ft.,
253 m

V A L L E Y

300 ft.,
91 m

DEATH VALLEY

NATIONAL PARK

178

To CA 127,
Shoshone

MAPTECH

◀ *Colorful badlands typify the landscape of Desolation Canyon.*

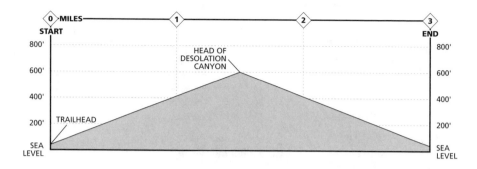

dry fall. Large and wide hand- and footholds make this an easy obstacle to surmount.

Above the dry fall the canyon opens up briefly and bends first to the left, then to the right. At the right-hand bend two washes diverge, one branching left (east) and the other, narrower wash branching right (south). Continue by following the narrower south-trending wash. A short distance above the fork, you reach another dry fall, this one only 6 feet high and easily ascended. The canyon ahead is wider and shallower than its middle reaches, allowing continuous views of the colorful badlands.

At 1.1 miles you reach another major confluence of washes separated by green- and red-shaded hills. From here follow the smaller wash to the right (southeast). The wash abruptly ends after 1.5 miles, where a high and impassable dry fall blocks the way.

From the dry fall, backtrack down the colorful canyon to the trailhead.

Key points

0.0 Trailhead.

1.5 Head of Desolation Canyon.

12 Natural Bridge Canyon

This outing is one of the most rewarding short hikes in Death Valley National Park. It features an exciting walk into a precipitous canyon that leads to a rare natural bridge, an arch of stone that spans the narrow canyon.

Start: The trail begins behind the interpretive sign.
General location: Southeast Death Valley National Park; 15 miles southeast of Furnace Creek Visitor center
Distance: 2.0-mile round-trip day hike
Approximate hiking time: 45 minutes–1 hour
Difficulty: Moderate
Trailhead elevation: 330 feet
High point: 1,200 feet
Land status: National park
Best season: November through April

Water availability: None available; bring your own
Maps: USGS Devils Golf Course; Death Valley National Park visitor map; USGS Death Valley National Monument and Vicinity, CA/NV (1:250,000 scale)
Fees and permits: No fees or permits required
Trail contact: Death Valley National Park, P.O. Box 579, Death Valley, CA 92328; (760) 786-2331; www.nps.gov/deva

---

Finding the trailhead: Follow driving directions for Hike 10 to reach the junction of California Highway 190 and Badwater Road, and turn south onto Badwater Road. After 13 miles, turn left (northeast) onto a dirt road signed NATURAL BRIDGE. This graded road is usually passable to cars, but expect it to very rough with severe washboards. The road ascends steadily, sometimes steeply, up an alluvial fan for 1.6 miles to the trailhead parking area at the foot of the Black Mountains.

The Hike

The short hike to Natural Bridge visits a rare rock span that arcs across the narrow, shady defile of lower Natural Bridge Canyon, one of myriad precipitous gorges on the west face of the Black Mountains in the southeast reaches of Death Valley National Park. The brief stroll to the bridge is an excellent leg stretcher for families touring the park, and hikers with extra energy are urged to hike as far as the impassable dry fall 1.0 mile from the trailhead.

An interpretive signboard at the trailhead offers insights into the fascinating geology of Natural Bridge Canyon. Hikers should read the sign; its information will greatly enhance your appreciation of the canyon and its rare natural bridge.

The well-worn trail leads east into the mouth of Natural Bridge Canyon from behind the interpretive sign. You quickly join the gravelly wash and turn left (northeast), heading upcanyon. The broken canyon walls are composed of the Furnace Creek Formation, the weathered fragments of which comprise the sand, gravel, and

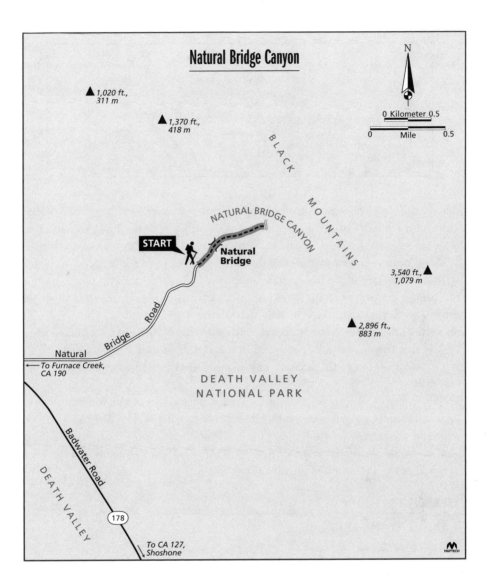

Natural Bridge Canyon

▲ 1,020 ft., 311 m

▲ 1,370 ft., 418 m

BLACK MOUNTAINS

NATURAL BRIDGE CANYON

START

Natural Bridge

0 Kilometer 0.5

0 Mile 0.5

N

▲ 3,540 ft., 1,079 m

▲ 2,896 ft., 883 m

Natural Bridge Road

← To Furnace Creek, CA 190

DEATH VALLEY NATIONAL PARK

Badwater Road

DEATH VALLEY

178

To CA 127, Shoshone

rocks in the bed of the wash. Dried mud coats the canyon walls like so much plaster, and water-polished chutes show where infrequent but often torrential runoff drains from the rockbound Black Mountains above.

After 0.4 mile, the natural bridge appears just ahead, an arch of stone that spans the canyon about 40 feet above the wash bottom. Although the canyon carries water

◀ *Natural Bridge spans the shadowed gorge of lower Natural Bridge Canyon in the Black Mountains.*

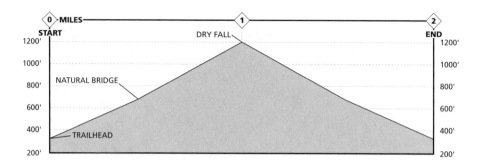

only in times of heavy precipitation, water was the principal sculptor of the bridge. You can see an ancient stream channel on the north side of the bridge; floodwaters once followed this channel around the resistant rock layer that comprises the bridge.

Most visitors return to the trailhead from the bridge, but hikers curious about what lies ahead are urged to continue upcanyon. Follow the wash upcanyon beyond the bridge, looking for fault caves and other evidence of rock movement on the canyon walls, including offset sedimentary strata, as you continue. About 0.3 mile above the bridge, gray bedrock appears and stair-steps up the wash, forming a series of low dry falls. These falls can be easily climbed, but at 1.0 mile you reach an impassable 20-foot dry fall that will stop all but determined hikers with rock climbing skills.

The notch in the canyon above the dry fall frames a dramatic picture of the rock-bound, precipitous west face of the Funeral Mountains, rising thousands of feet above. As you retrace your steps through the shadowed canyon back to the trailhead, you will enjoy occasional views of the Death Valley salt pan far below and the great east wall of the Panamint Mountains rising beyond.

Key points

0.0   Natural Bridge trailhead.
0.4   Natural Bridge.
1.0   Dry fall.

13 Sheephead Pass

This rarely used cross-country route, recommended for experienced desert hikers only, leads to the crest of the Ibex Hills in the southeastern corner of Death Valley National Park, where far-ranging vistas unfold across miles of rugged mountain ranges along the California–Nevada border.

Start: The cross-country route leads southeast from the parking area.
General location: Southeast Death Valley National Park; 45 miles southeast of Furnace Creek Visitor Center and 10 miles southwest of Shoshone
Distance: 4.4-mile round-trip day hike or overnighter; part cross-country
Approximate hiking time: 2 hours
Difficulty: Moderate
Trailhead elevation: 2,970 feet
High point: Sheephead Pass, 3,410 feet
Land status: National park

Best season: October through May
Water availability: None available; bring your own
Maps: USGS Salsberry Peak; Death Valley National Park visitor map; USGS Death Valley National Monument and Vicinity, CA/NV (1:250,000 scale)
Fees and permits: No fees or permits required
Trail contact: Death Valley National Park, P.O. Box 579, Death Valley, CA 92328; (760) 786-2331; www.nps.gov/deva

Finding the trailhead: There is no real trail to Sheephead Pass, nor is there a "trailhead." The directions below will guide you to a good and fairly easy-to-find starting point.

Follow driving directions for Hike 10 to reach the junction of California Highway 190 and Badwater Road, and turn south onto Badwater Road. Follow this road south through Death Valley, eventually leaving the valley and ascending to Jubilee Pass after 50.2 miles. The highway descends eastward from the pass and then begins ascending toward Salsberry Pass. You will reach Milepost 30, 7.7 miles from Jubilee Pass; 0.8 mile beyond the milepost, look for a dirt road that turns sharply southwest from a turnout on the south side of the highway, 0.1 mile below and west of the ELEVATION 3000 FEET sign. Turn onto this dirt road and follow it southwest for about 200 yards, where you can park in wide spots along the road shoulder.

Alternately, hikers approaching from the east via California Highway 127 should turn west onto California Highway 178, 26 miles south of Death Valley Junction and 1.5 miles north of Shoshone. Follow CA 178 generally west for 12.3 miles to Salsberry Pass. One mile west of the pass you reach Milepost 31; 0.2 mile beyond, you will find the southwest-branching dirt road, just below the ELEVATION 3000 FEET sign.

The Hike

The broad, low gap of Sheephead Pass separates the colorful rocky summits of Sheephead Mountain to the northwest, composed of calico volcanic rocks, from the broad, dark mass of Ibex Peak and the Ibex Hills to the southeast. This fine, pleasant

Vistas from Sheephead Pass stretch past the Ibex Hills Wilderness to distant mountains along the California/Nevada border.

day hike, cross-country much of the way, leads across open desert to a panoramic viewpoint on the southeast boundary of Death Valley National Park.

From your parking area follow a southeast course, heading toward the twin summits of Ibex Peak, rising on the distant skyline. The route ahead, leading east-southeast, is one of your own choosing, and you will dip into and rise out of innumerable gullies. Vegetation en route is dominated by creosote bush, which shares space with boxthorn, white bursage, and cheesebush.

Most hikers will reach Bradbury Wash, the main wash draining Sheephead Pass, in about twenty minutes. At this point adjust your course by following this shallow drainage generally eastward. Along the southern margins of the wash you may notice a faint, long-closed doubletrack. Although it is not essential to locate this track, it can help you stay on course. Be sure to continue generally east toward the low gap of Sheephead Pass, and avoid minor drainages that branch northeast toward Sheephead Peaks and southeast toward Ibex Peak. Consult your topo map frequently.

Views into the rugged Sheephead Peaks are excellent all along the way. As you gradually rise higher you will enjoy vistas to the Owlshead and Panamint Mountains to the southwest and west and to the basalt-capped Black Mountains to the northwest.

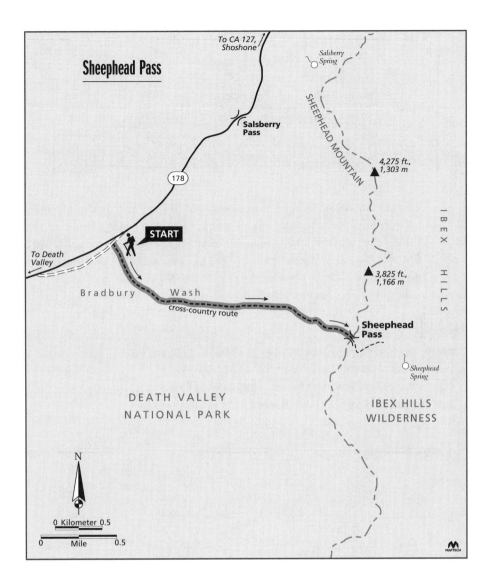

Sheephead Pass

To CA 127, Shoshone

Salsberry Spring

SHEEPHEAD MOUNTAIN

Salsberry Pass

178

4,275 ft., 1,303 m

START

To Death Valley

Bradbury   Wash
cross-country route

3,825 ft., 1,166 m

IBEX HILLS

Sheephead Pass

Sheephead Spring

DEATH VALLEY
NATIONAL PARK

IBEX HILLS
WILDERNESS

N

0 Kilometer 0.5

0   Mile   0.5

MAPTECH

As you approach the head of the wash, you will reach a fork at the western base of a prominent knob stacked with dark gray boulders and a cairn. From there follow the smaller wash to the left, curving around the north and east sides of the knob. Soon an old road becomes obvious as it exits the left (east) side of the wash and quickly leads you to the open ridge at Sheephead Pass, 2.2 miles from the trailhead, at 3,410 feet. Here you will find a low rock wall, rusty cans, bottles, and other relics left behind long ago by prospectors.

Vistas from the pass are memorable and include the multicolored Sheephead Peaks and the Black and Panamint Mountains. Yet the eastward views are truly the

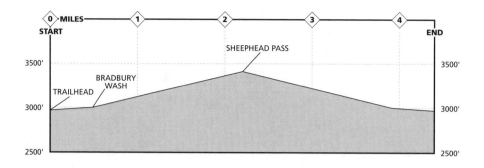

most spectacular. An unnamed canyon drops eastward through the BLM's Ibex Hills Wilderness, cutting a gorge past dark crags and a pair of bold rocky knobs. In the distant northeast, beyond the broad valley of the Amargosa Desert, is the rocky west wall of first the Nopah Range, then the Resting Spring Range, and finally the Spring Mountains in Nevada, crowned by 11,900-foot Charleston Peak.

From Sheephead Pass, carefully retrace your route to the trailhead.

Key points

0.0 Trailhead on CA 178 immediately west of and below 3,000 FEET elevation sign; begin hiking southeast toward Bradbury Wash.

0.5 Reach Bradbury Wash, then turn left (east), hiking up the wash.

2.2 Top out on the crest of the Ibex Hills at 3,410-foot Sheephead Pass.

Mojave National Preserve

The Mojave Desert—that vast expanse of rock, sand, and sparse vegetation that lies between Los Angeles and Las Vegas—is to many people a barren wasteland, a place to drive through as quickly as possible on the way to somewhere else. Yet the Mojave isn't as barren as it might first appear, and the diversity of landscapes here is unequaled in the deserts of the American West.

Perhaps the best of the Mojave, an area known as the East Mojave, has been protected within the confines of the 1.6-million acre Mojave National Preserve, an area administered by the National Park Service. The preserve is the third largest U.S. park unit outside Alaska. Only Death Valley and Yellowstone National Parks are larger. Nearly half of Mojave National Preserve, some 695,000 acres, are protected as wilderness. All but two of the hikes in this chapter are located inside that wilderness.

The preserve's modest elevations and dry weather make the area a superb destination from late fall through midspring, when higher mountain hiking areas are buried in snow. These hikes will lead you to rare groves of Rocky Mountain white fir trees, the world's largest Joshua tree woodland, and the California desert's most extensive area of sand dunes. You may see some of the diverse wildlife that dwells here, including feral burros, jackrabbits, antelope ground squirrels, mule deer, bighorn sheep, and roadrunners. Most of the hikes follow closed roads; the only three constructed foot trails in the preserve are also included in this chapter.

14 Lanfair Valley to Fort Piute

This interesting day hike leads to the only perennial stream in the eastern Mojave Desert. Part of the hike retraces the steps of westbound pioneers along the old Mojave Road.

Start: The trail begins at the east edge of the parking area, on the rim of Piute Gorge.
General location: Mojave National Preserve; 40 miles northwest of Needles
Distance: 4.7-mile loop day hike
Approximate hiking time: 2–2.5 hours
Difficulty: Moderate
Trailhead elevation: 3,450 feet
High point: Piute Hill, 3,600 feet
Land status: National preserve (administered by National Park Service)
Best season: October through May

Water availability: No potable water available; bring your own
Maps: USGS Signal Hill, Homer Mountain; Trails Illustrated Mojave National Preserve (Map 256)
Fees and permits: No fees or permits required
Trail contact: National Park Service, Mojave National Preserve, 222 East Main Street, Suite 202, Barstow, CA 92311; (760) 255-8801; www.nps.gov/moja

Finding the trailhead: Follow Interstate 40 for 108 miles east from Barstow or 34 miles west from Needles to the Goffs exit. Leave the freeway here and proceed 12 miles northeast to Goffs, your last source of gas and other services. Turn left (northwest) at Goffs onto Lanfair Road, which is paved for the first 10 miles and graded dirt thereafter. About 16 miles from Goffs, the signed Cedar Canyon Road branches left; 100 yards beyond, turn right onto an eastbound dirt road indicated by a small PT&T sign pointing east. Follow this fairly narrow graded dirt road, avoiding several lesser used roads branching right and left. After 5.6 miles bear left where a sign indicates the Rattlesnake Mine and a right-forking road. Ahead, your undulating road becomes narrower and rougher, simply a service road accessing a buried telephone cable. About 3.4 miles from the Rattlesnake Mine junction, the road crosses a sandy wash that may present an obstacle to vehicles with low clearance. As the road approaches the foot of the low Piute Range 9.5 miles from Lanfair Road, turn left onto a poor dirt road just before reaching a cattle guard. This road has a high center in places but is passable to carefully driven passenger cars. Proceeding north, pass the Mojave Road (the return leg of the loop) and a corral. In 1.3 miles reach the trailhead, a large turnout on the east side of the road overlooking Piute Gorge.

The Hike

Insights into natural history—from folding and faulting exposed in a rugged canyon to streamside, or riparian, vegetation (unique in the eastern Mojave Desert), to trailside petroglyphs along the Old Government (or Mojave) Wagon Road—are among the many attractions of this fine day hike.

Portions of this unique hike trace part of the Mojave Road. This route, established along old Indian trails, was a major travelway for settlers and mail carriers during the

A hiker ponders the meaning of trailside petroglyphs in Piute Canyon, located in the eastern reaches of Mojave National Preserve.

latter half of the nineteenth century between Prescott, Arizona, and Los Angeles. The route evolved into a wagon road, and its course took advantage of the few water sources scattered throughout the Mojave Desert. Since this route passed through Indian lands, there were inevitably conflicts between travelers and the native population. As a consequence, a series of five redoubts, or temporary forts, were constructed between Fort Whipple near Prescott, Arizona, and Camp Cady near Daggett, California.

"Fort Pah-Ute" was one such redoubt, located on a sun-baked hillside near the perennial waters of Piute Creek. This was the first stop for westbound travelers beyond the crossing of the Colorado River. This fort was occupied by as many as eighteen enlisted men between the fall of 1867 and the spring of 1868, who escorted travelers through Indian lands. By 1883, as the more southerly route of the Southern Pacific Railroad was completed, the Mojave Road had fallen into disuse.

Today a 130-mile segment of this historic route can be traced across the eastern Mojave Desert, and much of its course is popular with 4WD enthusiasts. But since much of this hike passes through a wilderness area closed to motor vehicles, hikers

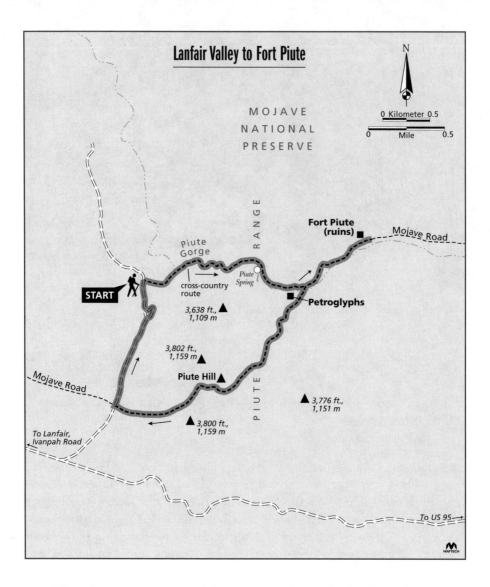

Lanfair Valley to Fort Piute

MOJAVE
NATIONAL
PRESERVE

Piute Gorge

PIUTE RANGE

Fort Piute
(ruins)

Mojave Road

START

cross-country
route

Piute
Spring

3,638 ft.,
1,109 m

Petroglyphs

3,802 ft.,
1,159 m

Piute Hill

3,776 ft.,
1,151 m

Mojave Road

3,800 ft.,
1,159 m

To Lanfair,
Ivanpah Road

To US 95

can follow the route at a wagon's pace, contemplating the hardships those hardy nineteenth-century pioneers faced daily on their long westward journeys.

This trip is a fine choice for a winter or spring day hike, when many other hiking areas remain buried in snow. Campsites are scarce, and those who choose to stay overnight should remember to camp at least 300 feet from water sources and that no camping is allowed within the fort ruins. Carry an ample water supply, and don't drink from Piute Spring unless you first purify the water.

Before beginning your hike, pause to enjoy the view before plunging into the canyon below. The broad expanse of Lanfair Valley stretches westward toward the unusual mesa of Table Mountain and northwest to the pinnacle-capped crest of the New York Mountains. To the north and south is the low volcanic ridge of the Piute Range, and below you Piute Gorge cuts northward into a scenic badlands landscape.

The trail descends eastward at first upon the resistant band of conglomerate that forms the rim of the gorge, quickly reaching a saddle littered with black volcanic boulders and decorated with creosote bush and bunchgrass. The trail then bends north, descending steeply into the dry wash of Piute Gorge; turn right, following the wash downstream. Almost at once, pass an obvious fault zone on the canyon wall, at a contact zone between volcanic breccia and gray volcanic rocks, where the strata dips downward toward the west.

Spring wildflowers that add color to the rugged, rocky canyon include Indian paintbrush and the yellow blossoms of hymenoxis. The canyon is quite narrow as you follow a serpentine course through the Piute Range. Broken cliffs and pinnacles of red and gray rock rise as much as 300 feet above, the strata sliced, offset, and contorted by numerous minor faults and folds. A particularly noticeable S-shaped fold offers insights into the dynamic geologic processes that created and continue to shape the landscape of the Mojave Desert.

The hiking is easy along the gravel and slickrock bed of the wash. Mojave yucca, beavertail, and barrel cactus dot the broken slopes above. As the canyon bends southeast, it suddenly becomes choked with tamarisk, willows, and desert willows. Also present are the tall, yellow flower stalks of prince's plume. A little bushwhacking lies ahead, and 1.0 mile from the trailhead you reach Piute Spring, where a vigorous flow of water issues from the canyon floor. Shaded by tall willows, the spring is a veritable oasis surrounded by parched desert.

To continue, hikers must forge their way through dense streamside vegetation along the trickling stream for 0.3 mile. Beyond this obstacle, the canyon opens up considerably where a southwest-trending canyon joins on the right. Hikers returning from the fort ruins should take the trail that leads south from this point to quickly join the Mojave Road.

Presently, cross the creek and follow the eastbound trail traversing the slope north of the wash, thus avoiding the thick vegetation that chokes the canyon bottom. Mojave yuccas, barrel cactus, cholla, and a variety of flowering shrubs clothe this sun-drenched south-facing slope. Soon the fort ruins come into view to the east. Piute Valley, framed by the slopes of Piute Canyon, stretches away beyond, while the Dead Mountains and hazy desert ranges in Arizona reach to the horizon.

About 1.7 miles from the trailhead, a row of volcanic boulders just south of the trail feature some fine petroglyphs; farther on, more carved boulders lie next to the trail. Soon thereafter the trail joins the end of the rough dirt road climbing up from Piute Valley, 1.8 miles from the trailhead. Two ruins of low rock walls are all that remain after more than one hundred years to remind us of the short-lived Fort Piute redoubt. The lower and larger rock wall of the corral lies just above the road end to the north. Above it lies the blockhouse, its walls built of native stone and slightly better preserved than the corral. With a little imagination one can visualize the lonely life soldiers led at this remote desert outpost. It is not surprising that the desertion rate was high. Not only was there the bleak, parched desert stretching away more than 100 miles in all directions, but the lure of nearby gold fields also must have been adequate inducement for many to abandon Army life.

From the fort, return 0.5 mile to the aforementioned canyon fork, and turn left (south), quickly joining the Mojave Road. Almost at once, wagon wheel ruts are visible where the road crosses a stretch of red rock. As you proceed southwest up the canyon, a boulder just south of the road features another fine petroglyph. Be sure not to disturb or deface any Indian artifacts you may encounter; leave them for others to appreciate.

Ahead the route alternates between the wash and open slopes but eventually abandons the wash and begins the steep climb over Piute Hill. The road is eroded and overgrown in places with creosote bush, but otherwise it has changed little since its heyday. Hiking the road allows you to contemplate the arduous journey of early settlers across the empty desert.

Views are somewhat limited by nearby slopes and ridges as you ascend, but you'll notice an increase in Mojave yucca on adjacent slopes. One mile from the fork of the canyon and 800 feet above the fort, the road tops out on the Piute Range at a saddle known as Piute Hill. From here broad vistas meet your gaze to the south, west, and north. The Mojave Road can be traced westward as it stretches away into the valley below.

From the hill the road winds steeply down the west slope amid abundant cholla and Mojave yucca. Hikers have the option of proceeding northwest cross-country for 1.0 mile to the trailhead, where cars are visible below, or following the Mojave Road for 0.5 mile to the edge of the valley, crossing a fenceline en route. From the juncture of the Mojave Road and the trailhead access road, turn right and stroll 0.9 mile to the trailhead, in spring enjoying the lavender blooms of beavertail cactus and the yellow flowers of hymenoxis along the way.

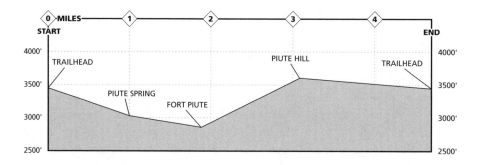

Key points

0.0 Trailhead.

1.0 Piute Spring.

1.3 Southwest-trending canyon opens up on the right. (Upon returning from Fort Piute, this is where you'll turn left (southwest) onto the trail leading to the Mojave Road.)

1.8 Fort Piute ruins.

2.3 Return to southwest-trending canyon and turn left (southwest).

3.3 Top out on Piute Hill.

3.8 Junction of Mojave Road and trailhead access road; turn right (north) to return to trailhead.

4.7 Trailhead.

15 Keystone Canyon to New York Peak

This rigorous but rewarding day hike leads you from a well-vegetated desert canyon to a remote granite crag in the New York Mountains. The peak features far-ranging vistas and supports a small grove of white fir trees, very rare in the Mojave Desert.

Start: The doubletrack trail continues west into Keystone Canyon from the suggested parking area.

General location: Northeast Mojave National Preserve; 50 miles northwest of Needles and 42 miles east of Baker

Distance: 4.5-mile round-trip day hike, part cross-country

Approximate hiking time: 3 hours

Difficulty: Strenuous

Trailhead elevation: 5,450 feet

High point: New York Peak, 7,463 feet

Land status: National preserve (administered by National Park Service)

Best season: Mid-April through mid-December (summers are hot but tolerable atop the peak)

Water availability: None available; bring your own

Maps: USGS Ivanpah; Trails Illustrated Mojave National Preserve (Map 256)

Fees and permits: No fees or permits required

Trail contact: National Park Service, Mojave National Preserve, 222 East Main Street, Suite 202, Barstow, CA 92311; (760) 255-8801; www.nps.gov/moja

Finding the trailhead: From Interstate 15, 37 miles northeast of Baker and 54 miles southwest of Las Vegas, Nevada, take the Nipton Road exit, also signed for Searchlight. This paved road leads southeast for 3.6 miles to its juncture with Ivanpah Road, signed for Cima. Turn right and proceed south here on Ivanpah Road, avoiding the right-forking Morning Star Mine Road after another 3.3 miles. Your road proceeds southeast toward the massive New York Mountains, eventually crossing the railroad tracks and jogging east. The pavement ends after another 8.6 miles, and the graded dirt road climbs over a low ridge. Bear right 4.7 miles from the pavement where Hart Mine Road branches left. A one-lane dirt road forks right (southwest) 1.2 miles farther, where Ivanpah Road begins a southeastward bend. Turning right onto this unsigned road, avoid a left-forking road almost at once, staying right on the wider road. Bear right again after 0.6 mile and reach a left-forking mining road 2.4 miles from Ivanpah Road just before dipping into the wash of Keystone Canyon. Another spur of the mining road forks left just past the wash. Since the main canyon road ahead is narrow with little parking space and is passable only to high-clearance vehicles, most hikers should consider turning left here and proceeding the short distance to a wide parking area.

The Hike

The scramble to New York Peak is not only a rewarding hike to vast panoramas on a mountain "island" in a desert "sea," it is also a trip into the past, where relict plant species survive from a time when the eastern Mojave Desert enjoyed a cooler and wetter climate.

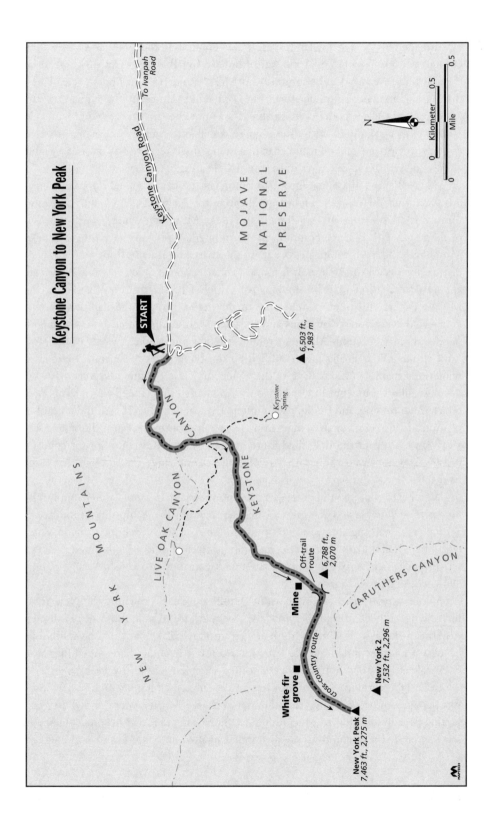

Keystone Canyon to New York Peak

START

Keystone Canyon Road

To Ivanpah Road

MOJAVE NATIONAL PRESERVE

▲ 6,503 ft., 1,983 m

Keystone Spring ○

KEYSTONE CANYON

LIVE OAK CANYON

○

NEW YORK MOUNTAINS

Off-trail route

▲ 6,788 ft., 2,070 m

Mine ■

Cross-country route

CARUTHERS CANYON

▲ New York 2 7,532 ft., 2,296 m

White fir grove ■

▲ New York Peak 7,463 ft., 2,275 m

N

0 Kilometer 0.5

0 Mile 0.5

Surrounded by vast lowlands, desert ranges such as the New Yorks rise high enough to capture substantial moisture from passing Pacific storms. In summer, as tropical moisture invades the region from Mexico and rises on updrafts created by the mountain masses, thunderstorms are generated. Although the climate of the Mojave Desert has become considerably drier since the last Ice Age (approximately 10,000 years ago), the moisture those ranges are able to milk from passing storms is enough to nurture plant species that have long since retreated to more favorable climes, such as the high ranges of southern California.

Silktassel and yerba santa, shrubs common on the damp coastal slopes of southern California, thrive in the higher elevations of the New York Mountains. But most unusual is the presence of a small stand of Rocky Mountain white fir near the crest of the range. This is a tree common in the montane forests in the southern Rocky Mountains, and a related species occurs in the coastal mountains from southern California northward to Oregon. It is found primarily above 6,000 feet where average annual precipitation may be double that which falls on the New Yorks. In the Mojave Desert, this tree is found only in the highest ranges: the Kingston, Providence, and New York Mountains and on Clark Mountain, which hosts the largest stand—about 1,000 trees. All the incredible biologic and scenic diversity of the New York Mountains is finally preserved behind the boundaries of federally designated wilderness, thanks to the passage of the California Desert Protection Act of 1994.

This hike should be undertaken only by hikers experienced in cross-country travel, route finding, and boulder scrambling. Experienced hikers can find a number of routes to the crest of the range, from where the summit is but a short scramble away. A variation of the described route goes by way of Keystone Spring, climbs a brushy draw southward to an east-trending limestone ridge, and follows that ridge west to the crest and on to the peak.

Whichever route you choose, carry a topo map and an ample water supply. The hike is most suitable as a day hike, as there are few possible campsites en route.

From the parking area, proceed up the rough road into Keystone Canyon. Vegetation here is abundant and diverse, including singleleaf piñon, Utah juniper, silktassel, turbinella oak, yerba santa, prince's plume, sagebrush, squawbush, Apache plume, cliffrose, and Mojave sage.

As the canyon turns south, imposing granite pinnacles crowning the New Yorks form a rugged backdrop to the wooded canyon. After 0.6 mile avoid an old mining road that forks right, leading south then west into Live Oak Canyon. One-tenth mile beyond is another junction. The left fork ascends a tributary canyon, ending after 0.25 mile at Keystone Spring, where another possible route to the peak begins.

Bear right, climbing higher into Keystone Canyon, which becomes increasingly wooded, presently including ceanothus, serviceberry, Mojave yucca, snowberry, and prickly pear in addition to previously cited flora. This old road becomes steep and severely eroded as it climbs to an abandoned small-scale copper mine and ends 1.5

miles from the trailhead. Old ore car tracks extend outward from the mine shaft, and the colorful copper ores of azurite (blue) and malachite (green) litter the ground nearby. Be sure not to drink the water seeping from this (or any other) mine shaft.

Ahead lies a strenuous but short, brushy scramble leading to the ridge above on the southwestern skyline. This area lies at the contact zone of the limestone that dominates the terrain to the east and the granite that is prevalent to the west. Two steep, southwest-trending gullies rise toward that ridge from the mine, and hikers can follow either to reach their objective.

The left-hand gully, cut into limestone, has remnants of an old mining trail and passes two more mine shafts, but it is a rough scramble on loose rock with much bushwhacking. The advantage of following the right-hand gully is that it climbs through granite, offering more stable footing, but the path is equally brushy.

Ascending either gully, hikers will enjoy a neck-stretching view of a prominent granite pinnacle looming boldly on the crest above. The climb ends after 0.2 mile, 500 feet above the mine, on a narrow saddle with a shallow prospect pit and more colorful copper ore. To gain the crest of the range, leave the limestone ridge, climbing steep slopes westward among granite boulders and gaining another 500 feet in 0.3 mile. The footing is good, making this climb less strenuous than the last.

Turbinella oak dominates the understory here, while in spring cryptantha adds a touch of fleeting color. Juniper persists, but two-needle (or Colorado) piñon has supplanted its singleleaf cousin. Botanists consider the two-needle piñon also to be a relict species in California; it's found only in the New Yorks and the Little San Bernardino Mountains in the California desert.

Finally, attain the crest of the range just south of the towering granite pinnacle. From here follow the crest southwest, scrambling over and around the boulders that dot the ridge. You'll likely be entertained by flocks of colorful violet-green swallows as they swoop and soar among the crags.

When the crest begins to trend more toward the south, begin looking for a shady north-facing slope on your right. Upon this slope you'll see a few of the thirty white firs that grow among the thick forest of piñons.

Ahead looms New York Peak (7,463 feet), and to its left lies New York 2 (7,532 feet). Hikers not inclined to scale those crags may want to terminate their hike here along the crest. To reach either summit, continue along the rugged ridge. Class 3 and 4 routes are required to attain both peaks. More challenging routes on these peaks and nearby crags should appeal to any rock climber.

While vistas from the summits are unsurpassed in all the Mojave Desert, those enjoyed from the crest are also far-reaching and panoramic. The broad Ivanpah Valley lies almost at your feet to the north, stretching past Ivanpah Dry Lake into Nevada. On the northern horizon are the Spring Mountains and lofty Charleston Peak in Nevada. Far to the northeast and more than 100 miles distant, the Virgin Mountains form the horizon near the Utah/Nevada/Arizona border.

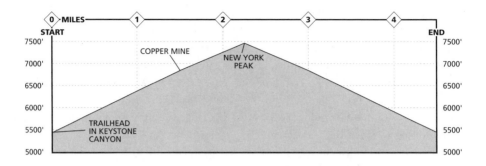

Eastward, beyond the invisible Colorado River trench, rise the desert mountains of western Arizona, including the Hualapai Mountains near Kingman, Arizona. Southeastward, ranks of low mountains march into the distant haze of the Colorado Desert. Toward the southwest, the San Jacinto, San Bernardino, and San Gabriel Mountains form the horizon 125 miles distant, seen over a sea of arid desert ranges. Cima Dome and Teutonia Peak lie closer at hand to the west. In the northwest rises the prominent bulk of Clark Mountain, and farther still are Telescope Peak and the Panamint Range in Death Valley National Park.

Hikers must eventually leave this rugged and remote range, carefully retracing their route to the trailhead.

Key points

0.0 Trailhead in Keystone Canyon; follow doubletrack westward, upcanyon.

0.3 Wilderness boundary.

0.6 Junction with southbound doubletrack leading to Live Oak Canyon; stay left (southeast).

0.7 Junction with southeast-branching doubletrack leading to Keystone Spring; bear right (southwest).

1.5 End of doubletrack at old copper mine; ascend steeply southwest, cross-country to the ridge crest above.

1.7 Top out on narrow saddle, then turn west, ascending to the New York Mountains' crest.

2.0 Crest of New York Mountains; turn left and follow crest southwest.

2.1 White fir trees on north slopes below crest.

2.25 New York Peak.

16 Cima Road to Teutonia Peak

This memorable short hike, one of the most popular in Mojave National Preserve, leads to a rockbound vista point high on the flanks of Cima Dome, the eroded remnants of an ancient mountain range.

Start: The trail begins behind the trail sign at the west edge of the parking area.
General location: North-central Mojave National Preserve; 25 miles east-northeast of Baker
Distance: 4.0-mile round-trip day hike
Approximate hiking time: 1.5 hours
Difficulty: Moderate
Trailhead elevation: 5,035 feet
High point: 5,700 feet
Land status: National preserve (administered by National Park Service)

Best seasons: March through May; October through mid-December
Water availability: None available; bring your own
Maps: USGS Cima Dome; Trails Illustrated Mojave National Preserve (Map 256)
Fees and permits: No fees or permits required
Trail contact: National Park Service, Mojave National Preserve, 222 East Main Street, Suite 202, Barstow, CA 92311; (760) 255-8801; www.nps.gov/moja

Finding the trailhead: From Interstate 15, 25 miles northeast of Baker, take the Cima exit and turn south onto Cima Road, quickly entering the Mojave National Preserve. This paved road climbs steadily southeastward up the Shadow Valley toward the broad hogback of Cima Dome. You reach the trailhead parking area on the right-hand (west) side of the road after 11.3 miles. If you reach a group of boulders on your left with a large white cross on them (Sunset Rock), you've gone 0.1 mile too far.

The Hike

This very scenic hike passes through the fringes of the most extensive and luxuriant Joshua tree forest on earth en route to the craggy prominence of Teutonia Peak, the high point of unique Cima Dome. Hikers will be delighted by the abundance of spring-blooming shrubs and wildflowers and will enjoy expansive vistas of much of the east Mojave Desert. Cima Dome is now protected as wilderness in the Mojave National Preserve, making the area a fine choice for a short desert backpack—but only if you pack in plenty of water and employ zero-impact practices to the fullest.

With so many volcanic landforms in the California desert, Cima Dome may at first glance appear to be just another volcanic cone, but it isn't. Encompassing 75 square miles, Cima Dome is an ancient mountain range in the advanced stages of old age. Erosion of this range has completely enshrouded it in its own detritus, forming a remarkably symmetrical, broad sloping alluvial surface known to geologists as a pediment. Teutonia Peak and a few residual crags forming a northwest-trending

A hiker pauses to contemplate Teutonia Peak in the eastern Mojave Desert.

ridge along the eastern margin of the dome are all that remain of the prominent mountain range that once stood here.

Carry an ample water supply for this hike; if you enjoy desert wildflowers, a good wildflower book will aid in identifying the diverse flora.

From the trailhead proceed southwest along an old doubletrack (closed to vehicles). Rising gently at first, pass among scattered granite boulders and a forest of picturesque Joshua trees. Among the abundant trailside flora you'll find Mojave sage, Mojave yucca, Indian paintbrush, Mormon tea, bladder sage, blackbrush, cholla,

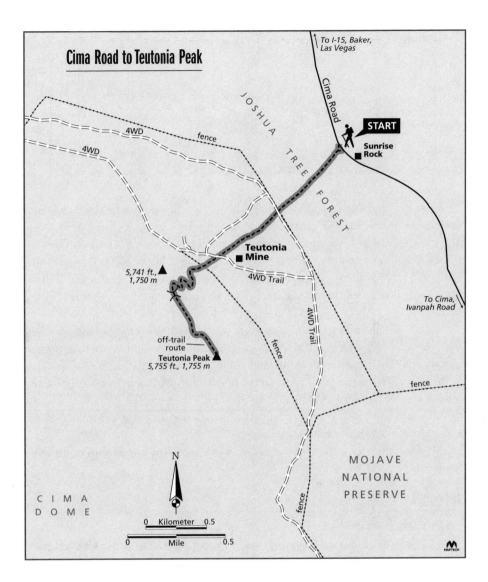

Cima Road to Teutonia Peak

rockcress, cliffrose, spiny menodora, and boxthorn. After 0.5 mile, reach a fenceline and a gate. Ignore the doubletrack that follows the fence to the left and right. From here the boulder-stacked summit of the peak looms 500 feet above toward the southwest.

Proceed along the doubletrack for another 0.5 mile, where you will reach another doubletrack forking right and left. Turn right, following the old road toward a fenced-off mine shaft. Soon the signed trail turns left (southwest) off the road, leading you to another fence, a gate, and another doubletrack.

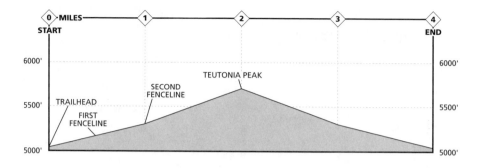

Cross the doubletrack and proceed to the foot of the dome, where, at 5,200 feet, you notice an increase in Utah junipers among the previously cited flora. Now negotiate several switchbacks to attain the summit ridge at 5,400 feet. The trail climbs southeastward along or near the ridge, ending at about 5,700 feet just short of the tall crags of the north peak, 2.0 miles from the trailhead. The actual summit lies a short distant south, and a Class 3 to 4 scramble is necessary to attain either summit.

Hikers not inclined to scale steep rock will nevertheless enjoy expansive vistas from the open ridge. Toward the southwest lies Cima Dome, and beyond are the San Jacinto and San Bernardino Mountains. Northwestward, Shadow Valley stretches toward the distant Kingston Range. To the north Clark Mountain rises abruptly, and eastward are the Ivanpah Mountains. To the southeast loom the New York Mountains. Toward the south notable landmarks include the Providence Mountains, the Kelso Dunes, and the Granite Mountains.

After soaking up the tremendous panorama, simply retrace your steps to the trailhead.

Key points

0.0 Teutonia Peak trailhead.

0.5 Cross fenceline and continue straight ahead, ignoring the doubletrack that forks right and left.

1.0 Second fenceline and gate.

2.0 End of trail immediately north of Teutonia Peak, at 5,700 feet.

17 Kelso Dunes

This unique half-day desert hike leads to the second tallest, but most extensive field of sand dunes in the California desert.

Start: Trails lead northwest to the base of the dunes from either parking area.
General location: Mojave National Preserve; 25 miles southeast of Baker
Distance: 3.0-mile round-trip day hike; no trail
Approximate hiking time: 1.5 hours
Difficulty: Moderate
Trailhead elevation: 2,590 feet
High point: 3,114 feet
Land status: National preserve (administered by National Park Service)

Best season: October through April
Water availability: None available; bring your own
Maps: USGS Kelso; Trails Illustrated Mojave National Preserve (Map 256)
Fees and permits: No fees or permits required
Trail contact: National Park Service, Mojave National Preserve, 222 East Main Street, Suite 202, Barstow, CA 92311; (760) 255-8801; www.nps.gov/moja

Finding the trailhead: From the Baker exit off Interstate 15, 63 miles northeast of Barstow and 91 miles southwest of Las Vegas, turn east onto signed Kelbaker Road. Another sign here indicates that Kelso is 35 miles ahead and warns that no services are available for 76 miles, so be sure to have a full tank of gas and plenty of water. Kelbaker Road, narrow but paved, eventually reaches the historic Kelso Depot built in 1924, after 34.75 miles. Ignore Kelso-Cima Road, which forks left just before you cross the Union Pacific Railroad tracks.

Ahead Kelbaker Road climbs a steady grade, passing the junction with the closed and unmaintained paved road leading southeast to the Vulcan Mine, an important source of iron ore during World War II. You reach a sign indicating Kelso Dunes Road 7.75 miles from Kelso and just north of a natural gas pipeline substation. Turn right (southwest) here onto the wide but rough dirt road and proceed 2.8 miles to a sign on the north (right-hand) side of the road indicating parking. Hikers can park here or in another turnout just ahead.

Alternatively, from Interstate 40 in the south, 52 miles west of Needles and 78 miles east of Barstow, take the Kelbaker Road/Amboy exit and follow Kelbaker Road northeast for 14.6 miles to the trailhead turnoff just beyond the power substation.

The Hike

To many persons, sand dunes represent the essential desert landscape, but dune systems are few and widely scattered in California's deserts. Most of these are administered by the National Park Service in Death Valley National Park and Mojave National Preserve.

Surprisingly, the vast, sandy expanse of the Kelso Dunes hosts vegetation, including many species growing solely in sandy environments. Colorful spring wildflowers and far-ranging vistas are major attractions of a hike in the Kelso Dunes, but the

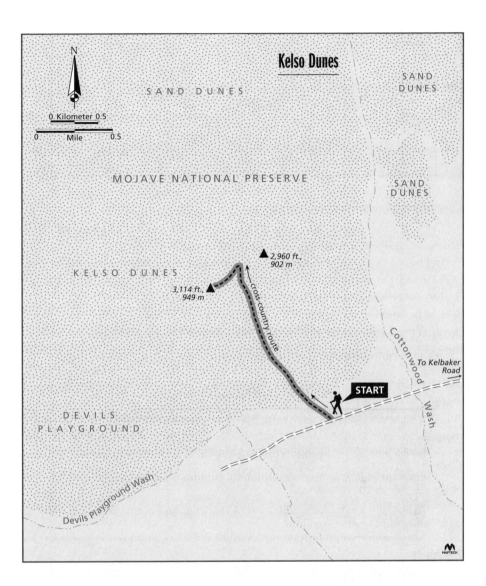

dunes' most interesting attribute is the booming or rumbling sound the sand makes as hikers create miniature sand avalanches while walking along the narrow crest of the dunes.

Nearly all the 100-square-mile Devils Playground dune field, of which Kelso Dunes are a part, was designated wilderness (save for a major railroad corridor) to protect this seemingly durable yet fragile environment. Access to off-road vehicles,

◀ *The Kelso Dunes, second highest of California's dune systems, contrast sweeping, wind-rippled slopes—brilliant white in the midday sun—with a backdrop of somber-hued mountain ranges.*

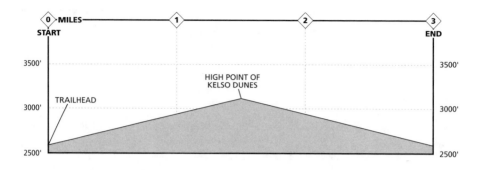

including mountain bikes, is prohibited in the Kelso Dunes area.

Even on a cool day, the sand reflects much light and heat, so carry plenty of water, wear a hat, and use sunscreen on this short but memorable jaunt.

Beginning from either parking area, well-worn trails lead northwest to the foot of the dunes. Once you reach the dunes, you can wander at will, enjoying the unique experience of hiking on sandhills.

For far-ranging vistas, the 3,114-foot high point of the dunes beckons. Avoid the direct route up the steep slip face. Instead, climb above the dunes' foothills to the skyline ridge just east of the high point, then follow the narrow sandy crest to the top.

This high point is a fine vantage point from which to appreciate the vast emptiness of the Mojave Desert. In the distant southwest horizon lies the San Gorgonio Wilderness, while closer are the barren Bristol Mountains. Stretching west to east are more dunes, and far to the northwest lies Soda Dry Lake, the sump for the Mojave River. In the northeast rise the broad slopes of Cima Dome and, farther still, the high point in the Mojave Desert, Clark Mountain. Eastward lies the immense wall of the Providence Mountains.

From the high point of the dunes, either retrace your route or glissade down the steep sandy slopes to the trailhead.

Key points

0.0 Kelso Dunes trailhead.
1.5 Reach apex of dunes on Point 3114.

18 Kelbaker Road to Peak 2451

This short but rewarding scramble leads to a commanding viewpoint on a rhyolite-capped ridge in the northern reaches of Mojave National Preserve.

Start: The doubletrack trail heads north opposite (east of) the parking area.
General location: Mojave National Preserve; 10.5 miles east of Baker
Distance: 2.4-mile round-trip day hike, cross-country
Approximate hiking time: 1–1.5 hours
Difficulty: Moderate
Trailhead elevation: 2,000 feet
High point: 2,451 feet
Land status: National preserve (administered by National Park Service)

Best season: October through April
Water availability: None available; bring your own
Maps: USGS Halloran Springs, Granite Spring; Trails Illustrated Mojave National Preserve (Map 256)
Fees and permits: No fees or permits required
Trail contact: National Park Service, Mojave National Preserve, 222 East Main Street, Suite 202, Barstow, CA 92311; (760) 255-8801; www.nps.gov/moja

Finding the trailhead: From the Baker exit off Interstate 15, 63 miles northeast of Barstow and 91 miles southwest of Las Vegas, turn east onto signed Kelbaker Road. Follow this paved road east-southeast for 10.8 miles to the first major curve in the road, then turn left onto a northbound dirt road. Follow this sandy track (a vehicle with high clearance and either front-wheel or four-wheel drive is recommended) due north along the foot of the rocky hills for 0.6 mile. At that point a low boulder-stacked hill rises immediately west of the road. Park on either the north or south side of the hill, where you may also car-camp.

The Hike

Rising along the western edge of the Cinder Cone Lava Beds, a low but prominent boulder-stacked ridge that stands out above the surrounding broad, gently sloping alluvial fans and bahadas. This ridge is one of the first outstanding landscape features seen by visitors who approach Mojave National Preserve from the north via Kelbaker Road. Kelbaker Road turns away from this ridge toward the Cinder Cone Lava Beds about 11 miles outside Baker and I–15, and the rocky prominence quickly fades from view in your rearview mirror.

The many hikers/visitors who speed past this ridge are passing up an excellent opportunity to explore a small corner of the preserve. From the crest of this craggy ridge, vistas unfold across the vast northern reaches of the Mojave Desert, contrasting images of the busy corridor of I–15 and Baker's small enclave of civilization with the raw and empty grandeur of desert mountains and valleys that stretch to the horizon in all directions.

Views from the summit of Peak 2451 stretch to the lava beds that define the northern reaches of Mojave National Preserve.

Although this hike is short and not very difficult, there is no trail. You'll be relying on your own routefinding skills to attain the crest of the ridge and return safely to the trailhead. Thus the trip is recommended only for hikers experienced in off-trail desert travel.

From the trailhead/car camping area, follow the dirt road generally north for several yards to a faint, long-closed road and turn right (northeast). The old doubletrack quickly becomes faint where it intersects a small wash. Simply continue northeast, following near the foot of the boulder-stacked ridge where, among desert-varnished rhyolite boulders, creosote bush and barrel cactus stud the slopes nearby.

Your route enters a prominent wash after 0.4 mile, and you follow its sandy course east through a notch between the north end of the ridge on the right and a boulder-covered hill on the left (northwest). After 0.8 mile you will join a much wider wash along the northeastern base of the ridge. Soon thereafter a small drainage opens up to the southwest, leading into the broad bowl on the eastern flanks of the ridge.

Turn right (southwest) into that bowl and soon reach a fork in the wash. Follow the shallow right fork of the wash, heading west toward a low saddle on the ridge

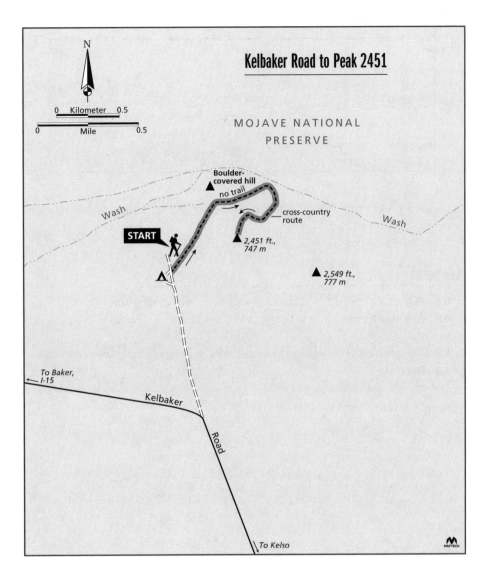

Kelbaker Road to Peak 2451

MOJAVE NATIONAL
PRESERVE

Boulder-covered hill
no trail

cross-country route

2,451 ft., 747 m

2,549 ft., 777 m

START

Wash

Wash

To Baker, I-15

Kelbaker

Road

To Kelso

ahead. Views from the saddle reach down a rocky draw toward the town of Baker and the vast dry bed of Soda Lake. The ascent ahead is short but exhilarating, leading southwest among boulders to the summit of Peak 2451.

Vistas from the peak are at their best on a clear, crisp winter or spring day. To the west and southwest, the vast alluvial surface of the eastern Mojave Desert, dissected by innumerable shallow washes and punctuated by ancient, profoundly eroded mountain ranges, stretches some 90 miles to the distant San Bernardino Mountains. In the east and southeast you'll see Club Peak crowning the Cinder Cone Lava Beds,

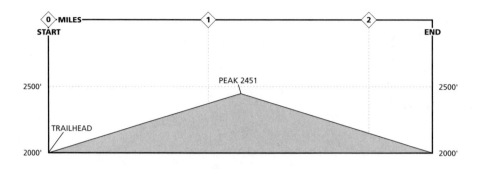

the jagged peaks of the New York Mountains, and the 4,000-foot western escarpment of the Providence Mountains.

From the peak, retrace your steps to the trailhead.

Key points

0.0 Begin hiking northeast on faint doubletrack from parking/camping area.

0.6 Pass immediately south of isolated boulder-covered hill, following broad wash east, then south.

0.9 Turn right (west), following tributary wash into the bowl on the eastern flanks of the ridge.

1.2 Peak 2451.

19 North Mid Hills Trail

This hike traces the northern half of the Mid Hills Trail, one of only three constructed trails in the preserve, along the eastern slopes of the granite-studded Mid Hills.

Start: The trail begins behind the trail sign at the southeast side of the parking area.
General location: Mojave National Preserve; 38 miles east-southeast of Baker and 49 miles northwest of Needles.
Distance: 7.2-mile round-trip day hike
Approximate hiking time: 3–3.5 hours
Difficulty: Moderate
Trailhead elevation: 5,500 feet
High point: 5,680 feet
Land status: National preserve (administered by National Park Service)

Best seasons: March through May; October through November
Water availability: None available; bring your own
Maps: USGS Columbia Mountain; Trails Illustrated Mojave National Preserve (Map 256)
Fees and permits: No fees or permits required
Trail contact: National Park Service, Mojave National Preserve, 222 East Main Street, Suite 202, Barstow, CA 92311; (760) 255-8801; www.nps.gov/moja

Finding the trailhead: From Baker on Interstate 15, take the Kelbaker Road exit and follow it for 34.75 miles to the Kelso Depot; turn left (northeast) onto Kelso-Cima Road. After 14.2 miles, turn right (east) onto Cedar Canyon Road, signed for various destinations, including Mid Hills and Hole-in-the-Wall.

You can also reach this junction from I-15 by taking the Cima exit 25 miles northeast of Baker and following Cima Road southeast for 17.6 miles to Cima (with a small store, post office, and pay telephone). Turn right (southwest) at Cima and follow Kelso-Cima Road for 4.6 miles to Cedar Canyon Road; turn left (east).

Cedar Canyon Road, paved for 2.4 miles and graded but rough thereafter, ascends steadily into the Mid Hills. After 6.1 miles, turn right (south) onto Black Canyon Road, also signed for Mid Hills and Hole-in-the-Wall. Follow this graded road south for 2.8 miles to the junction with the northern end of Wild Horse Canyon Road; turn right (southwest).

Hikers approaching from Interstate 40 in the south can reach that junction by taking the Essex Road exit, 46 miles west of Needles and 101 miles east of Barstow, and driving northwest on paved Essex Road for 10 miles to a junction. There turn right (north) onto Black Canyon Road. The pavement ends after another 9.6 miles, just beyond the turnoff to Hole-in-the-Wall Visitor Center and campground. From there follow graded Black Canyon Road north for another 6.4 miles to the junction with Wild Horse Canyon Road.

Drive southwest on Wild Horse Canyon Road for 2 miles, then turn left opposite the Mid Hills Campground entrance and park next to the windmill at the trailhead.

The Mid Hills Trail traverses a high divide through an open landscape, where continuous vistas highlight the contrast between trailside granite and more distant volcanic buttes and mesas.

The Hike

Near the center of Mojave National Preserve, and connecting the New York Mountains in the northeast with the Providence Mountains in the southwest, are the Mid Hills. Their name is misleading, however, since the Mid Hills are really more like mountains than hills. Prominent granite peaks rising nearly 6,000 feet punctuate the crest, and the higher terrain supports well-developed woodlands of piñon and juniper.

Linking Mid Hills Campground in the north with Hole-in-the-Wall in the south is the 8.5-mile Mid Hills Trail. This is one of only three constructed trails in the preserve, and it is arguably the most scenic. This trip leads you on an up-and-down course for 3.6 miles to a broad saddle on a granite ridge high above Gold Valley where far-ranging vistas unfold.

From the trailhead, the Mid Hills Trail begins a winding southeast course; ascend steadily upon the well-vegetated slopes. Cholla dominates the trailside flora, but

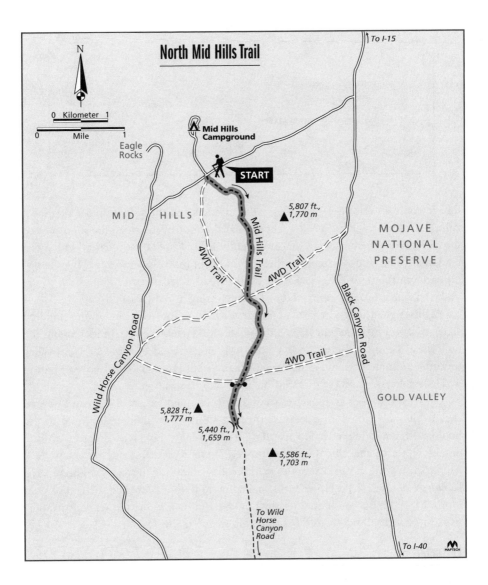

North Mid Hills Trail

you'll also see small piñons and junipers, sagebrush, cliffrose, Mormon tea, yucca, and hedgehog cactus. Soon the trail tops a saddle at 5,680 feet, and from there fine views open up to the southwest, stretching across the piñon- and juniper-studded expanse of Gold Valley to the rim of Wild Horse Mesa and to the Providence and Granite Mountains. On a clear day the vista reaches as far as the distant San Bernardino Mountains. In the northeast your view includes Round Valley and the rugged granite slopes of the New York Mountains.

From the saddle the trail begins descending south, following the sandy bed of a minor wash. Trailside slopes are clothed with desert almond, and that shrub's gray

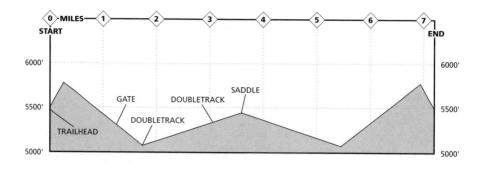

foliage contrasts with the green of nearby junipers and the yellow spines of cholla. After 1.2 miles, reach a gate in a fenceline at the foot of the ridge (be sure to close the gate). From there the trail descends gently for 0.4 mile to a junction with a dirt road in a broad, sandy wash. A sign here points right (northwest) to Mid Hills Campground. On the return trip you can take that road as an alternate route back to the trailhead, but it is quite sandy and not as interesting as the foot trail.

At the signed junction head southeast, following the wash for several hundred yards until you find the trail leaving the wash on the right (south). In increments the trail ahead begins ascending the southern, boulder-studded slopes of Gold Valley toward a prominent granite outcrop on the slopes of Peak 5828. Trailside vegetation is also less diverse, consisting of cliffrose, Mormon tea, and yucca.

Cross an old road and reach a second fenceline and gate at 3.1 miles. The trail ahead follows a closed road southeast, rising steadily for another 0.5 mile to the boulder-strewn saddle at 5,440 feet. From here granite boulders foreground more distant views of the Mid Hills, flat-topped Pinto Mountain, and the New York Mountains in the northeast. Southward are fine views of the volcanic-dominated landscape of lower Wild Horse Canyon, including Barber Butte and the rim of Wild Horse Mesa. Find a perch on a nearby boulder and soak in the tremendous panoramas, quiet, and solitude before backtracking to the trailhead.

Key points

0.0 Mid Hills trailhead.

1.2 Pass through gate in first fenceline.

1.6 Cross doubletrack; follow broad wash southeast, downstream.

3.1 Cross another doubletrack, then pass through gate in second fenceline.

3.6 Reach 5,440-foot saddle on ridge between Gold Valley and Wild Horse Canyon.

20 Eagle Rocks

This pleasant short hike, on an old road all the way, leads to the most prominent landmarks in the Mid Hills, the twin granite domes of Eagle Rocks.

Start: The doubletrack trail continues north from the parking area at the loop.
General location: Mojave National Preserve; 37 miles east-southeast of Baker and 50 miles northwest of Needles.
Distance: 1.4-mile round-trip day hike
Approximate hiking time: 45 minutes
Difficulty: Easy
Trailhead elevation: 5,600 feet
High point: 5,600 feet
Land status: National preserve (administered by National Park Service)

Best seasons: March through May; October through November
Water availability: None available; bring your own
Maps: USGS Mid Hills, Columbia Mountain; Trails Illustrated Mojave National Preserve (Map 256)
Fees and permits: No fees or permits required
Trail contact: National Park Service, Mojave National Preserve, 222 East Main Street, Suite 202, Barstow, CA 92311; (760) 255-8801; www.nps.gov/moja

Finding the trailhead: Follow driving directions for Hike 19 to reach the Mid Hills trailhead, then continue ahead on Wild Horse Canyon Road for another 0.7 mile to a sign indicating a left-hand curve. A dirt road branches right (northwest) here, but it is better to continue ahead for about 150 yards to a northbound dirt road and then turn right. Both roads join a short distance ahead.

This unimproved doubletrack, leading north through a piñon-juniper woodland, is narrow, with high centers in places. Drivers of cars should consider parking at the first junction, 0.2 mile from the main road, where there is room enough to park on the left (west) side of the road. With a high-clearance vehicle, you can continue along the right fork for another 0.3 mile and park in a loop, where the road ahead begins descending steadily. Parking is also available at a very good undeveloped campsite 0.2 mile south of the loop and 0.3 mile north of Wild Horse Canyon Road.

The Hike

This fun, short hike offers an easy opportunity to experience the high country of Mojave National Preserve. The trip surveys a diverse assemblage of high desert vegetation; from the crest of Mid Hills, panoramic views reach across much of the preserve's vast landscape.

From your parking area, follow the narrow dirt lane through a woodland of piñon and juniper. Soon you will begin a gradual northbound descent. Sharing space with the piñons and junipers on the slopes of the shallow draw are big sagebrush, Mormon tea, cliffrose, and Spanish bayonet yucca.

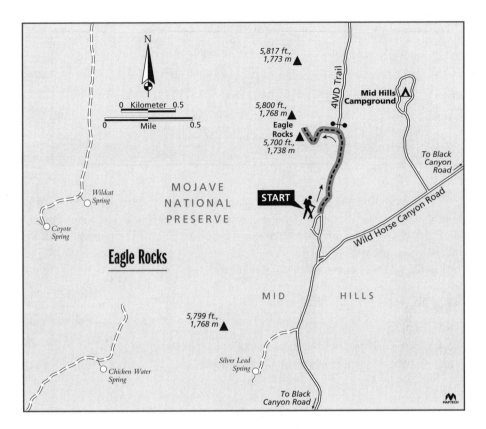

Shortly after a side drainage joins from the east, you reach a junction at 0.4 mile. The old road ahead leading downhill to the north is closed behind a wilderness boundary sign. Take the left fork to the west, heading uphill toward Eagle Rocks, looming just ahead on the western skyline. Your road is steep and badly eroded and becomes extremely steep after it bends southwest. Ignore a left-branching road leading downhill, and wind your way northwest to the road's end at the notch between Eagle Rocks.

Granite boulders litter the well-vegetated slopes here, where you will find Mojave yucca, silktassel, Joshua trees, and several varieties of cacti, including cholla, hedgehog, and old man prickly pear. The Eagle Rocks are a pair of domelike crags, one rising 200 feet above the notch to the north, the other rising more than 100 feet to the south. Although only skilled rock climbers can scale the rocks, there are ample opportunities for bouldering and scrambling nearby.

◀ *The granite crags of Eagle Rocks, crowning the Mid Hills between the Providence and New York Mountains, offer a fine destination for a short day hike plus the reward of far-ranging vistas across the eastern Mojave Desert.*

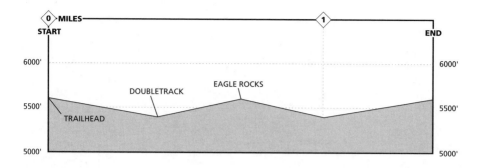

Vistas from the notch are exceptional, reaching northeast to the New York Mountains, east to the mesa of Table Mountain, and southwest to the Kelso Dunes, the Providence and Granite Mountains, and beyond across ranks of low, profoundly eroded desert mountain ranges.

From Eagle Rocks, return the way you came.

Key points

0.0   Trailhead.

0.4   Junction with steep westbound doubletrack; turn left (west).

0.7   End of doubletrack on saddle between Eagle Rocks.

21 Table Mountain

This challenging hike surveys landscapes of granite and volcanics en route to an isolated mesa, where unforgettable vistas unfold.

Start: The doubletrack trail begins on the east side of the borrow pit parking area.
General location: Mojave National Preserve; 40 miles east-southeast of Baker and 47 miles northwest of Needles
Distance: 6.2-mile round-trip day hike, mostly cross-country
Approximate hiking time: 3.5 hours
Difficulty: Strenuous
Trailhead elevation: 5,180 feet
High point: Table Mountain, 6,176 feet
Land status: National preserve (administered by National Park Service)

Best seasons: March through May; October through November
Water availability: None available; bring your own
Maps: USGS Columbia Mountain, Woods Mountains; Trails Illustrated Mojave National Preserve (Map 256)
Fees and permits: No fees or permits required
Trail contact: National Park Service, Mojave National Preserve, 222 East Main Street, Suite 202, Barstow, CA 92311; (760) 255-8801; www.nps.gov/moja

Finding the trailhead: Follow driving directions for Hike 19 to reach the junction of Black Canyon and Wild Horse Canyon Roads, and drive south on Black Canyon Road. Reach the summit of the road 0.8 mile from the junction, then descend another 0.8 mile to a cattleguard. Immediately north of the cattleguard, an eastbound spur leads a few yards into a borrow pit, where there is ample room to park.

Hikers approaching from Interstate 40 in the south can reach the trailhead by taking the Essex Road exit, 46 miles west of Needles and 101 miles east of Barstow, and driving northwest on paved Essex Road for 10 miles to a junction. There turn right (north) onto Black Canyon Road. The pavement ends after another 9.6 miles just beyond the turnoff to Hole-in-the-Wall Visitor Center and campground. From there follow graded Black Canyon Road north for another 4.8 miles to the borrow pit and trailhead.

The Hike

This interesting trip, part on dirt road and part cross-country, leads from open slopes to a granite-studded ridge and finally to Table Mountain, an isolated volcanic mesa rising between the Mid Hills and Lanfair Valley. Routefinding is straightforward, but don't attempt the hike unless you are comfortable scrambling up steep, boulder-covered slopes.

From the parking area, follow the poor doubletrack uphill to the southeast. Soon reach a level bench, then begin a gentle descent. After 0.3 mile pass through a gate in a fenceline (please close the gate) and continue your southeast course through the

The flat-topped volcanic butte of Table Mountain, crowning a granite-bound ridge, is a challenging and rewarding cross-country day hike in the central reaches of Mojave National Preserve.

yucca and boulder-dotted landscape. Your first goal is to reach the windmill visible in a draw to the north, but the old road follows a roundabout way to get there.

Table Mountain looms on the northeast skyline, and you can begin to visualize routes to the top. The ridge route follows the blocky granite ridge east from the windmill on a rugged up-and-down course. That route is very time-consuming and requires considerable scrambling. It is far easier to follow an eastbound course along the foot of the ridge. This way you will come to a draw that angles east/northeast to the crest of the ridge only 350 feet below the rim of Table Mountain.

At 0.6 mile, reach a junction and turn left (north) onto a sandy doubletrack; slog through the sand for 0.5 mile to the old windmill and corrals. Go through the corrals only if you intend to follow the ridge route. For the recommended lower route, stay on the south side of the fence and corrals and head east. You quickly come to a prominent boulder-stacked spur jutting south from the main ridge, and you should see a cairn at the foot of the spur.

Head generally eastward along the foot of the ridge, choosing your own way across mildly undulating terrain. Occasionally you will find cattle trails that will help

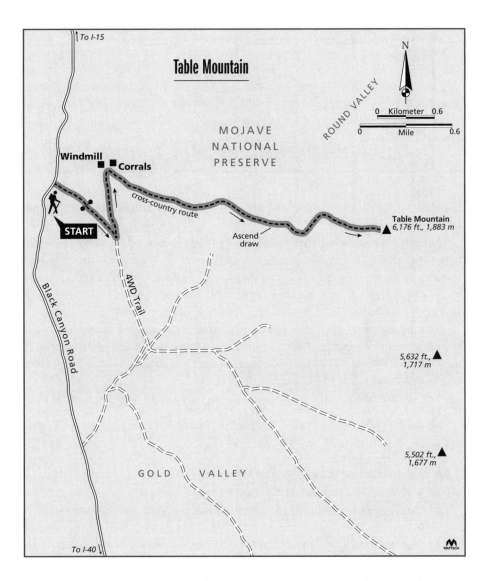

Table Mountain

To I-15

MOJAVE
NATIONAL
PRESERVE

N

ROUND VALLEY

0   Kilometer   0.6

0   Mile   0.6

Windmill   Corrals

cross-country route

START

Ascend
draw

Table Mountain
6,176 ft., 1,883 m

Black Canyon Road

4WD Trail

5,632 ft.,
1,717 m

5,502 ft.,
1,677 m

GOLD   VALLEY

To I-40

MAPTECH

speed your progress toward Table Mountain. About 1.0 mile from the windmill, you reach a fence; hug the very foot of the ridge and you can easily cross where the wires have been cut. Continue heading east and weaving a course among yucca, cliffrose, Mormon tea, and goldenbush.

Eventually you'll see where the base of the ridge turns briefly south and the crease of a minor draw rising east toward the top of the ridge. This draw, at 2.2 miles, is your route to the top. The south slopes of the draw are mantled with a thick stand of piñon, so the going is easier on the more open left (north) side. About halfway to the ridge, the draw begins to blend into slopes covered with granite

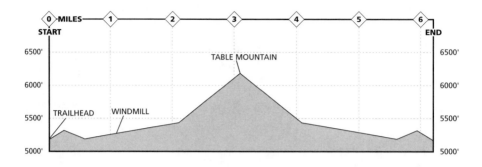

boulders. Continue to scramble steeply to the ridge crest at 5,800 feet, at the base of Table Mountain's mesa.

Although the mesa is encircled by a rim of low volcanic cliffs, there are breaks in the cliff band on either side of the western point of the mesa. Ascend steeply eastward up to the point, and head left (north) or right (south). Scramble up the breaks in the cliff and, at 3.1 miles, you've reached Table Mountain, where you can sit back and admire the view.

Far-ranging vistas reach east and northeast across legions of desert mountains stretching to the horizon in Nevada and Arizona. Views across the preserve include the Providence Mountains, Mid Hills, broad Cima Dome, the New York Mountains, Castle Peaks, and Clark Mountain.

After absorbing the vast desert panorama, carefully retrace your route to the trailhead.

Key points

0.0 Trailhead at borrow pit alongside Black Canyon Road.

0.6 Junction with northbound doubletrack; turn left (north).

1.1 End of doubletrack at windmill and corrals; turn right (east) and stay south of the fence-line.

2.2 Begin ascending a rocky draw, first east then northeast, toward Table Mountain ridge.

2.7 Reach the ridge immediately west of Table Mountain.

3.1 Top out on Table Mountain.

22 Hole-in-the-Wall

This short but unforgettable hike leads through a rugged slot canyon and onto yucca-studded flats surrounded by volcanic cliffs and buttes.

Start: The trail begins behind the interpretive sign at the parking area/picnic site.
General location: Mojave National Preserve; 42 miles east-southeast of Baker and 45 miles west-northwest of Needles
Distance: 2.0-mile round-trip day hike
Approximate hiking time: 1 hour
Difficulty: Moderate
Trailhead elevation: 4,280 feet
High point: 4,280 feet
Land status: National preserve (administered by National Park Service)

Best seasons: March through May; October through November
Water availability: None available; bring your own
Maps: USGS Columbia Mountain; Trails Illustrated Mojave National Preserve (Map 256)
Fees and permits: No fees or permits required
Trail contact: National Park Service, Mojave National Preserve, 222 East Main Street, Suite 202, Barstow, CA 92311; (760) 255-8801; www.nps.gov/moja

Finding the trailhead: From Interstate 40, 46 miles west of Needles and 101 miles east of Barstow, take the Essex Road exit and drive northwest on paved Essex Road for 10 miles to a junction. There turn right (north) onto paved Black Canyon Road. After 9.5 miles, reach the turnoff to Hole-in-the-Wall Visitor Center and picnic area; turn left (west). Follow the rough dirt road for 0.3 mile to the Hole-in-the-Wall Visitor Center, which is irregularly staffed; continue ahead for another 0.2 mile to the road's end at the Rings trailhead and picnic area. Tables, water, and trash cans are available here.

The Hike

This short hike may be the most exciting and spectacular in all Mojave National Preserve. The Rings Trail passes through a very narrow slot in a cliff of volcanic rock, descends to the ominously named gorge of Banshee Canyon, then opens up into lower Wild Horse Canyon, a beautiful valley embraced by volcanic cliffs and buttes.

Although the Rings Trail is potentially dangerous, it's not as difficult as it may first appear. Anyone with even a little scrambling experience will enjoy the exciting descent into Banshee Canyon. The route is, however, not recommended for small children.

The rock-lined trail begins behind the interpretive sign at the trailhead/picnic area and heads west. Very soon the trail ends and the only way to go is down. Much like in a narrow canyon in southern Utah or northern Arizona, you head steeply down the increasingly confined slot via chutes, occasionally boulder-hopping. The cliffs surrounding you rise nearly 200 feet above and are convoluted and pocked with vesicles—gas cavities that formed as molten lava solidified.

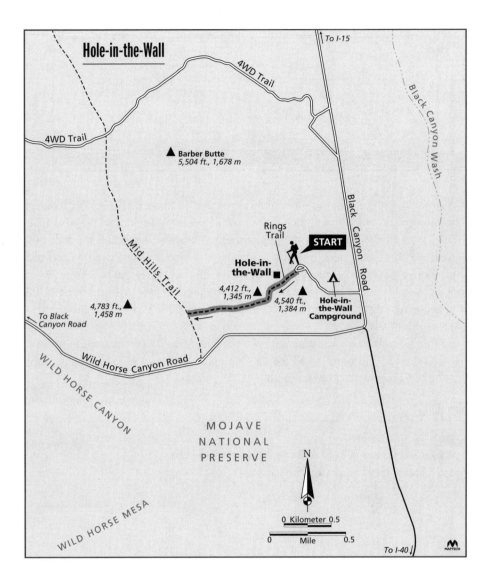

Soon reach the first set of large steel rings bolted onto the rock. Carefully descend through a steep, narrow chute just wide enough for one person to squeeze through. A short distance below is the second set of rings, this time leading you on a longer descent. Just beyond, you enter the boulder-strewn wash of Banshee Canyon. Many visitors simply wander around this short canyon and marvel at the erosional forms and soaring, colorful cliffs.

The Rings Trail through the volcanic cliffs at Hole-in-the-Wall is the shortest—and most exciting—trail in Mojave National Preserve.

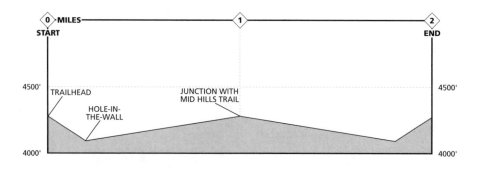

To continue, exit the mouth of the canyon and head west at 0.3 mile; cross an old doubletrack and you will pick up the westbound trail leading to the Mid Hills Trail. This well-defined but sometimes sandy trail leads west, skirting the foot of a lone butte of volcanic rock as it rises gradually on gentle slopes studded with cholla and Mojave yucca. Massive Wild Horse Mesa fills your view ahead. An array of rugged volcanic buttes appears to the north, dominated by Barber Butte rising 1,300 feet above. More distant views stretch southeast across wide Fenner Valley to the Old Woman Mountains.

After 1.0 mile, reach the junction with the Mid Hills Trail leading south to Wild Horse Trailhead and north to Mid Hills Campground. This is a good place to turn around and backtrack to the trailhead.

Key points

0.0 The Rings trailhead.

0.2 Reach the floor of Banshee Canyon below Hole-in-the-Wall.

1.0 Junction on left (south) with Mid Hills Trail.

23 Wild Horse Mesa

This rigorous, trail-less route leads very experienced desert hikers to one of the most remote and unique places in Mojave National Preserve; on clear days, 100-mile vistas unfold.

Start: The cross-country route leads southwest from parking areas alongside Wild Horse Canyon Road.
General location: Central Mojave National Preserve; 39 miles east-southeast of Baker and 48 miles west-northwest of Needles
Distance: 5.6-mile round-trip day hike, cross-country
Approximate hiking time: 4 hours
Difficulty: Strenuous
Trailhead elevation: 4,200 feet
High point: 5,610 feet
Land status: National preserve (administered by National Park Service)

Best seasons: March through May; October through November
Water availability: None available; bring your own
Maps: USGS Columbia Mountain; Trails Illustrated Mojave National Preserve (Map 256)
Fees and permits: No fees or permits required
Trail contact: National Park Service, Mojave National Preserve, 222 East Main Street, Suite 202, Barstow, CA 92311; (760) 255-8801; www.nps.gov/moja

Finding the trailhead: From Interstate 40, 46 miles west of Needles and 101 miles east of Barstow, take the Essex Road exit and drive northwest on paved Essex Road for 10 miles to a junction. There turn right (north) onto paved Black Canyon Road.

After 9.5 miles, reach the southern end of westbound Wild Horse Canyon Road, and turn left (west). This junction can be reached from the north by driving 8.5 miles south on Black Canyon Road from its junction with Cedar Canyon Road (see Hike 19).

Driving west on Wild Horse Canyon Road, pass the Wild Horse trailhead (the southern end of the Mid Hills Trail) after 1.0 mile. Continue ahead for another 0.5 mile, then park in a large undeveloped campsite on the north side of the road. If that site is occupied, continue ahead on Wild Horse Canyon Road for another 0.25 mile to a point where the road curves to the northwest. On the left (south) side of the road, there is a small turnout where you can park next to a WILDERNESS BOUNDARY sign.

The Hike

In the south-central reaches of Mojave National Preserve, between the limestone crags of the Providence Mountains and the granite ramparts of the Mid Hills, rises the 8-square-mile volcanic tableland of Wild Horse Mesa. This mesa is seemingly out of place among the profoundly eroded mountain ranges and broad valleys of the eastern Mojave Desert, and its landscape is more reminiscent of the canyon country of the Desert Southwest.

The Providence Mountains rise beyond the cactus- and juniper-studded tableland of Wild Horse Mesa.

This demanding cross-country hike, recommended for very experienced desert hikers only, follows the precipitous gorge of Saddle Horse Canyon to the volcanic rim of the mesa. Vistas from the mesa rim are panoramic, stretching far to the east into Arizona.

From either of the two parking areas off Wild Horse Canyon Road, proceed southwest into the broad mouth of Saddle Horse Canyon, crossing three dry washes and open flats studded with thorny catclaw, cholla, Mormon tea, and Mojave yucca. After 0.5 mile, pass a concrete guzzler and enter the lower reaches of Saddle Horse Canyon, embraced by the arms of the mesa that define the rim above. The flanks of the canyon rise in stairstep fashion, with cliff bands of tan, red, and gray volcanics separated by blocky talus slopes.

The route up the canyon ahead is of your own choosing, following the slopes above either side of the rocky, brush-fringed wash. The first major side canyon opens up on the right at 1.0 mile, slicing northwest into Wild Horse Mesa. Saddle Horse Canyon grows increasingly narrow ahead, with a scattering of piñon and juniper on the south slopes and yucca-studded slopes to the north. Views begin to expand eastward, stretching past the cliffbound labyrinth of Banshee Canyon near Hole-in-the-Wall to the volcanic Woods Mountains.

The canyon becomes much more constricted at 1.4 miles, where the first side canyon on your left (southwest) opens up. The way ahead is increasingly challenging where the wash, fringed with squawbush and live oak, is wedged between very

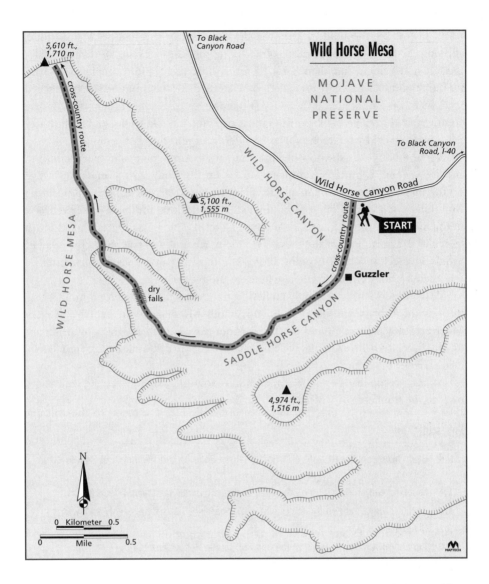

steep slopes. This stretch requires constant scrambling over and around the boulders that fill the wash. At 1.7 miles, the second southwest-trending side canyon opens up on the left; Saddle Horse Canyon bends northwest just beyond that confluence.

Bear right (northwest), staying in Saddle Horse Canyon. This is the toughest segment of the hike, and though the mesa top lies only 0.4 mile ahead, it may take another hour of scrambling to get there. It is easier at first to follow the right (southeast) side of the canyon, staying above the nearly impassable wash, but you should beware of the abundant yucca, cholla, prickly pear, and barrel cactus. It is a short but rigorous struggle to reach the first cliff band. There, where the canyon has cut through the cliff, you find a boulder jam that can be easily bypassed on the right (east). Just above the boulder jam, the drainage briefly slices through solid rock, affording better footing, but more obstacles lie just ahead. There are five dry falls, though none are higher than 8 to 10 feet. All of them afford ample hand- and footholds and can be easily ascended via Class 2 to Class 3 routes by experienced scramblers. Before ascending these dry falls, however, be absolutely sure that you are comfortable *descending* them on the return trip and are able to do so. The fifth dry fall is best skirted by scrambling over boulders on the right (east) side.

Above the dry falls, the now-shallow canyon supports a piñon-juniper woodland, and the walking is much less difficult for the final 0.5 mile to the mesa top. Once on the mesa top you can roam at will. The best vistas, of course, open up from the rims. Fine vistas can be enjoyed by following a mile-long southeastward extension of the mesa from the head of Saddle Horse Canyon. The mesa's high point, at 5,610 feet, is at the north end of the mesa, 1.0 mile north and 400 feet above the head of Saddle Horse Canyon. This point affords the most expansive views, but you'll be rewarded for your efforts from anywhere on the mesa rim.

Vistas stretch across seemingly endless horizons and include such prominent features as the Providence, New York, and Woods Mountains and Lanfair Valley in Mojave National Preserve and the Black Mountains in Arizona. Even more distant on the far eastern horizon are the Hualapai Mountains, 90 miles away near Kingman, Arizona.

After enjoying distant panoramas and quiet solitude, carefully retrace your route back to the trailhead.

Key points

0.0 Begin hiking southwest from Wild Horse Canyon Road toward the mouth of Saddle Horse Canyon.

1.4 First side canyon opens up on the left (southwest); continue straight ahead (west).

1.7 Second side canyon on the left (southwest); bear right, ascending steeply northwest.

2.1 Climb five dry falls.

2.8 Top out on Wild Horse Mesa at the head of Saddle Horse Canyon.

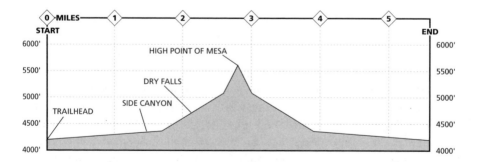

24 Quail Spring Basin

This trip follows a long-closed road into lonely Quail Spring Basin on the south slopes of the Providence Mountains; expansive views of much of the preserve can be enjoyed all along the way.

Start: The doubletrack trail begins at the WILDERNESS BOUNDARY sign and leads southeast.

General location: South-central Mojave National Preserve; 40 miles southeast of Baker and 55 miles west of Needles

Distance: 5.7-mile semiloop day hike

Approximate hiking time: 3 hours

Difficulty: Moderate

Trailhead elevation: 3,789 feet

High point: 4,462 feet

Land status: National preserve (administered by National Park Service)

Best seasons: March through May; October through November

Water availability: None available; bring your own

Maps: USGS Van Winkle Spring; Trails Illustrated Mojave National Preserve (Map 256)

Fees and permits: No fees or permits required

Trail contact: National Park Service, Mojave National Preserve, 222 East Main Street, Suite 202, Barstow, CA 92311; (760) 255-8801; www.nps.gov/moja

Finding the trailhead: For hikers approaching from the north, follow driving directions for Hike 17 to the junction of Kelbaker and Kelso Dunes Roads, then continue south on Kelbaker Road for another 4.9 miles. There a pair of easy-to-miss doubletracks fork right (southwest) and left (northeast). Turn left and follow the narrow tracks northeast for 0.9 mile to a loop turnaround next to the WILDERNESS BOUNDARY sign. This is a narrow and sometimes rough road, but carefully driven cars can make the trip. Be careful not to get too far off the road in the soft sand en route to and at the trailhead.

From Interstate 40 in the south, you can reach the trailhead by taking the Kelbaker Road/Amboy exit, 52 miles west of Needles and 78 miles east of Barstow. Follow the paved Kelbaker Road northeast for 8 miles to the summit at Granite Pass, then descend for 1.75 miles to the aforementioned junction with the northeastbound doubletrack.

The Hike

The trip to Quail Spring Basin on the south slopes of the Providence Mountains is one of the best hikes in Mojave National Preserve. It surveys landscapes ranging from open slopes studded with yuccas and cholla to a hidden high desert basin, and the ever-changing vistas take in much of the diverse landscapes present in the preserve. And since you follow closed doubletracks and gain only a modicum of elevation, it's a pleasant outing for even novice hikers.

The trail, a long-closed doubletrack, heads southeast past the wilderness boundary, carving a swath through a stand of tall creosote bush. Nearby slopes also support Mojave sage and cheesebush. Vistas are excellent from the start, reaching southwest

Quail Spring Basin, studded with granite knobs and Mojave yucca, spreads out at the southern foot of the Providence Mountains.

to the Granite Mountains and an array of domes, spires, and cliffs near Granite Pass. To the north and almost overhead are the southern peaks of the Providence Mountains. More distant features include Cima Dome, Clark Mountain, and the summit of Charleston Peak, far to the north in Nevada.

Your trail rises gradually but steadily; passing above 4,000 feet, the pattern of vegetation begins to change. Creosote bush becomes more widely scattered, and Mormon tea, blackbrush, Mojave yucca, pencil cholla, and deerhorn cholla begin to dominate nearby slopes. Stacks of granite boulders lie immediately north of the trail, arranged into a wide variety of shapes and forms.

Ignore two short northbound spur roads, leading to old car-camping areas, as you make your way southeastward to the saddle ahead that separates the Providence Mountains from the Horse Hills. Top the saddle at 4,462 feet, 1.9 miles from the trailhead, from where Quail Spring Basin spreads out before you. Avoid another northbound spur, unless you decide to explore the boulders just above. Instead begin descending eastward into the basin and quite soon reach a junction. Turn left (northeast) here; you will be returning via the right fork after looping through the basin.

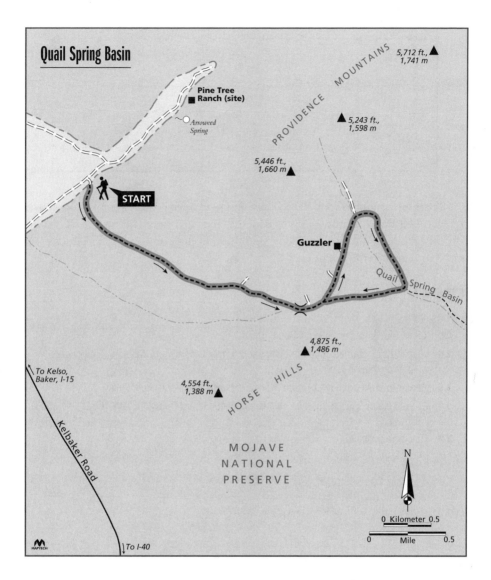

Quail Spring Basin

Pine Tree
Ranch (site)

Arroweed Spring

START

PROVIDENCE MOUNTAINS

5,712 ft.,
1,741 m

5,243 ft.,
1,598 m

5,446 ft.,
1,660 m

Guzzler

Quail Spring Basin

4,875 ft.,
1,486 m

To Kelso,
Baker, I-15

4,554 ft.,
1,388 m

HORSE HILLS

MOJAVE
NATIONAL
PRESERVE

Kelbaker Road

To I-40

N

0 Kilometer 0.5

0 Mile 0.5

The doubletrack leads northeast across the basin, passing two more short spur roads along the way. After 0.6 mile, reach the northernmost point in the basin, where the south wall of the Providence Mountains soars 1,300 feet above. Do not follow the more obvious track ahead (northwest). Instead follow the poorly defined doubletrack that turns right and heads east. Soon curve southeast and begin descending, crossing a small wash after 0.3 mile. At 0.6 mile, cross the main wash draining the basin immediately before climbing up the main doubletrack, the return leg of your loop. That last 0.6 mile is poorly defined, with vegetation slowly but surely reclaiming the old roadbed.

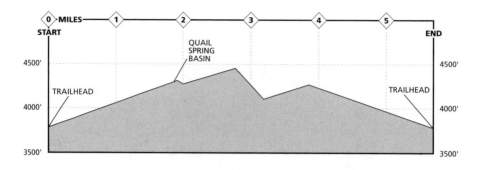

The road continues southeast, following Quail Spring Wash for 3.5 miles to the Hidden Hill Road, a route seldom used. But you turn right and head west, gradually ascending 0.6 mile to the saddle and then strolling downhill for a pleasant 1.9 miles to return to the trailhead.

Key points

0.0 Trailhead.

1.9 Cross saddle and enter Quail Spring Basin.

2.0 Junction with northeastbound doubletrack; turn left (northeast), following a clockwise loop around the basin.

3.2 Return to main doubletrack; turn right (southwest) and begin ascending.

3.7 Close the loop back at the first junction; continue straight ahead toward the saddle and trailhead.

5.7 Return to trailhead.

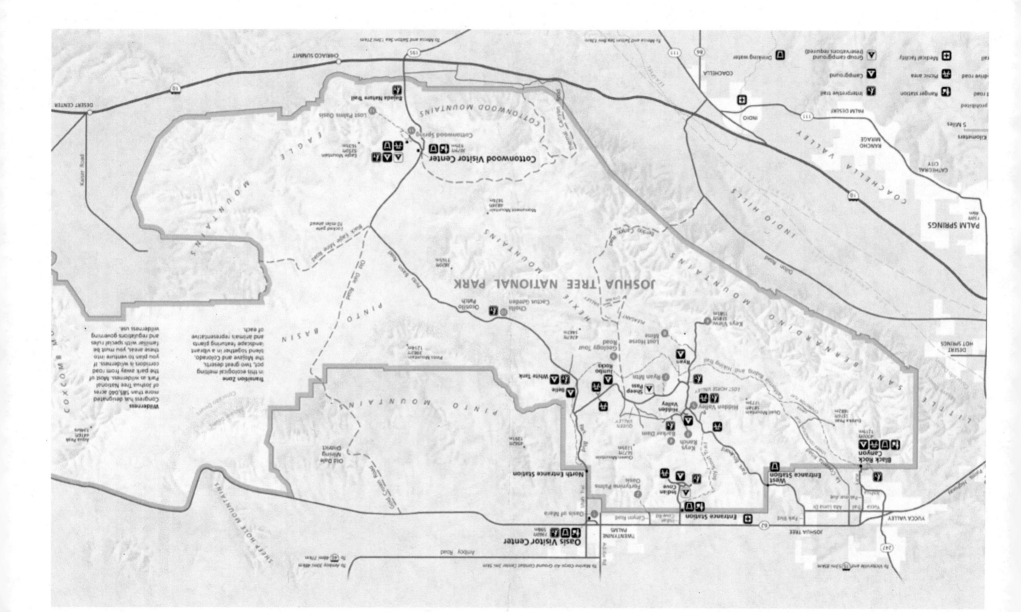

Schedule of Events:

Saturday, 1 and 3 PM at Rimrock Ranch:
Christy Gast performs "The Great Eenudation", (featuring the inflatable sculpture "Left Mitten")

Saturday, 6 to 9 PM Dinner at the Palms:
Musical entertainment by the Sibleys and Dick Slessig

Saturday, 8 PM Performance at the Palms:
Pentti Monkkonen

Sunday, 3 PM at Coyote Dry Lake:
"Dust Farming" by David Dodge and "Dingo Derby" by Feral Childe (Alice Wu + Moriah Carlson)

1. Rimrock Ranch
(HDTS Map distribution point)
Coming from the I-10 exit onto Hwy 62 proceed to Pioneertown Road in Yucca Valley. (Water Canyon Coffee Shop will be on your left) Turn LEFT and drive nine miles up through Pioneertown. The road will change names to Rimrock Road to Burns Canyon Road. At Powderhorn Pass (a dirt road) go left at the Rimrock Ranch sign. Enter through the ranch gate and head for the "remember to breath" sign.

Exhibition organized by Martha Otero
Kristin Botshekan
Performance by Christy Gast

5. Krblin Jihn Cabin
Backtrack to Aberdeen. Turn LEFT at Border. Turn RIGHT on Golden and then LEFT onto Sunburst. (You will be following the paved road) Drive about 1 mile to Crestview and take a LEFT, Drive 1.3 miles and take a RIGHT on Border again. Drive about one "block" - the Krblin Jihn Cabin will be on your left.

Eames Demetrios

9. Coyote Dry Lake:
Meet On Sunday afternoon at 3:00 on the dry lake for two performances. To get to Coyote Dry Lake turn off 29 Palms Hwy on Sunfair. Drive north (away from hills) 1.8 miles to Broadway. Turn LEFT at Broadway and drive 1.6 miles. The pavement will turn to dirt. When you get to the dry lake bed turn and drive LEFT for another .5 miles to end of the lake and look for a cluster of other cars.

Feral Childe (Alice Wu + Moriah Carlson)
David Dodge

10. Ecoshack
Continue north (away from hills) on Sunfair until it turns into a dirt road. Travel one mile up the dirt road to Olsen. Turn LEFT at Olsen and drive 1/4 mile to Sonora. Turn LEFT at Sonora. Ecoshack is 1/2 mile on the right (the green shack).

Stephanie Smith's Ecoshack will present finalists from the "Green Tent Competition"
Strawn/Sierralta(2) and Mark Soden/SCOW

2. Andy's Gamma Gulch Site
Leave Rimrock Ranch and drive back 1.8 miles to Pipes Canyon Road. Turn LEFT. Drive 2.2 miles to Gamma Gulch Rd., turn LEFT (do not drive above 25 mph on this road!!) Drive 1.6 miles to God's Way Love, turn RIGHT. Drive .4 miles to the green flagging tape on your right and the green rope directional arrow on the ground.

Chuck Moffit and Ingram Ober
Tracy Lea Hensley
Eddie Ruscha
Linda Taalman and Kathleen Johnson
Tao Urban
Wade Guyton
Kate Costello

6. Downtown Joshua Tree: HDTS HQ
Drive south (towards the hills) on Sunburst to 29 Palms Hwy (Hwy 62). Turn RIGHT and drive to Park Blvd. Turn LEFT. Look for a big white tent on the left side of the road (to the right of Coyote Corner and directly across the street from the Park Center and Park Cafe.) You can pick up maps, the publication and HDTS t-shirts here. Amy Yao's Art Swap Meet will feature products by an array of your favorite artists.

The Cake Society
Chris James
Amy Yao
Shannon Ebner
Lisa Anne Auerbach

11. Jasmine Little's House
Backtrack to 29 Palms Hwy and drive east. When entering 29 Palms you will pass the Stater Brothers and then Don's American BBQ. Turn RIGHT directly after this BBQ restaurant onto Estrella. Continue on Estrella past 3 stop signs, the last is Sullivan. Jasmine's house is the third on the RIGHT past Sullivan. The address is 6986 Estrella Ave.

14. The Palms
From Site 12 continue North on Iron Age Road until you come to pavement. Turn RIGHT on Godwin (dirt road). Continue about a mile to Indian Trail "T" Intersection. Stop. Get out at the "x" Look straight ahead North at Mountain. For additional info visit http://www.grnd0.com

Pentti Monkkonen

3. Noah Purifoy Foundation
From Gamma Gulch Road turn LEFT back onto Pipes Canyon Road. Pipes Canyon Road will terminate at Old Woman Springs Road. Turn RIGHT and drive a short distance to Aberdeen Drive where you will take a LEFT. Follow Aberdeen for several miles to the intersection of Border. Continue PAST Border to the end of Aberdeen and turn LEFT on Center (a dirt road) and then RIGHT again almost immediately on Blair Lane.

7. Behind the Bail Bonds:
From Park Blvd turn RIGHT onto 29 Palms Hwy. Drive one mile to the large yellow Bail Bonds Sign and turn RIGHT onto Neptune. Drive up Neptune towards the hills. Road will veer LEFT. Follow road about half a mile to the site (park before the turn around loop) and tune into micro radio channel.

Fabianne Lasserre and Christy Gast
Justin Beal
Justin Samson
Alex Slade
Sarah Vanderlip

12. Jim Skuldt on Hwy 62
From 29 Palms drive 20 miles east on Hwy 62. look for the big brown road sign and follow indications. Take an immediate right turn into Star's Way Out for a $1.75 beer.

15. Thom Merrick
From the Palms continue West on Amboy Road. Turn RIGHT on Godwin (dirt road). Continue about a mile to Indian Trail "T" Intersection. Stop. Get out at the "x" Look straight ahead North at Mountain. For additional info visit http://www.grnd0.com

4. Sunfair Parcel
From Noah's Site backtrack to Center (first dirt road). Turn RIGHT and drive about three desert blocks to Sunny Sands, turn RIGHT. Follow Sunny Sands for about one mile. It curve to follow the base of a hill (but do not make an actual left turn) Drive past wrecked cars and look for info.

AUDC
Austin Thomas

8. A-Z West:
From Site 5 you can walk up the hill toward A-Z West. The house is not open this week but you can follow the driveway as it turns right and wraps around the base of the hill. About halfway up the wash you will find Jon Hauptman's radically customized A-Z Wagon Station.

Jonas Hauptman

13. Iron Age Road
About three or four miles past Stars Way Out look for the sign for Iron Age Road. Turn L onto the dirt road right after the sign. Drive until you come to other cars.

Roxanne Barlett
Marie Lorenz
Skylar Haskard and Joel Kyack

16. Future Wal-Mart Super Store
As you leave town, stop and view the south corner at 29 Palms Hwy and Avalon. This is the proposed site of another Super Wal-Mart retail center which, if built, will homogenize character of our community and erode the economy of local small businesses.

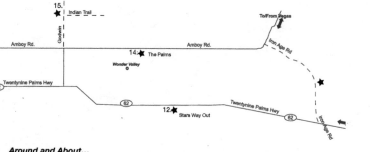

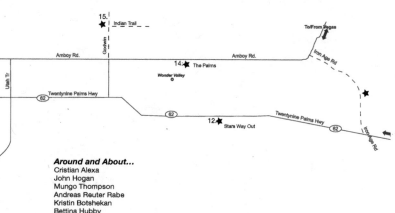

Around and About...
Cristian Alexa
John Hogan
Mungo Thompson
Andreas Reuter Rabe
Kristin Botshekan
Bettina Hubby
Due to the nature of Rainer Ganahl's work please ask about the location.

For artist's statements and further project info. visit www.highdeserttestsites.com

Directions: (all directions are from Hwy 62)

Andy's Gamma Gulch Parcel:
At the west end of Yucca Valley, next to Water Canyon Coffee Shop, turn Noth on Pioneertown Road. Follow road about 7 1/2 miles and turn right on Pipes Canyon Road. Go about 2 1/4 miles to Gamma Gulch, turn left. Drive about 1 1/2 miles past Cotton Tail and turn right on God's Way Love. Drive approx. 1/2 mile - parcel is on right side of road.===**Andy's Gamma Gulch Parcel**: Located on the large boulders in the middle of Andy Stillpas's Gamma Gulch Parcel, **"Grotto"** is an ongoing project by Kathleen Johnson and Linda Taalman. Other current projects include Giovanni Jance, Kate Costello,Tao Urban, and if you look hard you may still come across Wade Guyton's "X".
www.tkarchitecture.com

Noah Purifoy Foundation: 213-382-7516
At the West end of the town of Joshua Tree turn north at Sunburst. Follow the road as it curves right and the left again and turns into Border. Turn right on Aberdeen, then left on Center, then right on Blair. Drive approx. 1/4 mile.====**Noah Purifoy Foundation:** The Noah Purifoy Foundation is the site of an ongoing project by Noah Purifoy who created his own outdoor museum on this 7 and a half-acre parcel for over 13 years. Noah's site is open for viewing on an ongoing basis and is highly recommended to all high desert visitors.
www.noahpurifoy.com

Krblin Jihn Kabin:
At the West end of the town of Joshua Tree turn north at Sunburst. Take a right on Crestview and then take a right on Border. Go south on Border and it is on your left after a "block," before you go down into a stream bed. NB: Border does NOT intersect 62, no matter how many maps say it does! ====**Krblin Jihn Kabin:** (Eames Demetrios) The Krblin Jihn Kabin is part of Kymaerica. Like many of the cabins in the area, it was originally used to house defeated heretics. Jihn Wranglicans (a sect of Church of the California Christ) had their lives spared, but only on condition of a form of sectarian house arrest, where they could never leave their cabin and surrounding grounds. Food and water was brought to them by stedlers, young women whose families were unable to support them after the fighting and so were given to the faith. In his isolation, Krblin Jihn himself became an important Biblical translator. This site explores the history and context of this important structure and community, including the remnants of its remarkable compass wheel.
www.eamesdemetrios.com
www.kymaerica.com

Thom Merrick's Site:
Take Highway 62 East. Several miles fter 29 Palms turn left on Godwin (first paved road past airport). Go straight on Godwin at intersection through Amboy Rd. onto dirt road. Straight ahead on Godwin (about a mile) to Indian Trail "T" Intersection. Stop. Get out. Look straight ahead North at Mountain.==**Surprise, Terror, Superstition, Silence, Melancholy, Power, Strength:** A test site designated by Thom Merrick - it is a view of a twisted, jagged rock formation that he sees daily on the way to his studio. The site should be seen in relation to his interpretive map and web site of Wonder Valley at www.grnd0.com

25 Fir Canyon–Clark Mountain

This remote, seldom-visited hike leads into a cliffbound canyon on the north slopes of Clark Mountain, where you can view the Mojave Desert's largest stand of Rocky Mountain white fir trees.

Start: The doubletrack trail leads south behind the WILDERNESS BOUNDARY sign.
General location: Northern Mojave National Preserve; 37 miles northeast of Baker and 50 miles south-southwest of Las Vegas, Nevada
Distance: 3.8-mile round-trip day hike
Approximate hiking time: 2 hours
Difficulty: Moderate
Trailhead elevation: 4,900 feet
High point: 5,740 feet
Land status: National preserve (administered by National Park Service)

Best seasons: March through mid-June; mid-September through November
Water availability: None available; bring your own
Maps: USGS Clark Mountain; Trails Illustrated Mojave National Preserve (Map 256)
Fees and permits: No fees or permits required
Trail contact: National Park Service, Mojave National Preserve, 222 East Main Street, Suite 202, Barstow, CA 92311; (760) 255-8801; www.nps.gov/moja

Finding the trailhead: This trailhead is one of the most remote and seldom visited in all of Mojave National Preserve. Come prepared with plenty of fuel, water, and food—and a spare tire. In the event of vehicle problems or an emergency, you face a very long walk back to civilization.

From Interstate 15, 25 miles northeast of Baker, take the Cima exit and turn northwest onto the paved but unsigned Excelsior Mine Road. (Towing and a telephone are available at the exit, but fuel is not. The nearest available fuel can be obtained at Halloran Summit on I-15, 5 miles southwest of the Cima exit.) Follow Excelsior Mine Road for 8.7 miles to a power line corridor, where you will find a rough dirt road that turns northeast and follows the power line corridor. A 4WD vehicle is highly recommended to safely negotiate this rough and sometimes sandy road.

Follow this road for a long, slow 6 miles to the first junction with a southbound road, then turn right (south). There are no signs here, only a metal post painted red. Following the steadily rising road, cross a natural gas pipeline and enter Mojave National Preserve after 0.75 mile; the road enters a wash and follows the sand and gravel bed upstream. Beware of possible flash floods and flood damage on the doubletrack ahead. (If thunderstorms threaten or heavy rain is in the forecast, *do not* enter this canyon; save this trip for a sunny day.) After driving 2.5 miles from the power line road, a westbound 4WD road joins on the right. After another 0.4 mile, reach a faint doubletrack branching right (south) and blocked by steel posts and a WILDERNESS BOUNDARY sign. Park just below this doubletrack, on or near a short spur road above the main road/wash.

The Hike

Clark Mountain, highest in Mojave National Preserve, is located in a detached unit of the preserve, lying north of I–15's Cima exit, near Mountain Pass. This unit of the

Fir Canyon, home to a rare stand of Rocky Mountain white fir trees on the north slope of Clark Mountain, is one of the most remote locations in Mojave National Preserve.

preserve contains about 30,000 acres, of which more than 10,000 acres have been designated wilderness. Clark Mountain, due to its rugged inaccessibility, is one of the wildest and most pristine mountains in the Mojave Desert. A sizable population of bighorn sheep make their home among the dolomite cliffs of the mountain, and on the north slopes there are approximately 1,000 Rocky Mountain white fir trees, the largest stand in the Mojave (see Hike 15 for more about the white firs of the Mojave Desert).

This hike follows a closed doubletrack as it ascends into a deep, precipitous canyon on the north slopes of Clark Mountain. At the head of the canyon, tall white firs contrast with the dominant woodland of piñon and juniper. Since this is prime bighorn sheep habitat, pass quietly so that you don't disturb these sensitive animals. This quiet, seldom-visited canyon is a pleasing outing even in summer due to the shady woodland, moderately high elevation, and north-facing aspect.

From the trailhead the closed doubletrack immediately enters a wash behind the WILDERNESS BOUNDARY sign, then curves west around the shoulder of a ridge to enter the wide mouth of Fir Canyon. Far above, broken dolomite cliffs embrace an

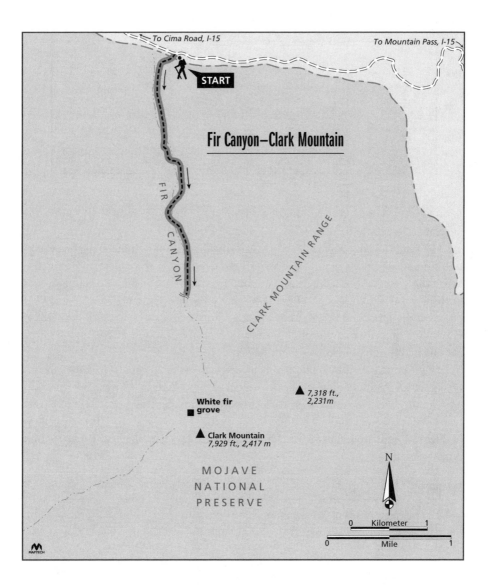

To Cima Road, I-15

To Mountain Pass, I-15

START

Fir Canyon–Clark Mountain

FIR CANYON

CLARK MOUNTAIN RANGE

▲ 7,318 ft., 2,231m

■ White fir grove

▲ Clark Mountain
7,929 ft., 2,417 m

MOJAVE
NATIONAL
PRESERVE

N

0   Kilometer   1

0   Mile   1

MAPTECH

immense amphitheater at the canyon's head. Even from a distance of about 2.0 miles, tall spire-shaped white firs stand out just below the mountain's crest on sheltered, north-facing slopes.

In the lower reaches of Fir Canyon, there is a mixing of vegetation from the Joshua tree woodland below and the piñon-juniper woodland above. Blackbrush dominates the lower slopes of the canyon, sharing space with desert almond, Spanish bayonet yucca, cliffrose, Apache plume, and Mormon tea. Also present are cholla, prickly pear, and hedgehog cactus, juniper, piñon, and a scattering of Joshua trees.

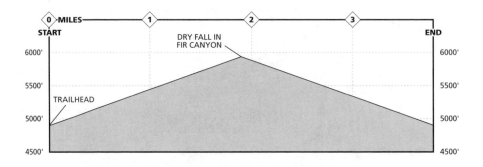

Soon enter a woodland dominated by piñon and juniper, the most dense and well-developed such woodland in Mojave National Preserve.

The old doubletrack affords a clear, easy-to-follow hiking route and gains elevation on a steady, moderate grade. As you head deeper into the canyon, piñon dominates the woodland, and sagebrush appears above 5,500 feet. Views reach far above into the great amphitheater, where bold gray cliffs of dolomite bound the rugged peaks on the mountain's crest. Above to the southeast rises the dome of Peak 7881. Crowning the center of the amphitheater is the pyramidal crag of 7,929-foot Clark Mountain, the apex of Mojave National Preserve.

After about 1.5 miles, cliffs begin to confine the increasingly narrow canyon; finally, at 1.9 miles, your way ahead is blocked by a high and impassable dry fall. You'll enjoy retracing your steps back down the canyon. Along the way are excellent views of the Mesquite Mountains, the Spring Mountains and Charleston Peak in Nevada, and mountains in the northern Mojave, including the Kingston and Nopah Ranges.

Key points

0.0 Trailhead at mouth of Fir Canyon.
1.9 Canyon blocked by dry fall.

The Mountainous Backbone of Southern California

This chapter, including twenty-six hikes, covers the mountainous heart of southern California, stretching from the mountains north of Ventura eastward through the San Gabriel and San Bernardino Mountains (the Transverse Ranges) to the Peninsular Ranges, which stretch south from near Palm Springs to the Mexican border. Two hikes, Skinner Peak (Hike 26) and Big Falls Canyon (Hike 27), were included because they offer exceptional scenery, even though they are located along the fringes of the imaginary line that separates southern and central California.

Hikers who reside in the Southland are fortunate to have so many wild places in which to briefly flee from the pressures of civilization. In fact, there is more federally designated wilderness—some 675,000 acres—adjacent to the greater Los Angeles area than there is near any other major urban area in the United States.

Trails in this chapter should appeal to hikers of all levels of ability and interests. The trips range from half-hour strolls to demanding multiday backpacks, and they survey some of the best wild country in southern California. These trails lead to the region's "big three" summits: 10,064-foot Mount San Antonio, 11,499-foot San Gorgonio Mountain, and 10,804-foot Mount San Jacinto. Hikers will also enjoy the trips to the world's largest Joshua tree and lodgepole pine, rare elephant trees and groves of California fan palms in the Sonoran desert, one of only two aspen groves in southern California, deep canyons, shady forests of pine and fir, chaparral-clad foothills, and high desert woodlands of piñon and juniper. The diversity of landscapes and ecosystems in this region is unsurpassed, and the rewards of hiking here are immeasurable.

26 Bird Spring Pass to Skinner Peak

This view-packed day hike follows the gently graded Pacific Crest Trail to a boulder-crowned summit in the extreme southern Sierra Nevada, where vistas stretch across the Mojave Desert to the distant San Gabriel Mountains.

Start: The trail begins on the north side of Bird Spring Pass, opposite the parking area.
General location: Kiavah Wilderness (Sequoia National Forest), in the extreme southern Sierra Nevada, 20 miles west of Ridgecrest
Distance: 8.2-mile round-trip day hike
Approximate hiking time: 3.5-4 hours
Difficulty: Moderate
Trailhead elevation: 5,355 feet
High point: Skinner Peak, 7,120 feet
Land status: National forest and BLM wilderness (Kiavah Wilderness)
Best seasons: Mid-April through mid-June;
mid-September through mid-November
Water availability: None available; bring your own
Maps: USGS Cane Canyon, Horse Canyon; Sequoia National Forest map
Fees and permits: No fees or permits required
Trail contact: Sequoia National Forest, Cannell Meadow Ranger District, 105 Whitney Road, Kernville, CA, 93238; (760) 376-3781 Bureau of Land Management, Ridgecrest Resource Area, 300 South Richmond Road, Ridgecrest, CA 93555; (760) 384-5400

Finding the trailhead: From California Highway 178, 59 miles east of Bakersfield and 29.2 miles west of the junction with California Highway 14, turn southeast in the hamlet of Weldon onto the signed Kelso Creek Road. Follow this good, paved two-lane road generally south up broad Kelso Valley. After 10.6 miles, immediately north of an isolated cluster of residences, turn left (east) onto a dirt road where a BLM sign indicates that Bird Spring Pass is 5.4 miles ahead.
   The road ahead, recommended for high-clearance vehicles only, is rough, narrow, rocky, subject to washouts, and quite steep in places. It ascends steadily for 6.6 miles to Bird Spring Pass, where the signed Pacific Crest Trail crosses the road. Parking is available in the turnout on the right (south) side of the road.

The Hike

The Pacific Crest Trail north of Bird Spring Pass is seldom used, save for PCT through-hikers in late spring. This segment affords the fastest access to the plateau top of the Scodie Mountains and brings hikers within easy striking distance of the Scodies' highest point, 7,120-foot Skinner Peak. The hike is rigorous, gaining nearly 1,800 feet of elevation, though the trail maintains moderate grades.

The sandy tread of the PCT, sometimes trod by grazing cattle, follows a moderate grade northwest from the pass among Joshua trees and a variety of shrubs, including big sagebrush, Mormon tea, brittlebush, and hop-sage. These south-facing slopes are ablaze with wildflowers in springtime.

The Pacific Crest Trail traverses the granite slopes of Skinner Peak, studded with piñon and juniper and decorated with spring wildflowers, affording panoramic vistas all along the way.

After bending out of a precipitous draw, the trail contours out to the broken granite shoulder of a ridge. The trail ascends into the realm of the piñon woodland at 6,200 feet; at 6,520 feet, after 2.5 miles, the trail tops out on the Sierra crest. Here you have your first look at Skinner Peak, a granite knob on the northwest skyline, lying atop a blocky, piñon-studded crest.

The trail ahead stays just below and west of the crest, carving a swath among piñons, scrub oak, Mormon tea, beavertail cactus, and yucca. More switchbacks ahead lead back to the crest, and you proceed briefly northwest to a small notch northwest of Point 6931.

When the PCT leaves the crest and begins a traverse, leave the trail and ascend the crest northwest, weaving a way among the thick oak and piñon woodland for 0.4 mile to 7,120-foot Skinner Peak, where you'll find a register can atop the summit boulder. The biggest attraction of Skinner Peak, aside from its remote location, is the far-ranging vistas of the southern Sierra, the western reaches of the Mojave Desert, and, on clear days, the San Gabriel Mountains.

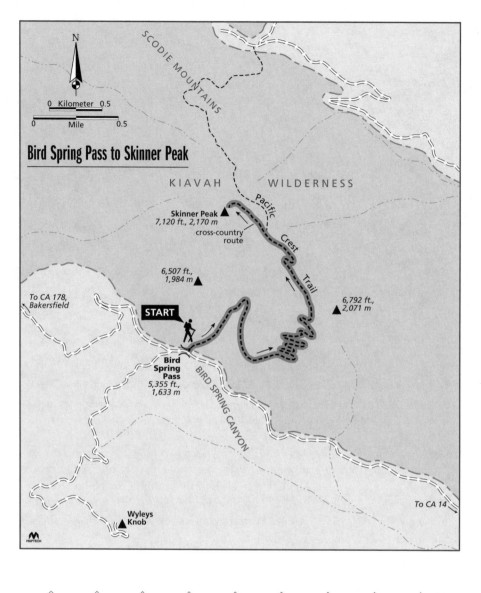

Bird Spring Pass to Skinner Peak

SCODIE MOUNTAINS

KIAVAH   WILDERNESS

N
0 Kilometer 0.5
0   Mile   0.5

Skinner Peak
7,120 ft., 2,170 m

cross-country route

Pacific Crest Trail

6,507 ft., 1,984 m

To CA 178, Bakersfield

START

6,792 ft., 2,071 m

Bird Spring Pass
5,355 ft., 1,633 m

BIRD SPRING CANYON

To CA 14

Wyleys Knob

MAPTECH

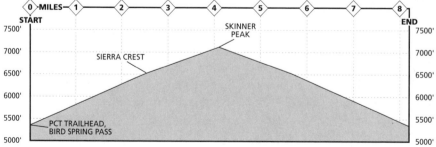

0 MILES 1   2   3   4   5   6   7   8
START   END

7500'   7500'
                    SKINNER PEAK
7000'   7000'
        SIERRA CREST
6500'   6500'

6000'   6000'

5500'   5500'
    PCT TRAILHEAD,
    BIRD SPRING PASS
5000'   5000'

Key points

0.0 PCT trailhead at Bird Spring Pass.

2.5 Trail tops out on Sierra crest at 6,520 feet.

3.7 Leave PCT and follow crest northwest.

4.1 Skinner Peak.

27 Big Falls Canyon

This short, pleasant day hike leads to a beautiful cascading creek in the South Coast Ranges.

Start: The trail begins on the east side of the parking area, immediately above Lopez Canyon Creek.
General location: Santa Lucia Range, Santa Lucia Wilderness (Los Padres National Forest), in the extreme southern reaches of the South Coast Ranges, 10 miles southeast of San Luis Obispo
Distance: 2.5-mile round-trip day hike
Approximate hiking time: 1 hour
Difficulty: Easy
Trailhead elevation: 800 feet
High point: 1,080 feet
Land status: National forest wilderness (Santa Lucia Wilderness)
Best season: Mid-October through May

Water availability: Available from Big Falls Canyon Creek; treat before drinking, or bring your own
Maps: USGS Lopez Mountain; Los Padres National Forest map (Monterey and Santa Lucia Ranger Districts)
Fees and permits: Wilderness Permits are not required. A California Campfire Permit is required for open fires and backpack stoves. A National Forest Adventure Pass is required to park at the trailhead.
Trail contact: Los Padres National Forest, Santa Lucia Ranger District, 1616 North Carlotti Drive, Santa Maria, CA 93454; (805) 925-9538

Finding the trailhead: From U.S. Highway 101 in Arroyo Grande, 15 miles south of San Luis Obispo and 15 miles north of Santa Maria, take the Lopez Lake exit and go east on California Highway 227, following signs pointing to Lopez Lake. After driving 0.9 mile from US 101, turn right and leave CA 227 where a sign points to Lopez Lake. Your paved road eventually crosses Lopez Lake's dam and follows above its southern shoreline. Just before entering the Lopez Lake Recreation Area, turn right onto Hi Mountain Road, 10.3 miles from CA 227. Turn left onto Upper Lopez Canyon Road after another 0.8 mile. The Hi Mountain Road continues straight ahead, reaching Arroyo Grande Station (Forest Service) after 1.1 miles.

Proceed north, then west on Upper Lopez Canyon Road, bearing right after another 6.3 miles where a sign points to Lopez Canyon. The pavement ends 0.1 mile beyond; proceed up the canyon, crossing and recrossing shallow Lopez Canyon Creek fifteen times. This section of road may be impassable after hard rains.

Reach the signed trailhead after driving 3.6 miles from the end of the pavement. Parking is somewhat limited here.

The Hike

The Santa Lucia Wilderness lies near the southern end of the Santa Lucia Range east of San Luis Obispo. Few trails penetrate into this small but rugged wild area. Due to the dense chaparral that blankets the hillsides, off-trail travel is generally impossible.

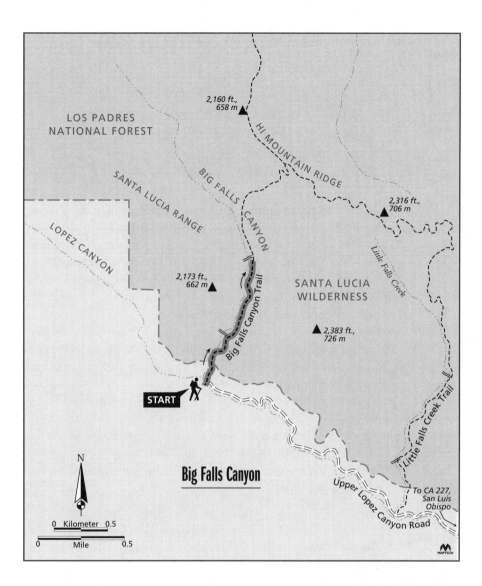

Big Falls Canyon

The trail up Big Falls Canyon penetrates a major westward-flowing tributary of Lopez Canyon and ascends to the crest of the range. The many large, deep pools in this canyon host a healthy population of small trout, although fishing is poor. Newts are also commonly seen in portions of the creek.

Portions of this route are sometimes overgrown with poison oak, so exercise reasonable caution to avoid irritation. The Forest Service periodically clears the poison oak from the trail, so consider following the trail beyond the upper falls and climbing to the crest of the range, where good views of the surrounding countryside unfold.

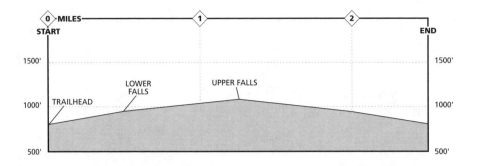

From the trailhead, follow the path downstream a short distance; boulder-hop across Lopez Canyon Creek, turn northeast, and enter lower Big Falls Canyon and the Santa Lucia Wilderness. Soon after crossing to the south bank of Big Falls Canyon Creek, pass an information sign and recross to the north bank. Your trail, shaded by live oak and California sycamore, is frequently lined with poison oak.

As you ascend northeasterly along the bottom of shady Big Falls Canyon, you pass several deep, lovely pools—excellent swimming holes.

Soon climb up and around the impressive lower falls, passing several trails leading to the falls themselves. At this point, the fragrant California bay begins to contribute shade to the already well-shaded canyon. Deep pools near the lower falls are excellent for cooling off after completing the hike.

Ascend past the upper falls, where the creek tends to dry up early in dry years or in midsummer during years of normal precipitation. Soon the trail, decked with thickets of poison oak, climbs beyond this point to Hi Mountain Ridge, the crest of the range in another 1.2 miles. Hikers with ample time and energy might choose to loop back to Lopez Canyon via the southbound trail along that ridge and the trail descending into Little Falls Canyon.

From this point, most hikers will backtrack to the trailhead.

Key points

0.0 Big Falls Canyon trailhead.

0.5 Lower falls.

1.25 Upper falls.

28 Mount Pinos to Grouse Mountain

This pleasant day hike follows the crest of a high, conifer-clad mountain range south of the San Joaquin Valley. Vistas reach across the flat expanse of the San Joaquin Valley to the distant peaks of the Sierra Nevada.

Start: The trail begins at the Mount Pinos Trail sign on the west side of the parking area.

General location: Western Transverse Ranges, Chumash Wilderness (Los Padres National Forest), 9 miles west of Frazier Park

Distance: 6.6-mile round-trip day hike or overnighter

Approximate hiking time: 3 hours

Difficulty: Moderate

Trailhead elevation: 8,800 feet

High point: Mount Pinos trailhead, 8,800 feet

Land status: National forest wilderness (Chumash Wilderness)

Best season: Late May through October

Water availability: None available; bring your own

Maps: USGS Sawmill Mountain (trail not shown on quad); Los Padres National Forest map, south portion (Santa Barbara, Ojai, and Mount Pinos Ranger Districts)

Fees and permits: Wilderness Permits are not required. A California Campfire Permit is required for open fires and backpack stoves. A National Forest Adventure Pass is required to park at the trailhead.

Trail contact: Los Padres National Forest, Mount Pinos Ranger District, 34580 Lockwood Valley Road, Frazier Park, CA 93225; (805) 245-3731

Finding the trailhead: From Interstate 5, 3 miles north of Gorman and 41 miles south of Bakersfield, take the Frazier Park exit and follow the main paved road, Frazier Park–Cuddy Valley Road, west. Avoid a southbound road to Lockwood Valley after driving 8 miles west from I-5. After driving 11.7 miles from I-5, bear left where the sign indicates Mount Pinos; Mill Potrero Road branches right and leads northwest to California Highway 166.

The paved road now begins a steady climb to Mount Pinos, passing two Forest Service campgrounds en route. After 8.2 miles, at the large parking area for the Chula Vista walk-in campground, turn left onto the very rough road leading to Mount Pinos. After driving another 1.8 miles, reach the trailhead and parking area at the Condor Observation Site, just beyond a right-branching spur road leading to the summit microwave tower. Low-powered and low-clearance vehicles may have a difficult time negotiating this very rough 1.8 miles of dirt road.

The Hike

Mount Pinos, the high point of a major east–west ridge about 15 to 20 miles west of Tejon Pass, lies in a region where the South Coast Ranges, the Transverse Ranges, and the Tehachapi Mountains coalesce. Geologically, the Mount Pinos area is part of the South Coast Ranges. However, due to its east–west alignment, it appears to be more closely associated with the Transverse Ranges, which include the San Gabriel and San Bernardino Mountains.

The Mount Pinos high country west of Interstate 5 supports cool forests of pine and fir.

The entire region is mantled in a thick conifer forest and laced with numerous trails and streams. Several trail camps throughout the Mount Pinos Ranger District beckon overnight campers.

This ridgetop hike traverses the Mount Pinos high country and ends with an easy cross-country jaunt to a seldom-visited mountain covered by a thick Jeffrey pine forest. Grouse Mountain's central location on this high ridge offers an isolated destination for city-weary hikers. Few people ascend the gentle forested slopes of this mountain, so this satisfying leg-stretcher provides an easy opportunity to enjoy nature's solitude.

Backpackers willing to carry water will find ample opportunity for camping along much of this route, though most backpackers choose to camp at Sheep Camp and Lilly Meadows along the North Fork Lockwood Creek.

From the parking area, your hike begins at the Mount Pinos Trail sign. The trail starts out as a paved path, passing several gnarled and twisted Jeffrey and limber pines. You soon branch left onto the trail proper; the paved path continues a short distance to a bench-furnished viewpoint.

You are accompanied by panoramic vistas as you switchback down the west slope of Mount Pinos and enter the Chumash Wilderness. These vistas include the southern

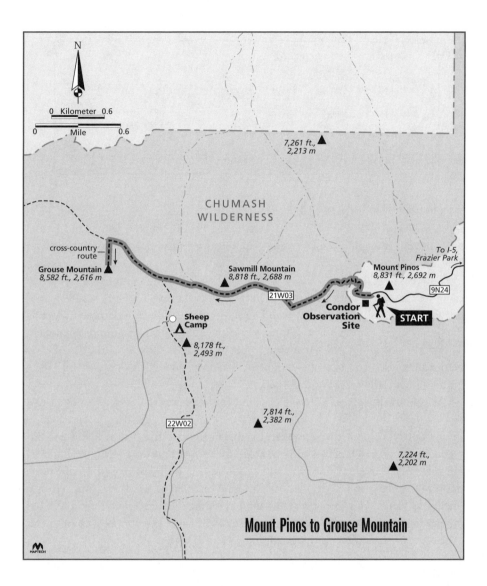

Mount Pinos to Grouse Mountain

Sierra Nevada and the alpine peaks of the Great Western Divide to the north, lying beyond the patchwork of farmlands in the southern San Joaquin Valley. To the southeast, south, and southwest lies the forested terrain of the western Transverse Ranges, beckoning hikers to explore their intriguing landscape.

The west slope of Mount Pinos is subalpine in character, and as you follow switchbacks down the mountain you pass many stunted limber pines. The trail is decked in spring and early summer with western wallflower and Indian paintbrush. You soon enter a stand of white fir and Jeffrey pine; after 0.8 mile the trail bottoms out at an 8,350-foot saddle. You then begin a moderate ascent up the east ridge of Sawmill Mountain in a forest dominated by Jeffrey pine.

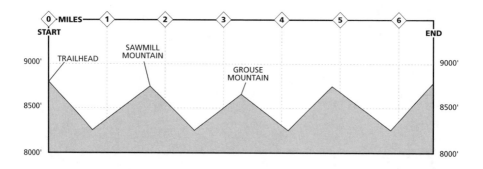

The trail eventually levels off on the summit plateau of Sawmill Mountain. A short walk north to the 8,750-foot high point, clad in stunted Jeffrey and limber pines, reveals sweeping views of the San Joaquin Valley and the southern Sierra Nevada.

The trail next descends west to join Trail 22W02, leading south past the two trail camps in the North Fork Lockwood Creek. Backpackers will want to turn left here, but day hikers will stay right, descending to another saddle at 8,350 feet. The trail then rises once again along the forested northeast shoulder of Grouse Mountain. This mountain is not labeled on the topo map but is shown on the Los Padres National Forest map; it is the mountain between Sawmill Mountain and Cerro Noroeste (also known as Mount Abel).

At a point almost due north of Grouse Mountain, where the trail begins a slight descent, leave the trail and head southwest until you reach the flat summit ridge of the mountain. (Use of the topo map for this portion of the hike is highly recommended.) Upon reaching the summit ridge, turn south and walk along the undulating ridgetop through a pleasant, parklike forest. In a little less than 0.5 mile, reach the south summit and high point of Grouse Mountain at 8,650 feet, marked by a small rock cairn. Views are somewhat limited because of the Jeffrey pine forest, but the peaceful nature of this isolated mountain easily makes up for the lack of vistas.

Eventually backtrack to the trailhead.

Key points

0.0 Mount Pinos trailhead.

1.7 Sawmill Mountain.

2.2 Junction with Trail 22W02 leading south to North Fork Lockwood Creek; continue straight ahead (west).

2.8 Leave the trail on the northeast shoulder of Grouse Mountain; head south cross-country along the ridge.

3.3 Summit of Grouse Mountain.

29 Pine Mountain

This rewarding day hike follows the lofty crest of Pine Mountain through a cool pine and fir forest. Vistas reach into the wild backcountry of the Sespe Wilderness.

Start: Follow the closed road east from the parking area for 0.2 mile to the Pine Mountain Trail on the east side of the road.

General location: Western Transverse Ranges, Sespe Wilderness (Los Padres National Forest), 35 miles north of Ventura

Distance: 7.2-mile round-trip day hike or overnighter

Approximate hiking time: 3.5 hours

Difficulty: Moderate

Trailhead elevation: 6,975 feet

High point: 7,431 feet

Land status: National forest wilderness (Sespe Wilderness)

Best season: Late May through mid-November

Water availability: None available; bring your own

Maps: USGS Reyes Peak, Lion Canyon, San Guillermo Mountain; Los Padres National Forest map, south portion (Santa Barbara, Ojai, and Mount Pinos Ranger Districts)

Fees and permits: Wilderness Permits are not required. A California Campfire Permit is required for open fires and backpack stoves. A National Forest Adventure Pass is required to park at the trailhead.

Trail contact: Los Padres National Forest, Ojai Ranger District, 1190 East Ojai Avenue, Ojai, CA 93023; (805) 646-4348

Finding the trailhead: From California Highway 33—the Jacinto Reyes Scenic Byway—about 25 miles south of its junction with California Highway 166 (7 miles east of New Cuyama) and 47 miles north of Ventura, turn east where a sign indicates the Pine Mountain Recreation Area. Follow this narrow oiled road eastward. The oiled surface ends after about 6 miles; continue east on dirt road for one more mile to the dead end at the Pine Mountain trailhead. There are two no-fee campgrounds available on Pine Mountain for car campers: Pine Mountain has eight sites, and Reyes Peak has seven sites. Neither campground provides water.

The Hike

West of the San Gabriel Mountains and Interstate 5, the Transverse Ranges rise to impressive heights before fading into the lower ranges at the extreme western terminus of the province near Point Arguello. From Pine Mountain in the south to Frazier Mountain in the east to the Mount Pinos massif in the north, this high, well-watered region, covered by many square miles of conifer forest, sees much fewer visitors than do other thickly forested high country areas of southern California.

This hike along Pine Mountain ridge leads to Peak 7431, the easternmost 7,000-foot peak on this high ridge. However, backpackers may want to descend north into Beartrap Creek or take advantage of several trail camps along Piedra Blanca Creek to the east of Pine Mountain (see the Los Padres National Forest map for trail camp locations). Campsites in those canyons are shaded by ponderosa and Jeffrey pine,

The sandstone cliffs on the south slope of Pine Mountain in the Sespe Wilderness are reminiscent of the Southwest's canyon country.

juniper, and piñon pine. Water is usually available, though backpackers should contact the Ojai Ranger District office in Ojai to inquire about water availability.

Those who arrange a car shuttle can hike out to Sespe Creek at the southern foot of Pine Mountain—a point-to-point hike of about 12.5 miles. Backpackers who carry an adequate supply of water will find almost unlimited campsite possibilities in the open, parklike forest that characterizes this ridgeline hike.

Where the road is blocked to further access for vehicles, begin hiking eastward along the south slopes of Peak 7109 via the retired road. After hiking about 0.2 mile, leave the road where it bends southeast and pick up eastbound Pine Mountain Trail just beyond the berm on the east side of the road.

The trail begins traversing north-facing slopes, soon entering the Sespe Wilderness on the north slopes of Reyes Peak, at 7,510 feet the highest point on Pine Mountain. The old Reyes Peak quadrangle shows the north slopes of Pine Mountain barren of vegetation. However, as you will immediately notice, these north slopes are cloaked in a thick pine-and-fir forest.

The undulating trail, shaded the entire distance by Jeffrey, ponderosa, and sugar pine and white fir, stays on or just north of the ridgecrest. On your eastward course you often have good views northwest into the Cuyama Valley, north to the highly eroded sandstone hills surrounding the upper Cuyama River, and beyond to the Mount Pinos massif. You also obtain occasional conifer-framed views eastward to the

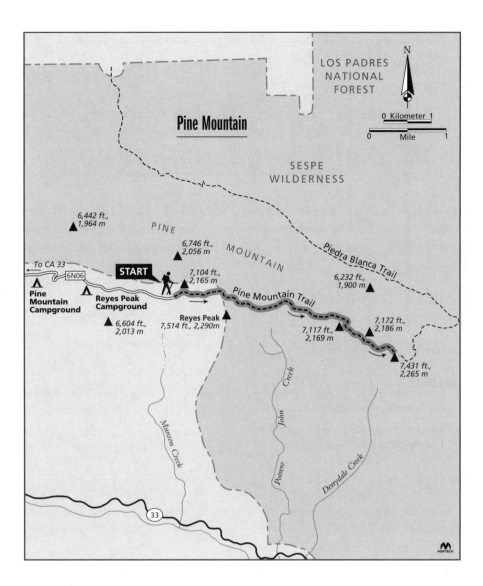

Pine Mountain

LOS PADRES
NATIONAL
FOREST

SESPE
WILDERNESS

PINE

MOUNTAIN

6,442 ft.,
1,964 m

6,746 ft.,
2,056 m

7,104 ft.,
2,165 m

Piedra Blanca Trail

6,232 ft.,
1,900 m

Pine Mountain Trail

To CA 33

6N06

START

Pine
Mountain
Campground

Reyes Peak
Campground

6,604 ft.,
2,013 m

Reyes Peak
7,514 ft., 2,290m

7,117 ft.,
2,169 m

7,172 ft.,
2,186 m

7,431 ft.,
2,265 m

Munson Creek

Potrero John Creek

Derrydale Creek

33

MAPTECH

thickly forested terrain of the western Transverse Ranges province. When the trail touches the crest at occasional ridgetop saddles or gaps, your gaze reaches southward to the chaparral-choked hillsides that plunge deep into Sespe Creek.

After rounding the north slopes of Peak 7114, about 1.9 miles from the trailhead, you have views into the headwaters bowl of Potrero John Creek. Here, under Peak 7306, lie broken sandstone cliffs, reminiscent of Utah's canyon country. On the more open stretches of trail, you cross grassy slopes decorated by currant, yellow lupine, western wallflower, and snowplant in late spring and early summer.

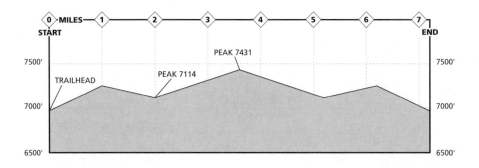

A short distance beyond an inverted orange triangle attached to a metal post, round a minor boulder-covered, north-trending ridge. Descend slightly to a small saddle, and then negotiate a few switchbacks. Just beyond, where the trail and ridge begin steadily descending to the east, leave the trail and scramble a short distance south to the boulder-heaped summit of Peak 7431. Views are somewhat limited due to the thick Jeffrey pine forest.

From this peak, either retrace your route to the trailhead or, if equipped for an overnight stay, follow the trail northeast into Piedra Blanca Creek, where good, conifer-shaded campsites await.

Key points

0.0   Pine Mountain trailhead.

0.2   Turn left (east) onto Pine Mountain Trail.

3.6   Peak 7431.

30 Sierra Pelona

This rewarding day hike leads to a windswept ridge offering far-ranging vistas stretching from the San Gabriel Mountains to the southern Sierra Nevada.

Start: The trail begins on the south side of Bouquet Canyon Road, immediately east of an ICY road sign.

General location: Western Transverse Ranges, Angeles National Forest, 12 miles west of Palmdale and 15 miles northeast of Newhall

Distance: 4.4-mile round-trip day hike

Approximate hiking time: 2–2.5 hours

Difficulty: Moderate

Trailhead elevation: 3,200 feet

High point: 4,550 feet

Land status: National forest

Best season: Mid-October through May

Water availability: Available at 1.2 miles from Big Oak Spring; purify before drinking, or bring your own

Maps: USGS Sleepy Valley; Angeles National Forest map

Fees and permits: Wilderness Permits are not required. A California Campfire Permit is required for open fires and backpack stoves. A National Forest Adventure Pass is required to park at the trailhead.

Trail contact: Angeles National Forest, Saugus Ranger District, 30800 Bouquet Canyon Road, Saugus, CA 91350; (805) 296-9710

Finding the trailhead: From the junction of Spunky Canyon and Bouquet Canyon Roads at the upper (east) end of Bouquet Reservoir, 18 miles southeast of Saugus, proceed east on Bouquet Canyon Road for 2.1 miles. The trailhead lies just east of an ICY road sign, on the south side of the road.

The trailhead can also be reached from California Highway 14 in Palmdale. Follow Los Angeles County Road N2 west for about 8.2 miles, then turn south onto Bouquet Canyon Road and drive 4.2 miles to the trailhead.

The Hike

The Sierra Pelona is one of several long hogback ridges lying between the San Gabriel Mountains to the southeast and Interstate 5 to the west. This hike follows the north slopes of the central Sierra Pelona massif, ascending to the crest through chaparral and scattered oaks. The outstanding feature of Sierra Pelona is the superb, 360-degree panorama that unfolds from the summit ridge.

The hike is usually open year-round but can be uncomfortable during the heat of summer. Strong Santa Ana winds also buffet this exposed mountain occasionally, especially in autumn.

From the trailhead your path leads southwest through chaparral consisting of birchleaf mountain mahogany, scrub oak, chamise, buckwheat, and an occasional canyon live oak. As you gain elevation you also gain vistas of Bouquet Canyon, Bouquet Reservoir, and the surrounding mountains.

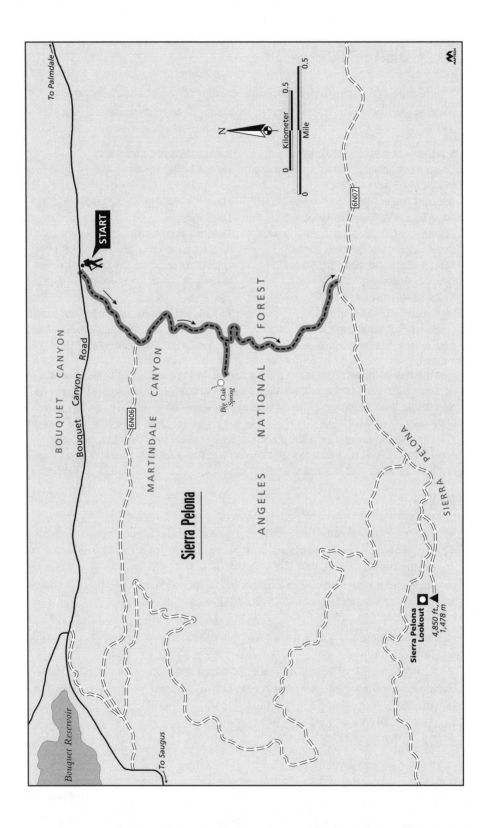

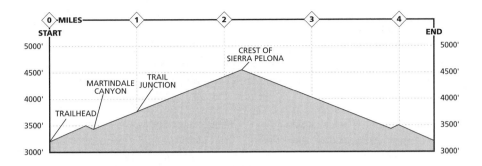

After hiking 0.4 mile, crest a minor east–west ridge and cross Forest Road 6N06. Beyond the road, the trail descends slightly to cross Martindale Canyon's dry streambed, then resumes climbing north-facing slopes.

After hiking 0.6 mile from FR 6N06, meet a short spur trail in a live oak stand. This spur leads 0.2 mile west to Big Oak Spring, a possible campsite and the site of what was formerly the world's largest canyon live oak. Unfortunately, that tree was destroyed by a brushfire.

The trail continues southward, ascending grassy slopes decorated in spring by lupine, western wallflower, and some Mariposa tulip. After another 1.2 miles of moderate ascent, you reach the crest of Sierra Pelona and a junction with Forest Road 6N07, where sweeping vistas are revealed. A short jaunt east or, especially, west reveals the best panoramas.

To reach Peak 4850, the former site of the Sierra Pelona fire lookout tower, hike 1.6 mile west along FR 6N07, staying left at two junctions and gaining 300 feet of elevation en route. The finest vistas on the mountain are obtained from the lookout. Wind gusts as high as 100 miles per hour have been recorded here.

After reveling in the superb panorama, you will reluctantly descend back to the trailhead.

Key points

0.0 Trailhead on Bouquet Canyon Road.

0.4 Cross FR 6N06.

1.0 Junction with westbound spur to Big Oak Spring; stay left (southeast).

2.2 Junction with FR 6N07 on the crest of Sierra Pelona.

31 Devils Chair

This memorable hike leads into the intriguing rock formations of the Devils Punchbowl at the northern foot of the San Gabriel Mountains.

Start: The trail begins on the west side of the hikers' parking area, immediately above South Fork Big Rock Creek.
General location: North-central San Gabriel Mountains, Angeles National Forest, 20 miles southeast of Palmdale
Distance: 5.0-mile round-trip day hike or overnighter
Approximate hiking time: 2-2.5 hours
Difficulty: Moderate
Trailhead elevation: 4,600 feet
High point: Devils Chair, 5,050 feet
Land status: National forest
Best season: Mid-September through May

Water availability: Available from Holcomb Canyon's creek at 1.9 miles; purify before drinking, or bring your own
Maps: USGS Valyermo; Angeles National Forest map
Fees and permits: Wilderness Permits are not required. A California Campfire Permit is required for open fires and backpack stoves. A National Forest Adventure Pass is required to park at the trailhead.
Trail contact: Angeles National Forest, Valyermo Ranger District, P.O. Box 15, 29835 Valyermo Road, Valyermo, CA 93563; (661) 944-2187

Finding the trailhead: There are several ways to reach the trailhead, all of them beginning from California Highway 138. Probably the best and most straightforward route is 165th Street East, also known as Bobs Gap Road, which turns south from CA 138 about 4.5 miles east of Pearblossom and 26 miles west of Interstate 15. Follow this road south across the desert and over a low range of hills into a farming area along the San Andreas Rift Zone. After driving 7.5 miles south of CA 138, turn left onto Big Pines Highway and proceed eastward for 0.3 mile. Turn right (south) and follow paved Forest Road 4N11 along Big Rock Creek, passing the Sycamore Flats Campground. After 2.5 more miles turn right (south) once again onto dirt Forest Road 4N11A leading to South Fork Campground. After 1 mile turn right into the hikers' parking area, just below the campground.

The Hike

The Devils Punchbowl is another of California's many striking rock formations. Lying at the northern foot of the San Gabriel Mountains along the San Andreas Rift Zone, this unusual, highly eroded sandstone-conglomerate-shale formation is especially interesting. The trail leads hikers to its best viewpoint, the Devils Chair, where the entire hellish landscape of the Punchbowl spreads out to the north, with the barrens of the Mojave Desert fading into the distance beyond.

This hike can be taken as a leisurely overnighter. Backpackers will find good campsites in Holcomb Canyon next to the creek.

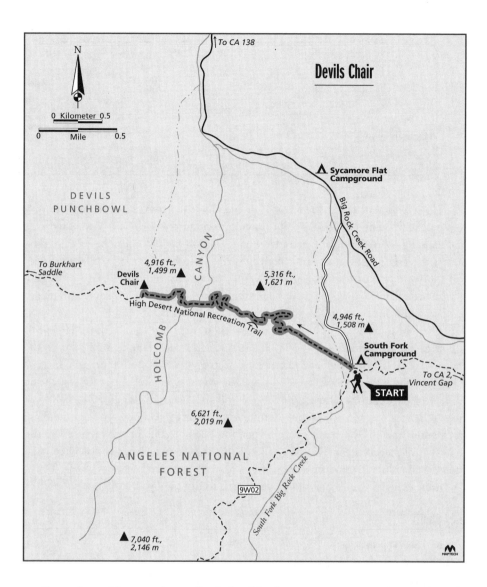

From the parking area, immediately boulder-hop your way across the South Fork Big Rock Creek and find the northwestbound High Desert National Recreation Trail on the west side. Runoff in this canyon can be substantial during the spring snowmelt period; caution is advised when crossing this creek during high water.

From the west side of the creek, the trail switchbacks up to the low gap visible on the western skyline, through scrub oak, manzanita, mountain mahogany, and some piñon pine. From the gap you have good views east and west along the north slopes of the San Gabriel Mountains. A portion of the Devils Punchbowl is visible to the west across Holcomb Canyon.

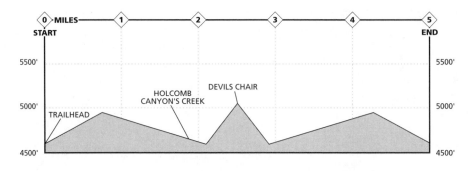

The trail then descends 400 feet into the depths of Holcomb Canyon via chaparral-covered slopes. The perennial stream flowing through this canyon is shaded by large oaks and big-cone Douglas firs, under which pleasant campsites can be located. Hop across this creek (which also runs high in spring) and begin a steep 480-foot ascent up the west wall of the canyon. Above this ascent, the trail heads west through a piñon woodland, where you will be rewarded with good views across the highly eroded sandstone hills and canyons of the Devils Punchbowl.

The trail hugs the rim of the formation, then turns north for a short descent to the rock point of the Devils Chair. Handrails help steady fainthearted hikers—the near-vertical slopes of slippery, rotten rock drop precipitously away on all sides.

The Devils Punchbowl lies along the San Andreas Fault. You might notice the similarity between the Devils Punchbowl and the Mormon Rocks, which lie just west of I–15 along CA 138, about 20 miles east of the Punchbowl. At one time these formations may have been a single formation, but horizontal movement along the fault has displaced them. The west side of the San Andreas Fault is slowly moving northward, while the east sideslips southward.

After enjoying this unusual area, backtrack to the trailhead.

Key points

0.0   South Fork trailhead.

1.9   Cross Holcomb Canyon's creek.

2.5   Devils Chair.

32 Twin Peaks

This rigorous trail leads experienced and well-conditioned hikers deep into the high country of the San Gabriel Wilderness, where vistas unfold across a maze of rugged canyons and ridges.

Start: The signed Mount Waterman Trail begins on the west side of Angeles Crest Highway, opposite the parking area.

General location: Central San Gabriel Mountains, San Gabriel Wilderness (Angeles National Forest), 15 miles north of Azusa

Distance: 9.6-mile round-trip day hike or overnighter

Approximate hiking time: 5 hours

Difficulty: Strenuous

Trailhead elevation: 6,800 feet

High point: East Twin Peak, 7,761 feet

Land status: National forest wilderness (San Gabriel Wilderness)

Best season: Late May through November

Water availability: None available; bring your own

Maps: USGS Waterman Mountain; Angeles National Forest map

Fees and permits: Wilderness Permits are not required. A California Campfire Permit is required for campfires and backpack stoves. A National Forest Adventure Pass is required to park at the trailhead.

Trail contact: Angeles National Forest, Arroyo Seco Ranger District, Oak Grove Park, Flintridge, CA 91011; (626) 790-1151

Finding the trailhead: The trailhead is located in the Buckhorn Flat area, about 1 mile east of Cloudburst Summit on the Angeles Crest National Scenic Byway (California Highway 2), 33 miles east of La Canada and 22 miles west of Big Pines. Park in the turnout on the east side of the highway directly above the Buckhorn Forest Service Guard Station.

The Hike

This strenuous trip tours the San Gabriel Wilderness high country, passing through parklike forests and traversing boulder-dotted slopes. This is bighorn sheep country, and the quiet and observant hiker may spot one or more of these magnificent animals scampering among the granitic boulders, cliffs, and outcrops that characterize this wild and rugged corner of the San Gabriels.

From the trailhead, cross the highway and find the trail behind the MT. WATERMAN TRAIL sign. Turn left (south) onto this well-graded trail, avoiding a doubletrack climbing directly up the slope to the west.

Proceeding south along the Mount Waterman Trail, cross a closed dirt road after 0.25 mile and resume hiking the trail across the road. Soon hop across a small creek and climb to the crest of the range through an open pine-and-fir forest. At the crest are a rope tow and a ski run a few yards east of the trail. Here turn right (west) and climb moderately along or near the ridge, meeting the Mount Waterman Summit

The Twin Peaks Trail ascends to the 7,761-foot summit of east Twin Peak, seen in this view from west Twin Peak. JOHN REILLY PHOTO

Trail 1.75 miles from the trailhead. A 0.75-mile (one-way) side trip can take you from here to the boulder-stacked summit of Waterman Mountain—at 8,038 feet, the high point of the San Gabriel Wilderness. The north slope of the mountain is the location of a small ski area.

From this junction begin your long descent to Twin Peaks Saddle. Twin Peaks loom boldly in the south across the deep gash of the saddle. After negotiating several switchbacks, reach another junction, 3.0 miles from the trailhead. Straight ahead (west) is Three Points and the Angeles Crest Highway, 5.0 miles away. Turn left here, where the sign reads TWIN PEAKS SADDLE–1, NO TRAIL BEYOND SADDLE.

The trail presently contours in an easterly direction, soon crossing a small creek, the headwaters of Devils Canyon, offering a year-round source of water. Continue descending, finally reaching 6,550-foot Twin Peaks Saddle. Contrary to the sign at

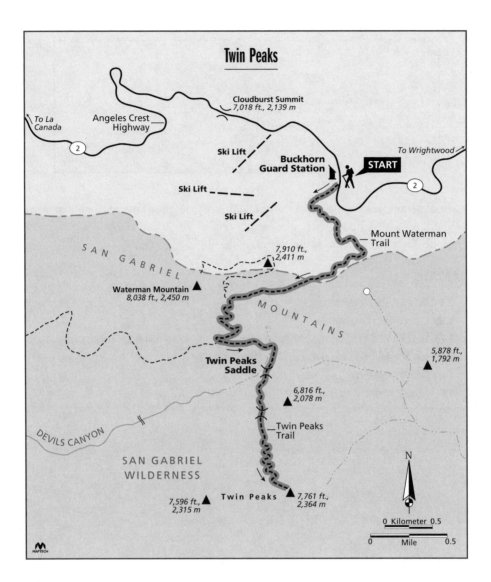

Twin Peaks

Cloudburst Summit
7,018 ft., 2,139 m

Angeles Crest Highway

To La Canada

2

Ski Lift

Buckhorn Guard Station

START

To Wrightwood

2

Ski Lift

Ski Lift

Mount Waterman Trail

S A N   G A B R I E L

7,910 ft., 2,411 m

Waterman Mountain
8,038 ft., 2,450 m

M O U N T A I N S

5,878 ft., 1,792 m

Twin Peaks Saddle

6,816 ft., 2,078 m

DEVILS CANYON

Twin Peaks Trail

N

SAN GABRIEL WILDERNESS

7,596 ft., 2,315 m

Twin Peaks

7,761 ft., 2,364 m

0 Kilometer 0.5

0 Mile 0.5

MAPTECH

the last junction, there is a trail beyond the saddle. The route contours in a southerly direction across smooth, openly forested slopes to another saddle, this one slightly higher than the last. From here it's a 1,200-foot climb up the north slope of Twin Peaks via a very steep unmaintained path. The cool forest of Jeffrey and sugar pine and white fir provides adequate shade during this strenuous climb. The switchbacks on this trail make a weak attempt to ease the grade. At last you reach the summit ridge and walk southeastward to the 7,761-foot summit of east Twin Peak.

On this boulder-littered peak, enjoy inspiring views into the San Gabriel Wilderness with its deep, brush-choked canyons and rugged topography. Most of the San

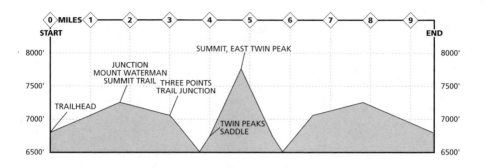

Gabriel Mountains are visible to the east and west; the sprawling metropolitan areas of the Los Angeles Basin lie at your feet more than 7,000 feet below.

From here retrace your route to the trailhead.

Key points

0.0 Mount Waterman trailhead.

0.25 Cross closed dirt road.

1.75 Junction with Mount Waterman Summit Trail; bear left (west) and begin descending.

3.0 Junction with westbound trail to Three Points; bear left (east).

4.0 Twin Peaks Saddle.

4.8 Summit of east Twin Peak.

33 Smith Mountain

The Bear Creek Trail traverses the chaparral-clad eastern reaches of the San Gabriel Wilderness and features panoramic vistas into the heart of the San Gabriel Mountains.

Start: The signed Bear Creek Trail begins at the northwest end of the parking area.
General location: Central San Gabriel Mountains, San Gabriel Wilderness (Angeles National Forest), 10 miles north of Azusa
Distance: 6.8-mile round-trip day hike
Approximate hiking time: 3–3.5 hours
Difficulty: Moderate
Trailhead elevation: 3,300 feet
High point: Smith Mountain, 5,111 feet
Land status: National forest
Best season: Mid-October through late May

Water availability: None available; bring your own
Maps: USGS Crystal Lake; Angeles National Forest map
Fees and permits: Wilderness Permits are not required. A California Campfire Permit is required for open fires and backpack stoves. A National Forest Adventure Pass is required to park at the trailhead.
Trail contact: Angeles National Forest, Mount Baldy Ranger District, 110 North Wabash Avenue, Glendora, CA 91741; (909) 335-1251

Finding the trailhead: From Interstate 210 in Azusa, turn north onto California Highway 39 (Azusa Avenue); the sign indicates NATIONAL FOREST RECREATION AREAS. Drive north through Azusa and into the foothills along the San Gabriel River Canyon. After driving 14.5 miles from I-210, bear left where East Fork Road crosses the river via a bridge.

You reach the signed Bear Creek Trailhead 6.2 miles from East Fork Road. Park in the large turnout on the west side of CA 39, across the road from the Valley of the Moon Penny Pines Plantation.

The Hike

The San Gabriel Wilderness encompasses more than 36,000 acres of extremely rugged terrain, ranging from chaparral-choked canyons and ridges to rich conifer forests in the high country. Only a few trails penetrate its margins; the interior remains a vast, wild region where black bear, mule deer, and mountain lion make their home. Since the area lies so close to the millions who live in the Los Angeles Basin, it is remarkable that a true wilderness experience can be found and enjoyed here in the heart of the San Gabriel Mountains.

Smith Mountain is the southernmost 5,000-foot peak on a long south-trending ridge separating the North Fork San Gabriel River from Bear Creek and the San Gabriel Wilderness. From its open summit, a large portion of the San Gabriel Mountains and the rugged depths of the San Gabriel Wilderness meet your gaze.

Smith Mountain, at left center, affords panoramic vistas on the east boundary of the rugged San Gabriel Wilderness. JOHN REILLY PHOTO

(Information and California Campfire Permits for backpackers can be obtained Friday through Sunday at the San Gabriel Entrance Station, located at the mouth of San Gabriel Canyon, or at Glendora Ranger Station during the week.)

The trail begins at the northwest end of the large parking area. It traverses east-facing slopes, proceeding in a southerly direction high above the highway. You soon cross a low ridge and enter the Lost Canyon drainage. The rich chaparral vegetation you'll see along the first 3.0 miles includes buckwheat, chamise, white sage, yucca, scrub oak, ceanothus, yerba santa, birchleaf mountain mahogany, silktassel, and holly-leaf cherry.

The trail bends in and out of several draws that funnel runoff into Lost Canyon. These gullies are shaded by canyon live oak, California bay, willow, California sycamore, and big-leaf maple—attesting to the availability of moisture in these usually dry watercourses and to the cooler microclimate that prevails there.

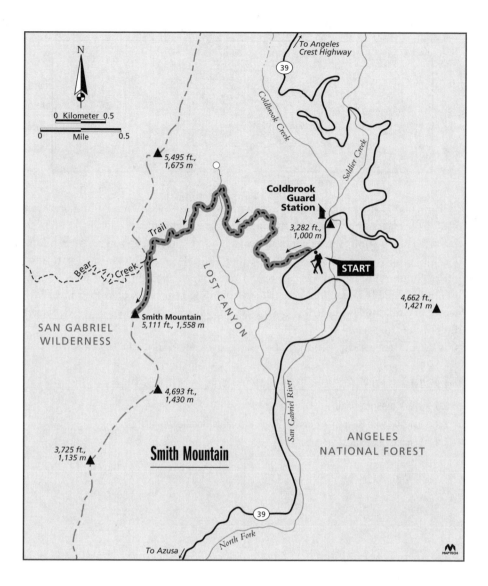

Reach 4,300-foot Smith Mountain Saddle after hiking 2.8 miles from the trailhead. The ridge to the north and south delineates the eastern boundary of the San Gabriel Wilderness.

The Bear Creek Trail descends westward from here into the depths of Bear Creek Canyon. But turn left (south) and begin climbing the steep north ridge of Smith Mountain. The trail, a boot-worn path ascending an overgrown firebreak, climbs steeply for 800 feet through scrub oak and manzanita.

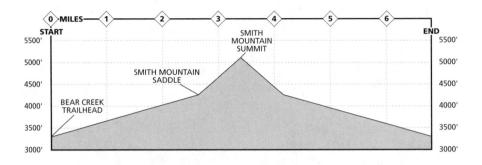

Big-cone Douglas firs soon appear on sheltered northwest-facing slopes just west of the ridge. Scrambling over or around a few granitic outcrops adds excitement to this often-steep climb. Views continue to expand as you gain elevation. After hiking 0.6 mile from the Bear Creek Trail, you find yourself standing atop the open summit of Smith Mountain, with an unobstructed view in all directions. The summit itself is crowned by a small boulder; the surrounding vegetation consists primarily of manzanita, silktassel, scrub oak, buckwheat, and chamise. Blue penstemon decorates the peak in the spring.

On your return trip, simply amble back down the trail to the highway.

Key points

0.0 Bear Creek trailhead.

2.8 Junction with Bear Creek Trail at Smith Mountain Saddle; turn left (south).

3.4 Summit of Smith Mountain.

34 Mount Baden-Powell

This high-elevation day hike leads to a windswept, subalpine summit in the northern reaches of the Sheep Mountain Wilderness, where far-ranging vistas unfold.

Start: The trail begins 150 yards east of Dawson Saddle, across (south of) a large turnout on Angeles Crest Highway.
General location: Northeast San Gabriel Mountains, Sheep Mountain Wilderness (Angeles National Forest), 20 miles northeast of Azusa
Distance: 8.2-mile round-trip day hike or overnighter
Approximate hiking time: 4 hours
Difficulty: Moderate
Trailhead elevation: 7,903 feet
High point: Mount Baden-Powell, 9,399 feet
Land status: National forest
Best season: Late May through mid-November

Water availability: None available; bring your own
Maps: USGS Crystal Lake (route from trailhead to Pacific Crest Trail not shown on quad); Angeles National Forest map
Fees and permits: Wilderness Permits are not required. A California Campfire Permit is required for open fires and backpack stoves. A National Forest Adventure Pass is required to park at the trailhead.
Trail contact: Angeles National Forest, Valyermo Ranger District, P.O. Box 15, 29835 Valyermo Road, Valyermo, CA 93563; (661) 944-2187

Finding the trailhead: Drive to Dawson Saddle, the high point of the Angeles Crest National Scenic Byway (California Highway 2), 47 miles east of La Canada and 10 miles west of Big Pines. The trail begins 150 yards east of Dawson Saddle, across the highway and south of a large turnout.

The Hike

At 7,903 feet, Dawson Saddle provides the second-highest trailhead in the San Gabriel Mountains, affording easy access to the high country. A trail was constructed in the early 1980s that bypasses the old path going over 9,138-foot Throop Peak. This new trail joins the Pacific Crest Trail on the crest of the range and makes the ascent to Mount Baden-Powell much easier and yet less popular than the traditional route starting at Vincent Gap.

After locating the beginning of the trail, ascend two switchbacks while rounding the point directly above Dawson Saddle. The trail then proceeds in a southerly direction, on or near the ridgeline, in a forest of Jeffrey, sugar, and lodgepole pines and white fir. At times you will see traces of the old path leading up to Throop Peak.

After traversing the north slope of Throop Peak, and 1.6 miles from the trailhead, intersect the Pacific Crest Trail at an elevation of about 8,850 feet. Turn left

Mount Baden-Powell rises beyond cloudy San Gabriel Canyon west of Mount San Antonio.
CRAWFORD M. JUDGE PHOTO

(east), descend along the ridgecrest, then climb up and around 8,997-foot Mount Burnham, where you enter a lodgepole and limber pine forest. Descend once again, round the north slopes of Hill 9086, and soon thereafter meet the Mount Baden-Powell Trail. Turn right (south) and ascend the final subalpine slopes for 0.1 mile to the summit, passing some wind-tortured limber pines, distinguished by needles in bundles of five. Some of these trees are believed to be as old as 2,000 years.

On the summit is a small concrete monument erected by the Boy Scouts in honor of their founder, Lord Baden-Powell. Views are excellent and far-ranging, rivaling those from Mount San Antonio.

From the summit, retrace your steps to Dawson Saddle. If you have a car waiting, you can descend the Mount Baden-Powell Trail for 4.0 miles to the Vincent Gap trailhead, 5.0 miles east of Dawson Saddle on the Angeles Crest National Scenic Byway.

Key points

0.0   Dawson Saddle trailhead.
1.6   Junction with Pacific Crest Trail (PCT); turn left (east) onto the PCT.
4.0   Junction with Mount Baden-Powell Trail; turn right (south).
4.1   Summit of Mount Baden-Powell.

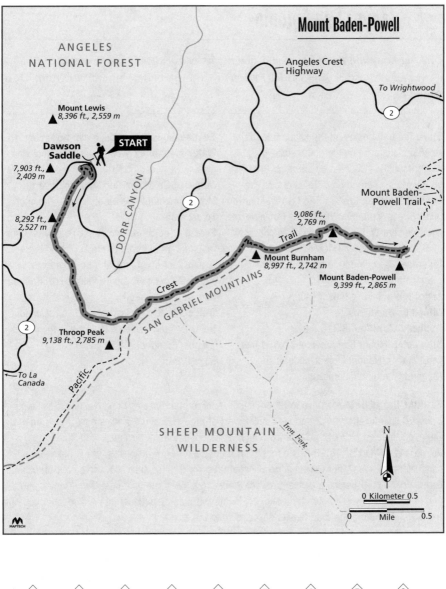

Mount Baden-Powell

ANGELES
NATIONAL FOREST

Angeles Crest
Highway

To Wrightwood

2

Mount Lewis
▲ 8,396 ft., 2,559 m

**Dawson
Saddle**
▲

START

Mount Baden-
Powell Trail

7,903 ft.,
2,409 m

DORR CANYON

8,292 ft., ▲
2,527 m

2

9,086 ft.,
2,769 m
▲

Trail

Mount Burnham
▲ 8,997 ft., 2,742 m

▲

Crest

SAN GABRIEL MOUNTAINS

Mount Baden-Powell
9,399 ft., 2,865 m

2

Throop Peak
9,138 ft., 2,785 m ▲

Pacific

→ To La
Canada

Iron Fork

SHEEP MOUNTAIN
WILDERNESS

N

0 Kilometer 0.5

0   Mile   0.5

MAPTECH

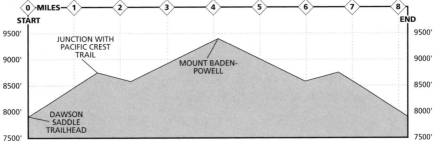

35 Mount San Antonio

This rigorous and exciting up-and-down trip leads experienced hikers to the highest mountain in the San Gabriel Mountains, the timberline summit of Mount San Antonio.

Start: The trail begins on the south side of the small parking area on the south slope of Wright Mountain, marked by elevation 8,310 on the Mount San Antonio USGS quad.
General location: Eastern San Gabriel Mountains, Sheep Mountain Wilderness (Angeles National Forest), 5 miles south of Wrightwood and 15 miles north of Ontario
Distance: 8.0-mile round-trip day hike or overnighter
Approximate hiking time: 5 hours
Difficulty: Strenuous
Trailhead elevation: 8,310 feet
High point: Mount San Antonio, 10,064 feet
Land status: National forest wilderness (Sheep Mountain Wilderness)

Best season: June through mid-November
Water availability: None available; bring your own
Maps: USGS Mount San Antonio; Sheep Mountain Wilderness map; Angeles National Forest map
Fees and permits: Wilderness Permits are not required. A California Campfire Permit is required for open fires and backpack stoves. A National Forest Adventure Pass is required to park at the trailhead.
Trail contact: Angeles National Forest, Mount Baldy Ranger District, 110 North Wabash Avenue, Glendora, CA 91741; (909) 335-1251

Finding the trailhead: Drive to Blue Ridge Summit on the Angeles Crest National Scenic Byway (California Highway 2), about 2 miles west of Big Pines and 53 miles east of La Canada. There, on the east side of the large Inspiration Point parking area, turn east onto Blue Ridge Road (Forest Road 3N06). This is a rough dirt road, quite narrow in places, but is passable to carefully driven cars. After driving generally southeast for 6 miles, bear left where right-branching Forest Road 3N39 begins a descent toward Prairie Fork. Continue east past Guffy Campground and in 1.75 miles you'll reach the trailhead, located at a small parking area on the south side of the road, just before the road begins descending to the east.

The Hike

From the loftiest summit in the San Gabriel Mountains, hikers are rewarded with vistas of a vast sweep of coastal, desert, and mountain scenery encompassing a great portion of southern California. Hikers completing this strenuous up-and-down trek on a steep, unmaintained trail will fully understand what John Muir meant when he called the San Gabriel Mountains "more rigidly inaccessible than any other I ever attempted to penetrate." This is prime bighorn sheep habitat, and the wary hiker is likely to see one or more of these agile, majestic creatures.

Crystalline skies during a winter sunrise on Mount San Antonio provide far-ranging vistas of distant southern California mountains and valleys, views normally obscured by smog and haze. JOHN REILLY PHOTO

From the trailhead, immediately descend to a saddle at 8,200 feet, then climb a ridge up and over Point 8555 on a narrow path resembling a game trail. A difficult stretch of uphill trail awaits after you have descended to another saddle. From this point, scramble up a sharp-edged ridge; precipitous rocky slopes fall abruptly more than 1,000 feet on either side. This is the most difficult and dangerous segment of the hike and should be attempted only by very experienced hikers.

Beyond that loose and slippery pitch, the trail becomes much easier to follow, soon climbing toward 9,648-foot Pine Mountain through a cool forest of lodgepole pine, where scattered clumps of chinquapin compose the only ground cover. The trail contours around Pine Mountain, staying about 130 feet below the summit, then drops steeply to an open, brushy saddle at 9,151 feet. A short distance above that saddle, pass a lightly used southwest-branching trail descending into Fish Fork. Instead of taking this path, begin a moderate, southbound ridgetop ascent through subalpine

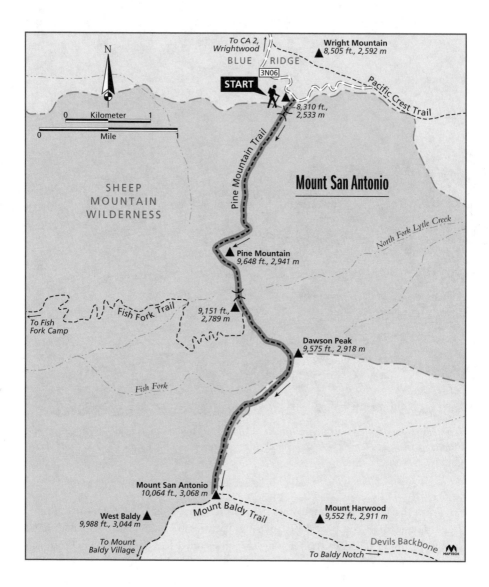

forest to the upper-west slopes of 9,575-foot Dawson Peak. You can easily reach the summit of Dawson Peak, which lies but a few hundred yards east of the trail.

The trail descends steeply from Dawson Peak to a saddle at 8,800 feet, passing a few Jeffrey pines en route. From there the trail climbs more than 1,200 feet upon the north ridge of Mount San Antonio. Footing is often bad on this very steep section of trail, but hikers are rewarded with a sense of accomplishment as they labor up the last few feet to the open summit of Mount San Antonio, the only peak in the San Gabriel Mountains rising above 10,000 feet.

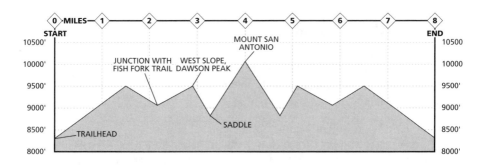

The summit stands just above timberline; the stunted and weather-beaten lodge-pole pines a short distance downslope attest to the severe winds and deep snow drifts that are prevalent here for half the year. The entire San Gabriel Mountains are visible, as are the other major mountain ranges of southern California. On a very clear day (which unfortunately is quite rare in southern California), you can see the Sierra Nevada as far north as the Mount Langley area, far to the northwest. Telescope Peak, towering above Death Valley, can be seen in the north, and far to the northeast rises Charleston Peak near Las Vegas. The vast, seemingly barren landscape of the Mojave Desert sprawls northward from the foot of the San Gabriel Mountains. The urban areas of southern California, stretching to the Pacific coast, are visible to the south and west. Such an all-encompassing vista is worthy of the highest summit in the range.

After absorbing the magnificent panorama, carefully reverse your strenuous up-and-down route to the trailhead.

Key points

0.0 Trailhead.

2.1 9,151-foot saddle and junction with trail descending into Fish Fork; stay left (south) and begin ascending.

2.8 West slope of Dawson Peak.

3.3 8,800-foot saddle between Dawson Peak and Mount San Antonio.

4.0 Summit of Mount San Antonio.

36 Cucamonga Peak

This rewarding trip takes hikers from the upper reaches of San Antonio Canyon through the heart of the Cucamonga Wilderness to the landmark pyramid of Cucamonga Peak, where panoramic vistas unfold.

Start: The signed trail begins at the end of a paved lane 100 yards east of the parking area.
General location: Eastern San Gabriel Mountains, Cucamonga Wilderness (Angeles and San Bernardino National Forests), 10 miles northeast of Ontario
Distance: 14.2-mile round-trip day hike or overnighter
Approximate hiking time: 7 hours
Difficulty: Strenuous
Trailhead elevation: 5,000 feet
High point: Cucamonga Peak, 8,859 feet
Land status: National forest wilderness (Cucamonga Wilderness)
Best season: Late May through mid-November
Water availability: Available from Cedar Springs at 2.25 miles; treat before drinking, or bring your own

Maps: USGS Mount Baldy, Telegraph Peak, Cucamonga Peak (Chapman Trail not shown on quads); Cucamonga Wilderness map; Angeles National Forest map
Fees and permits: A Wilderness Permit is required and can be obtained at the Mount Baldy Ranger District office in Glendora or at the Forest Supervisor's office in Arcadia. A California Campfire Permit is required for open fires and backpack stoves. A National Forest Adventure Pass is required to park at the trailhead.
Trail contact: Angeles National Forest, Mount Baldy Ranger District, 110 North Wabash Avenue, Glendora, CA 91741; (909) 335-1251

Finding the trailhead: Proceed to Mount Baldy Village in San Antonio Canyon, about 11 miles north of Interstate 10 in Ontario via Euclid or Mountain Avenue, both of which join Mount Baldy Road in the foothills. Mount Baldy Village is also 10 miles north of Claremont via Padua or Mills Avenue, which also join Mount Baldy Road in the foothills above San Antonio Dam. From the village, continue up Mount Baldy Road for 1.5 miles and turn right, proceeding 0.1 mile to the large parking area at the mouth of Icehouse Canyon.

The Hike

The San Gabriel Mountains are part of California's Transverse Ranges province. These ranges extend east–west across the framework of California's predominantly northwest–southeast–trending mountains and valleys. The Transverse Ranges province is approximately 300 miles long, stretching from the Eagle and Pinto Mountains of Joshua Tree National Park in the east to Point Arguello near Santa Barbara in the west. Typically, the highest terrain lies near the eastern terminus of each of the mountain ranges constituting this province.

Etiwanda Peak (8,662 feet) rises a mile northeast of Cucamonga Peak in the eastern San Gabriel Mountains. JOHN REILLY PHOTO

Cucamonga Peak stands high on the eastern end of the San Gabriel Mountains, soaring out of the deep gash of the San Andreas Rift Zone. This flat-topped "volcano-shaped" mountain is a familiar landmark to many southern Californians and is one of the most remote mountains in the range. The shortest route to its lofty summit involves a minimum 6 miles of hiking and thousands of feet of elevation gain. But hikers who complete this strenuous trip are rewarded with sweeping vistas of a large portion of southern California.

The subalpine forest of weather-beaten lodgepole pine on this flat, sandy summit offers a cool respite from oppressive summertime heat in the valleys below. Hikers relaxing on the summit often see a variety of soaring raptors riding the strong thermals that often sweep the slopes of the peak.

Usually taken as a day hike, this trip can be extended by an overnight stay in Cedar Glen or Kelly Camp, both of which have water.

From the parking area walk 100 yards east along a paved lane to the trailhead. En route you will pass a large concrete foundation, all that remains of the old Icehouse

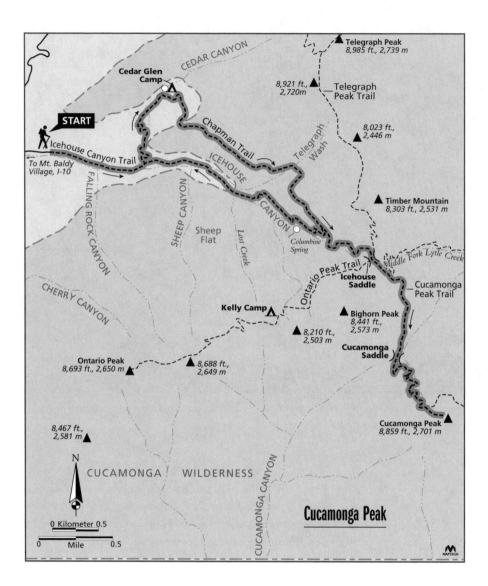

Lodge, which was consumed by a fire in 1988. Proceed up the canyon on the steadily ascending, sometimes rocky trail, passing the remains of several cabins. The route leads through a forest of partially burned big-cone Douglas fir, canyon live oak, incense-cedar, and white alder, passing several wildflower-cloaked springs.

Reach a junction after hiking 1.0 mile from the trailhead. The Icehouse Canyon Trail continues straight ahead, rejoining the route about 0.75 mile below Icehouse Saddle. That trail offers a shorter but somewhat more strenuous route to Icehouse Saddle and is better suited for the return trip if you choose to follow it.

Turn left onto the Chapman Trail, where a sign indicates that Cedar Springs is 1.25 miles and Cedar Glen is 1.5 miles ahead. This trail climbs up and out of Icehouse Canyon and begins ascending the lower reaches of Cedar Canyon, home of a major Icehouse tributary. Occasionally crossing Cedar Canyon's intermittently flowing stream, reach reliable Cedar Springs, the last source of water on the trail, after hiking 1.25 miles through a partially burned forest. You reach 6,400-foot Cedar Glen in another 0.25 mile, shaded by a cool stand of Jeffrey pine and white fir, but curiously there are no cedars here. This spot is an excellent choice for an overnight stay but is heavily used on many weekends throughout the year.

Beyond Cedar Glen, the trail rounds a spur ridge emanating from Telegraph Peak, enters the small (13,000 acres) but beautiful Cucamonga Wilderness, and begins a protracted traverse through stands of pine and fir and across open talus slopes, with ever-more-frequent views back down Icehouse Canyon to the mountains beyond. To the south, directly across Icehouse Canyon, rises the forested north slope of Ontario Peak.

About 1.8 miles from Cedar Glen, the Icehouse Canyon Trail joins your route on the right. Climb the final 0.7 mile through a parklike forest to 7,600-foot Icehouse Saddle, a major trail junction. The northbound trail leads to Baldy Notch and the Mount Baldy Ski Area via Timber Mountain, Telegraph Peak, and Thunder Mountain. The southwestbound trail leads to Kelly Camp a mile away, the last campsite with water, and then on to Ontario Peak. Take the southeastbound trail, where a sign indicates CUCAMONGA PEAK. The eastbound trail descending to the Middle Fork Lytle Creek quickly departs to your left as you begin traversing the eastern slopes of Bighorn Peak. The trail soon passes a few abandoned mine shafts, and after 1.0 mile you reach Cucamonga Saddle at 7,654 feet. From there the trail climbs 1,200 feet in little more than a mile to the summit of Cucamonga Peak, passing through a thick north-slope forest of pine and fir. Above 8,600 feet, the forest is dominated by lodgepole pine.

Eventually reaching the short path leading to the summit, turn right; the main trail (rarely used) continues east and ends at a trailhead at the head of South Fork

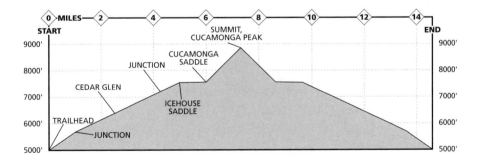

Lytle Creek. This trailhead is the former site of the largest living conifer in southern California—a 7-foot, 8-inch-diameter sugar pine dedicated to Joe Elliot, early supervisor of the San Bernardino National Forest.

Turning right, ascend the final sandy slopes to the 8,859-foot summit of Cucamonga Peak, where a magnificent vista unfolds. Massive 11,499-foot San Gorgonio Mountain, the highest point in southern California, dominates the eastern horizon 30 miles distant. At your feet lies the San Bernardino Valley, 7,500 feet below and 4 miles away.

Keep a sharp eye out on the precipitous slopes south and east of the peak; you may be lucky enough to spot one of the many Nelson bighorn sheep that inhabit the most rugged and remote reaches of the range.

After taking in the absorbing vista, doubleback to the trailhead.

Key points

0.0 Icehouse Canyon trailhead.

1.0 Junction of Icehouse Canyon and Chapman Trails; turn left (west) onto Chapman Trail.

2.25 Cedar Springs.

2.5 Cedar Glen.

4.3 Junction with Icehouse Canyon Trail; turn left (southeast).

5.0 Junction at Icehouse Saddle; turn right and follow the southeastbound trail toward Cucamonga Peak.

6.0 Cucamonga Saddle.

7.0 Junction with eastbound Cucamonga Peak Trail; turn right (southeast) and ascend toward the peak.

7.1 Summit of Cucamonga Peak.

37 Cajon Mountain

This hike, following dirt roads throughout, leads to a commanding vista point on the western edge of the San Bernardino Mountains high above Interstate 15 and Cajon Canyon.

Start: The southbound dirt road begins behind the locked gate at Cleghorn Pass.
General location: Western San Bernardino Mountains (San Bernardino National Forest), 5 miles north of San Bernardino
Distance: 8.0-mile round-trip day hike
Approximate hiking time: 3–3.5 hours
Difficulty: Moderate
Trailhead elevation: 4,545 feet
High point: Cajon Mountain, 5,310 feet
Land status: National forest

Best season: October through May (avoid the area during periods of substantial snow)
Water availability: None available; bring your own
Maps: USGS Cajon; San Bernardino National Forest map
Fees and permits: A National Forest Adventure Pass is required to park at the trailhead.
Trail contact: San Bernardino National Forest, Cajon Ranger District, Star Route, Box 100, 1209 Lytle Creek Road, Fontana, CA 92336-9704; (909) 887-2576

Finding the trailhead: From California Highway 138 above the western end of Silverwood Lake, 11 miles east of Interstate 15 and 11 miles northeast of Crestline Junction on California Highway 18, take the Cleghorn Road exit (Forest Road 2N49) and drive west up the canyon. The pavement ends after 1 mile and becomes a rough dirt road for the remaining 3.2 miles to Cleghorn Pass. Park in the large clearing at the pass. If the gate at the pass is open, it is possible to drive south on the dirt road for another 2.3 miles to the westbound Cajon Mountain Road. This will eliminate 4.6 miles of hiking and 455 feet of elevation gain.

The Hike

This leisurely day hike, on dirt road all the way, provides an unparalleled view of Cajon Canyon and the San Andreas Rift Zone, through which I–15 passes. The area may be closed periodically due to fire danger. Conditions vary each year, so be sure to consult the Cajon Ranger District of the San Bernardino National Forest to find out if the area is open to travel.

From Cleghorn Pass the road traverses north- and east-facing slopes, staying close to the ridgeline. You pass through areas of chaparral broken intermittently by grassy slopes. Among the trees along this stretch are black oak, its yellowing leaves offering virtually the only fall color in southern California's mountains. You will also notice both big-cone Douglas fir and incense-cedar, which is typically found in canyon bottoms.

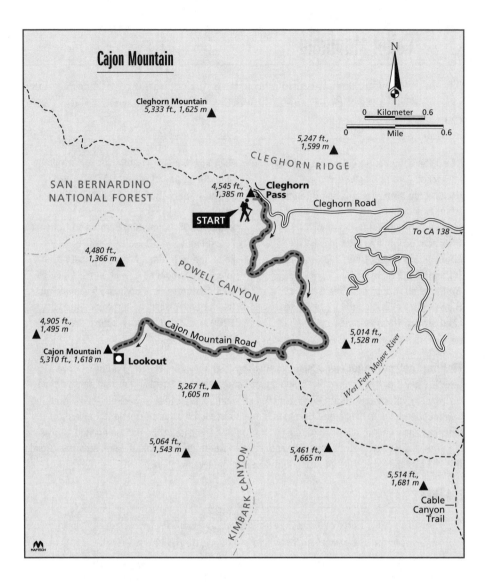

Cajon Mountain

After strolling 2.3 miles, you reach the westbound Cajon Mountain Road. Turn right (west) at that junction, passing the always-locked gate, and begin traversing north-facing slopes covered with canyon live oak, big-cone Douglas fir, incense-cedar, and some California bay.

After 1.7 miles, reach the summit of Cajon Mountain, capped with fire lookout and microwave towers. Your attention may well be diverted immediately from these works of man, however, since the spectacular vistas rival those obtained from an airplane.

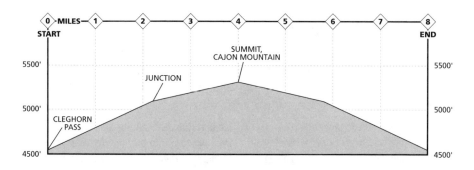

The high eastern peaks of the San Gabriel Mountains skyrocket above the deep cleft of Cajon Canyon. Also visible are portions of the San Bernardino Valley to the south and the western peaks of the San Bernardino Mountains.

From the peak, retrace your route to the trailhead.

Key points

0.0   Cleghorn Pass.

2.3   Junction with Cajon Mountain Road; turn right (west).

4.0   Summit of Cajon Mountain.

38 Delamar Mountain

This short trip, part cross-country, leads to a tree-crowned viewpoint north of Big Bear Lake.

Start: The signed Pacific Crest Trail (PCT) begins heading southeast from the south side of Forest Road 3N12, opposite the parking area.
General location: East-central San Bernardino Mountains, San Bernardino National Forest, 2 miles north of Fawnskin
Distance: 1.2-mile round-trip day hike
Approximate hiking time: 1 hour
Difficulty: Moderate
Trailhead elevation: 7,750 feet
High point: Delamar Mountain, 8,398 feet

Land status: National forest
Best season: Late May through mid-November
Water availability: None available; bring your own
Maps: USGS Fawnskin (route not shown on quad); San Bernardino National Forest map
Fees and permits: A National Forest Adventure Pass is required to park at the trailhead.
Trail contact: San Bernardino National Forest, Big Bear Ranger District, P.O. Box 290, North Shore Drive, Highway 38, Fawnskin, CA 92333; (909) 866-3437

Finding the trailhead: From Fawnskin on the north shore of Big Bear Lake, turn northwest onto Rim of the World Drive (Forest Road 3N14), where a sign indicates HOLCOMB VALLEY. Follow this road for 1.8 miles (the pavement ends after 0.4 mile), avoiding several signed spur roads, to northbound FR 3N12, where a sign indicates that Holcomb Valley is 6 miles ahead. Follow FR 3N12 northeast, passing several signed spur roads, for 1.7 miles to the trailhead. Park on the north side of the road, just east of the junction with northwestbound Forest Road 3N94 and across the road from an inconspicuous PCT marker.

The Hike

This seldom-visited yet easily accessible mountain, mantled in a pine and fir forest, provides views of Big Bear Lake and the San Gorgonio Wilderness and offers a refreshing (if brief) escape from civilization.

From your car, walk southeast across the road and proceed eastward along the Pacific Crest Trail. After walking 150 yards along the PCT through an open forest of Jeffrey pine and white fir, leave the trail where it makes a southeastward bend, then climb steeply up the small trail-less ridge in a southerly direction. After climbing for about 50 yards, cross an old bulldozer trail, created years ago when this forest was selectively logged.

About 100 yards above that track, encounter another bulldozer trail. Follow it in a southerly direction on or near the ridgeline. This route dwindles to a singletrack as you gain elevation. Upon reaching the small, rounded summit area, the trail disappears completely, and you must make your way a short distance south through a

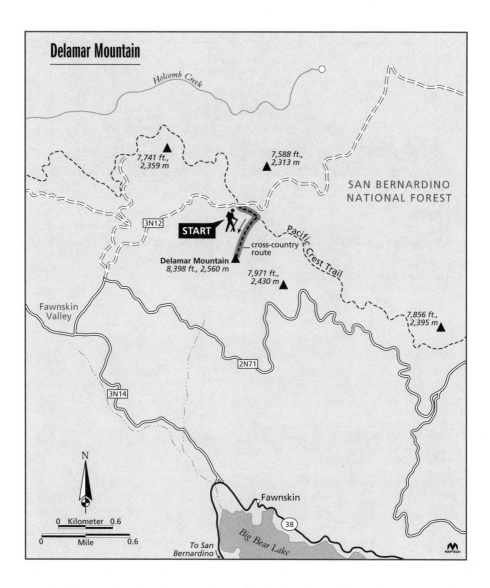

Delamar Mountain

Holcomb Creek

7,741 ft., 2,359 m

7,588 ft., 2,313 m

SAN BERNARDINO
NATIONAL FOREST

3N12

START

cross-country route

Pacific Crest Trail

Delamar Mountain
8,398 ft., 2,560 m

7,971 ft., 2,430 m

7,856 ft., 2,395 m

Fawnskin
Valley

2N71

3N14

N

0   Kilometer   0.6

0   Mile   0.6

Fawnskin

38

Big Bear Lake

To San
Bernardino

patch of mountain whitethorn to the rock pile that forms the high point of Delamar Mountain.

Here, in a cool conifer forest, you have good views south across Big Bear Lake to the San Gorgonio Wilderness on the southeastern skyline. Views are also good to the north across the green spread of Holcomb Valley.

After enjoying this pleasant mountain, carefully retrace your route back to the trailhead.

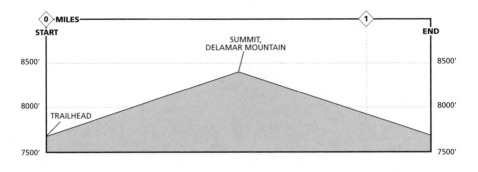

Key points

0.0 Trailhead; follow Pacific Crest Trail east for 150 yards, then turn south and ascend the trail-less ridge.

0.6 Summit of Delamar Mountain.

39 Champion Lodgepole Pine

This very easy stroll through the conifer forests of the San Bernardino Mountains leads to the world's largest-known lodgepole pine.

Start: The Lodgepole Pine Trail begins past the trail sign and picnic table at the north side of the parking area.
General location: East-central San Bernardino Mountains, San Bernardino National Forest, 1.5 miles south of Big Bear Lake
Distance: 0.6-mile round-trip
Approximate hiking time: 20 minutes
Difficulty: Easy
Trailhead elevation: 7,680 feet
High point: 7,680 feet

Land status: National forest
Best season: Mid-May through mid-November
Water availability: None available; bring your own
Maps: USGS Big Bear Lake; San Bernardino National Forest map
Fees and permits: A National Forest Adventure Pass is required to park at the trailhead.
Trail contact: San Bernardino National Forest, Big Bear Ranger District, P.O. Box 290, North Shore Drive, Highway 38, Fawnskin, CA 92333; (909) 866-3437

Finding the trailhead: From California Highway 18 on the south shore of Big Bear Lake, 2 miles west of Big Bear Lake Village, turn south onto Mill Creek Road (Forest Road 2N10). Stay on this road for 4.8 miles (the pavement ends after 1.1 miles), following signs indicating CHAMPION LODGEPOLE PINE at numerous junctions. After driving 4.8 miles, turn right (west) onto Forest Road 2N11 and proceed west for 1 mile to the signed Lodgepole Pine Trail.

The Hike

Between the Santa Ana River Canyon in the south and Big Bear Lake in the north rises a well-watered, thickly forested plateau reminiscent of the Tahquitz Creek plateau in the San Jacinto Mountains. Lush meadows and several small, willow-clad streams enrich this interesting plateau. This leisurely downhill walk leads hikers to the largest-known lodgepole pine, standing at the edge of the largest meadow on the plateau.

Lodgepole pines—easily identified by needles in bundles of two and by their scaly, light-orange to light-brown bark—are usually found on dry, well-drained slopes above the 8,500-foot level in southern California's mountains but occasionally invade wet meadows at lower elevations. The lodgepole pines on this plateau are among the finest specimens anywhere.

From the trailhead, the route leads past a TRAIL sign and picnic table, then descends north through a forest of Jeffrey pine and white fir along a small grass-fringed creek. The surrounding boulder-dotted slopes are interrupted at times by clumps of chinquapin and mountain whitethorn.

The world-champion lodgepole pine, rising at left center, thrives in the gentle meadow and forest landscape in the heart of the San Bernardino Mountains.

The trail soon levels off near a meadow, where lodgepole pines join the forest, and you soon reach a junction with a westbound trail leading to Siberia Creek. Turn right (north) and within 50 feet skirt the edge of a large, forest-rimmed meadow and immediately afterwards reach the fenced-in champion. This impressive tree stands 110 feet high, with a circumference of 20 feet.

After enjoying this peaceful locale, retrace your route to the trailhead.

Key points

0.0   Lodgepole Pine trailhead.
0.3   Champion lodgepole pine.

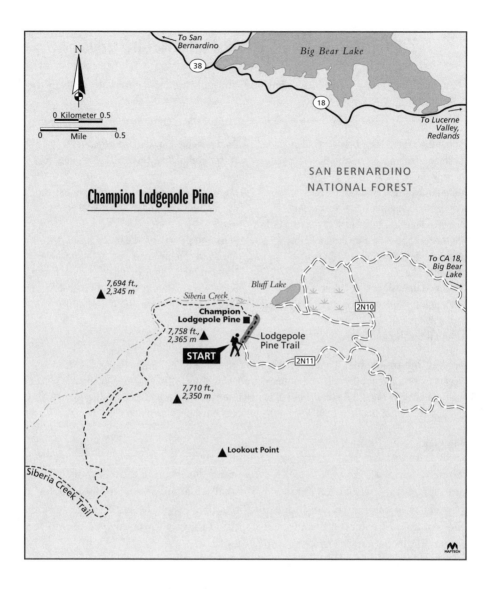

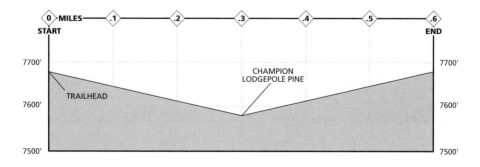

40 Ponderosa and Whispering Pines Nature Trails

These two very easy interpretive trails lead through the rich, peaceful forests of the San Bernardino Mountains.

Start: The signed trails begin on either side of California Highway 38 next to their respective parking areas.

General location: East-central San Bernardino Mountains, San Bernardino National Forest, 4 miles east of Angelus Oaks

Distance: 0.75-mile loop nature trails

Approximate hiking time: 45 minutes

Difficulty: Easy

Trailhead elevation: 6,400 feet

High point: Ponderosa Trail, 6,450 feet; Whispering Pines Trail, 6,550 feet

Land status: National forest

Best season: May through November

Water availability: None available; bring your own

Maps: USGS Big Bear Lake (trails not shown on quad); San Bernardino National Forest map

Fees and permits: A National Forest Adventure Pass is required to park at the trailhead.

Trail contact: San Bernardino National Forest, San Gorgonio Ranger District, 34701 Mill Creek Road, Mentone, CA 92359; (909) 794-1123

Finding the trailheads: The trailheads are on either side of CA 38 (the Rim of the World Scenic Byway), about 50 yards west of the western end of Jenks Lake Road, and about 25 miles east of Redlands and 23.5 miles south of the highway's junction with California Highway 18 at the eastern end of Big Bear Lake. Park in the turnouts on either side of the highway.

The Hike

These nature trails are well suited for a leisurely stroll through the mountains and are especially beneficial for families with small children or anyone looking for a relaxing walk through a cool mountain forest. Small signs along the way interpret the workings of nature in this pleasant transition forest, allowing newcomers to the mountains to better appreciate this fine country.

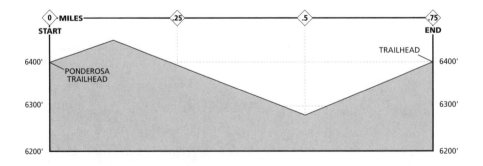

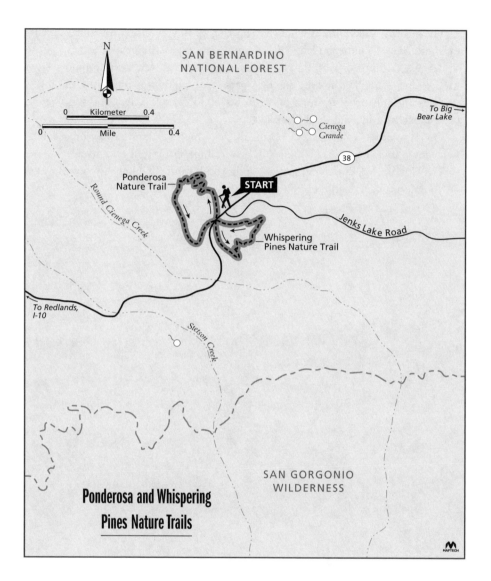

N

SAN BERNARDINO
NATIONAL FOREST

Cienega
Grande

To Big
Bear Lake

0   Kilometer   0.4

0   Mile   0.4

Ponderosa
Nature Trail

START

38

Round Cienega Creek

Jenks Lake Road

Whispering
Pines Nature Trail

To Redlands,
I-10

Stetson Creek

SAN GORGONIO
WILDERNESS

**Ponderosa and Whispering
Pines Nature Trails**

MAPTECH

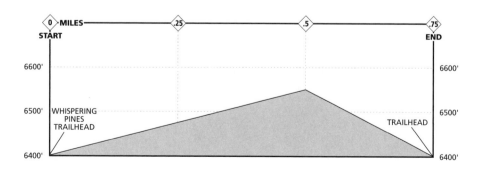

0 MILES   .25   .5   .75
START   END

6600'   6600'

6500' WHISPERING   6500'
       PINES   TRAILHEAD
       TRAILHEAD

6400'   6400'

These short walks should whet the appetites of novice hikers for longer excursions into one of southern California's finest hiking areas, the nearby San Gorgonio Wilderness. The Whispering Pines Trail, south of the highway, has interpretive signs that are also in braille, allowing sightless persons to enjoy this refreshing mountain world. Both trails travel through open forests of ponderosa, Jeffrey, and sugar pines, white fir, canyon live oak, and black oak.

The Ponderosa Trail proceeds north from the highway, crests a low hill, switchbacks down to a small flat, then ascends gentle slopes back to the highway.

The Whispering Pines Trail gently climbs south from the highway, tops out on a hill, then loops back to the trailhead.

41 Anderson Peak

This excellent backpack trip tours the north slopes and high western divides of the San Gorgonio high country, offering many fine places to camp and far-ranging vistas stretching across southern California's wildest mountain country.

Start: The signed Forsee Creek Trail begins heading southeast from the road's end.
General location: East-central San Bernardino Mountains, San Gorgonio Wilderness (San Bernardino National Forest), 5 miles east of Angelus Oaks
Distance: 19.1-mile loop backpack, suitable for a 2- to 3-day trip
Approximate hiking time: 2–3 days
Difficulty: Strenuous
Trailhead elevation: 6,760 feet
High point: Anderson Peak, 10,864 feet
Land status: National forest wilderness (San Gorgonio Wilderness)
Best season: Mid-June through October
Water availability: Available from Forsee Creek at Mile 3.0; at Mile 3.2; from Limber Pine Spring at Mile 6.8; from Trail Fork Springs

at Mile 12.3; and from Jackstraw Springs at Mile 14.6; and again at Forsee Creek at Mile 16.1
Maps: USGS Forest Falls, Big Bear Lake (route from trailhead to San Bernardino Peak Divide Trail not shown on quad); San Bernardino National Forest map; San Gorgonio Wilderness map
Fees and permits: A Wilderness Permit is required. California Campfire Permit is required for campfires and backpack stoves. National Forest Adventure Pass is required to park at the trailhead.
Trail contact: San Bernardino National Forest, San Gorgonio Ranger District, 34701 Mill Creek Road, Mentone, CA 92359; (909) 794-1123

Finding the trailhead: From Redlands, drive east on California Highway 38 (the Rim of the World Scenic Byway) for 25 miles to Jenks Lake Road, just east of the Ponderosa and Whispering Pines trailheads. Follow Jenks Lake Road east for 0.3 mile, then turn right (south) onto Forest Road 1N82 where a sign points to the trailhead. Follow this rough dirt road for 0.5 mile to its end at the Forsee Creek trailhead.

The Hike

This excellent loop trip explores the western end of the San Gorgonio Wilderness and includes an ascent of the highest peak west of Dollar Lake Saddle. The unmaintained trail leading past Johns Meadow to the San Bernardino Peak Divide offers a refreshing change of pace from more popular, sometimes crowded San Gorgonio Wilderness trails.

From the parking area walk south for 0.4 mile, then turn right onto the Johns Meadow Trail (you will be returning via the Forsee Creek Trail on the left). The trail traverses north-facing slopes in a westerly direction, beneath a canopy of white fir, incense-cedar, and Jeffrey and ponderosa pines. During this gentle traverse, you

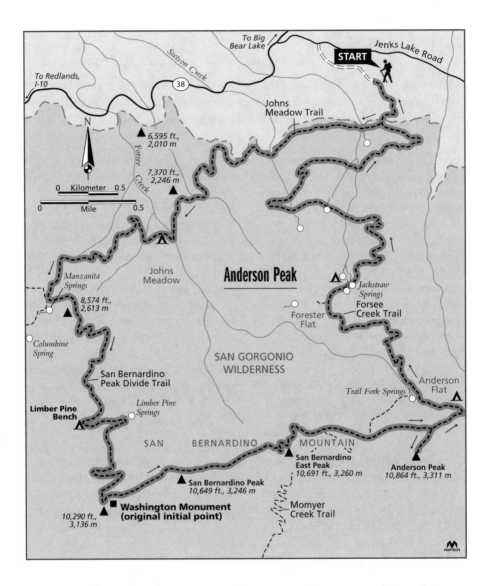

obtain occasional forest-framed views northward to Sugarloaf Mountain and the Big Bear–Santa Ana River Divide.

After 2.7 miles pass through a low saddle and descend for 0.3 mile to a ford of Forsee Creek, then proceed westward through a forest of Jeffrey pine and white fir, soon passing the Johns Meadow campsites, where the trail becomes faint.

From Johns Meadow continue west, cross a grass-lined creek, turn right, and then make your way through a grassy area in a northwesterly direction above the creek. Avoid the left-branching path that climbs steeply immediately after crossing the creek.

The trail rises via switchbacks upon the north slopes of the San Bernardino Peak Divide through a forest of pine and fir, crossing a few small creeks and willow-choked gullies en route. Intersect the San Bernardino Peak Divide Trail after hiking 4.8 pleasant miles from the trailhead, and turn left (east). As you rise above the 8,600-foot level, lodgepole pine begins to dominate the forest. Reach the excellent campsites on Limber Pine Bench after 1.7 miles; 0.3 mile beyond that, pass reliable Limber Pine Spring.

Continuing to ascend, pass just below the Washington Monument, about 0.5 mile west of San Bernardino Peak. The site of the monument offers a more sweeping panorama than the peak itself. This monument was erected in 1852 as an initial baseline triangulation point, and subsequent land surveys for southern California were based on calculations obtained from this initial point.

The trail continues east, passing just north of San Bernardino Peak and San Bernardino East Peak, both easy climbs from the trail. About 3.7 miles from Limber Pine Spring, you pass southeastbound Momyer Creek Trail, climbing 5,300 feet out of Mill Creek Canyon in 6.0 miles, on your right.

You next meet a northeastbound trail descending 0.5 mile to Trail Fork Springs, a reliable and very cold piped spring at 10,400 feet. Bear right, continuing east for 0.4 mile, then turn right (south) and ascend the steep north slopes of Anderson Peak via a faint trail for 0.2 mile to the 10,864-foot summit, which is surrounded by granitic boulders and stunted lodgepole pines. Vistas are excellent from here, especially eastward to the highest peaks of the San Gorgonio Wilderness.

From the summit, backtrack to the San Bernardino Peak Divide Trail, turn right, and hike east for 0.3 mile to a trail junction in Anderson Flat. Turn left (northwest) onto the Forsee Creek Trail and descend 0.4 mile to Trail Fork Springs. Continue to descend along the headwaters of Forsee Creek and past Jackstraw Springs at 9,300 feet and its associated campsites after another 2.3 miles.

Below 8,600 feet, Jeffrey and sugar pines and white fir become the dominant forest trees. Intersect the Johns Meadow Trail about 4.1 miles below Jackstraw Springs, and backtrack the final 0.4 mile to the trailhead.

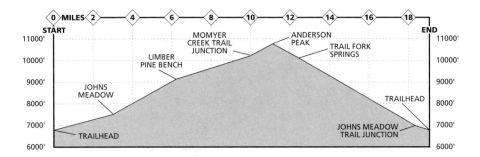

Key points

0.0 Forsee Creek trailhead.

0.4 Junction with Forsee Creek Trail (the return leg of the loop) and the Johns Meadow Trail. Turn right (west) onto the Johns Meadow Trail.

3.0 Forsee Creek.

3.2 Johns Meadow campsites.

4.8 Junction with San Bernardino Peak Divide Trail; turn left (east).

6.5 Limber Pine Bench.

6.8 Limber Pine Springs.

8.1 Washington Monument.

10.5 Junction with southeastbound Momyer Creek Trail; continue straight ahead (east).

10.8 Junction with northeastbound trail leading to Trail Fork Springs; continue straight ahead (east).

11.2 Junction with trail to Anderson Peak; turn right (south).

11.4 Summit of Anderson Peak.

11.6 Return to San Bernardino Peak Divide Trail; turn right (east).

11.9 Junction with Forsee Creek Trail; turn left (northwest) and begin descending.

12.3 Trail Fork Springs.

14.6 Jackstraw Springs.

18.7 Junction with Johns Meadow Trail; retrace your steps back to the trailhead.

19.1 Return to the trailhead.

42 San Gorgonio Mountain

This memorable trip is perhaps the finest backpack route in southern California, touring the region's most scenic high-mountain landscape.

Start: The signed South Fork Trail begins on the south side of the parking area.
General location: East-central San Bernardino Mountains, San Gorgonio Wilderness (San Bernardino National Forest), 11 miles southeast of Big Bear Lake
Distance: 21.3-mile semiloop backpack
Approximate hiking time: 2–3 days
Difficulty: Strenuous
Trailhead elevation: 6,900 feet
High point: San Gorgonio Mountain, 11,499 feet
Land status: National forest wilderness (San Gorgonio Wilderness)
Best season: Late June through mid-October
Water availability: South Fork Meadows at Mile 3.75; at Dollar Lake, 0.6 mile east of the

junction with the Dollar Lake Trail at Mile 5.75; at Dry Lake at Mile 15.8; and again at South Fork Meadows at Mile 17.8
Maps: USGS Moonridge, and San Gorgonio Mountain; San Bernardino National Forest map; San Gorgonio Wilderness map
Fees and permits: A Wilderness Permit is required. A California Campfire Permit is required for campfires and backpack stoves. A National Forest Adventure Pass is required to park at the trailhead.
Trail contact: San Bernardino National Forest, San Gorgonio Ranger District, 34701 Mill Creek Road, Mentone, CA 92359; (909) 794-1123.

Finding the trailhead: From Interstate 10 in Redlands, turn north onto California Highway 38 and follow signs pointing to Barton Flats. You reach the Mill Creek Ranger Station (where Wilderness Permits are available) after driving 9 miles from I-10.

Continue following CA 38 (the Rim of the World Scenic Byway) to Jenks Lake Road (25 miles from I-10), and then turn right and follow this good paved road, ignoring the left turn to Jenks Lake. After 2.5 miles reach the large hikers' parking area at the South Fork trailhead.

The Hike

Glacial cirques, virgin forests, windswept alpine ridges, two subalpine lakes, a lush meadow, and panoramic vistas make this one of the finest and most memorable hikes in southern California.

From the trailhead, the initial 2.25 miles of the hike leads you past brushy Horse Meadows, across the long-closed Poopout Hill Road, and into the San Gorgonio Wilderness. Beyond the old road you climb a moderately steep draw and top out on a 7,800-foot saddle. Shortly thereafter, the old trail from Poopout Hill joins the trail on the left. Begin a gentle ascent toward South Fork Meadows, passing through a cool forest of pine and fir.

Prostrate limber pines high in the San Gorgonio Wilderness attest to the harsh weather conditions that prevail in this highest region of southern California. RICK MARVIN PHOTO

After 3.5 miles of hiking, avoid an eastbound trail leading to Grinnell Ridge Camp. Instead, climb moderately for 0.25 mile along the South Fork Santa Ana River to a junction in South Fork Meadows. You will be returning via the left fork where the sign points to Dry Lake.

Turning right, quickly climb out of the lush oasis of South Fork Meadows, leaving ferns, grasses, and abundant water behind. The trail ascends via switchbacks through pine-and-fir forest; crosses an open, brushy slope choked with manzanita and chinquapin; and meets the left-branching Dollar Lake Trail about 2.0 miles from the meadows. Dollar Lake has been so heavily used in the past that the Forest Service has closed the lake to camping. It is recovering nicely and makes a pleasant spot for a lunch break. The lake is about 0.6 mile off the main trail, and if you need water, there is a good spring about 200 feet above the south end of the lake. This is your last easily accessible water for more than 10 miles. Hikers who plan on camping on San Gorgonio Mountain, or anywhere along the high divide between Dollar Lake and Dry Lake, are advised to pack ample water for a dry camp—at least one gallon per person.

Bearing right at the Dollar Lake Trail junction, ascend 0.75 mile to 10,000-foot Dollar Lake Saddle and reach a four-way trail junction. The westbound trail traverses the crest of San Bernardino Mountain, passing High Meadow Springs after 0.9 mile. The southbound trail descends past Plummer Meadows to Mill Creek Canyon. Turn left (east) onto the San Bernardino Peak Divide Trail, and cross the south and west slopes of Charlton and Little Charlton Peaks, reaching Dry Lake View Trail Camp (no water) after 1.5 miles. The trail then rounds the west ridge of Jepson Peak, where the limber pine forest becomes stunted and ground-hugging. Unobstructed vistas begin opening up to the west and south.

The most turbulent weather in southern California occurs along this high ridge—battered trees offer the most vivid evidence of violent, unrestrained winds and blowing and drifting snow.

After following the contours of Jepson Peak's southern slopes on a tread of granite sand, reach a saddle at the 11,050-foot level from which you can see Dry Lake Basin and, in wet years, the "semipermanent" snowfields that cling to the north slopes of this high ridge. The trail soon rounds Point 11,171 and meets the trail coming up from Vivian Creek on the right. After another 0.2 mile meet the right-branching Sky High Trail, your route of return. But for now continue straight ahead (east) and hike 0.4 mile to the highest point in southern California, crossing barren alpine fell fields.

Due to the broad, nearly flat nature of San Gorgonio Mountain, you must traverse the rim of the summit plateau for views in all directions. The view from the summit area is impressive, encompassing the eastern end of the San Gorgonio Wilderness and extending north to Big Bear Lake and beyond. The hazy coastal valleys to the southwest, with their sprawling urban areas and millions of people, evoke an especially keen sense of appreciation for the San Gorgonio Wilderness and its promise of escape (even if temporary) from the fast-paced, hectic lifestyle that characterizes southern California.

From the summit, backtrack 0.4 mile to the Sky High Trail and turn left (south), traversing the west then south slopes of San Gorgonio Mountain. After less than 1.0 mile, amid thickening forest you get a glimpse of the dry lakebed of The Tarn, 400 feet downhill to the south. If you're lucky, you might even spot bighorn sheep in this area—they are fairly common in the rugged, trail-less headwaters of the Whitewater River.

Beyond The Tarn, begin descending switchbacks down east-facing slopes, passing the twisted wreckage of an airplane en route. About 4.5 miles from the summit of San Gorgonio Mountain, reach another major trail junction at 9,936-foot Mine Shaft Saddle. The eastbound trail leads to Fish Creek; another trail branches right from that trail after 0.25 mile, descending to North Fork Meadows, one of the least-used trails in the wilderness.

Turn left and begin a 2.0-mile descent to moraine-dammed Dry Lake. The descent is shaded by lodgepole pines, with clumps of chinquapin making up the understory. About 0.5 mile before reaching Dry Lake, which is dry only during years of scant precipitation, begin crossing the eastern edge of a moraine that was created when the large (by southern California standards) glaciers occupying the north slopes of Jepson Peak and San Gorgonio Mountain began to recede, slowly dumping their load of debris quarried from the upper slopes of the two peaks.

After reaching the west shore of Dry Lake at 9,065 feet—the largest lake in the wilderness—bear left at the junction with the eastbound trail leading 0.4 mile to

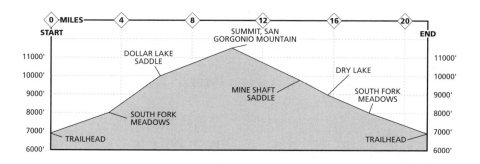

Lodgepole Spring and its adjacent campsites. Your route hugs the west shore of the lake, crosses its outlet, and follows this creek downstream.

Soon begin descending via switchbacks into South Fork Meadows, emerging from lodgepole pines into a stand of Jeffrey pine and white fir. After the trail levels out, hop across Dry Lake's outlet creek, then cross the infant South Fork Santa Ana River before reaching the South Fork Meadows Trail junction. From there, turn right and retrace your route to the trailhead.

Key points

0.0 South Fork trailhead.

3.5 Junction with eastbound trail to Grinnell Ridge Camp; continue straight ahead (south).

3.75 Junction in South Fork Meadows; turn right (southwest).

5.75 Junction with Dollar Lake Trail; bear right (southwest).

6.5 Junction at Dollar Lake Saddle; turn left (south) onto the San Bernardino Peak Divide Trail.

8.0 Dry Lake View Trail Camp.

9.8 Junction with southwestbound Vivian Creek Trail; continue straight ahead (east).

10.0 Junction with Sky High Trail; bear left (southeast) toward San Gorgonio Mountain.

10.4 Summit of San Gorgonio Mountain.

10.8 Return to Sky High Trail junction and turn left (south).

13.8 Junction at Mine Shaft Saddle; bear left (northwest) and descend along the Dry Lake Trail.

15.8 Dry Lake and the junction with the eastbound trail to Lodgepole Spring; bear left (north).

17.8 Junction in South Fork Meadows; turn right (northwest) and retrace your steps to the trailhead.

21.3 South Fork trailhead.

43 Fish Creek Aspen Grove

This short but rewarding hike leads through conifer forest on the northeastern edge of the San Gorgonio Wilderness to southern California's largest grove of quaking aspen.

Start: The Aspen Grove Trail begins on the west side of Forest Road 1N05, at the saddle marked "7410" on the Moonridge USGS quad.
General location: East-central San Bernardino Mountains, San Gorgonio Wilderness (San Bernardino National Forest), 9 miles southeast of Big Bear Lake
Distance: 0.8-mile round-trip
Approximate hiking time: 30 minutes
Difficulty: Easy
Trailhead elevation: 7,410 feet
High point: 7,410 feet
Land status: National forest
Best season: Late May through mid-November

Water availability: Available from Fish Creek at the aspen grove; treat before drinking, or bring your own
Maps: USGS Moonridge; San Bernardino National Forest map
Fees and permits: A Wilderness Permit is required. A California Campfire Permit is required for campfires and backpack stoves. A National Forest Adventure Pass is required to park at the trailhead.
Trail contact: San Bernardino National Forest, San Gorgonio Ranger District, 34701 Mill Creek Road, Mentone, CA 92359; (909) 794-1123

Finding the trailhead: From California Highway 38 (the Rim of the World Scenic Byway), 32 miles east of Redlands and 14.5 miles south of Big Bear City, turn south onto Forest Road 1N02, where a sign points to Heart Bar Campground, Coon Creek-6, and Fish Creek-8. Follow this dirt road southeast for 1.25 miles to a junction with FR 1N05, where you turn right. Follow this road for 1.5 miles to the signed Aspen Grove trailhead.

The Hike

The San Bernardino Mountains have by far the most diverse plant life in southern California. The fascinating collection of plants in this range includes almost everything from desert and coastal to alpine species. These mountains harbor the largest-known Joshua tree and lodgepole pine. They also support some rare species found nowhere else in southern California. In Holcomb Creek, for example, near long-abandoned beaver dams, lies an isolated stand of narrowleaf cottonwood, a Rocky Mountain species. And quaking aspens are found in two separate groves—one stands in upper Arrastre Creek, not far from the champion Joshua tree, and the other along the lower reaches of Fish Creek, on the northern boundary of the San Gorgonio Wilderness.

This short stroll leads you to the aspens of Fish Creek, where the laughing stream and the shimmering leaves of aspens create a most peaceful and unique southern

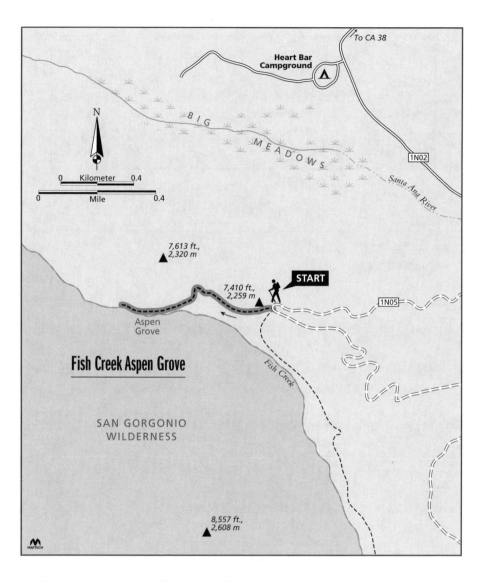

California setting. This walk is especially attractive after the first frosts of autumn, when the aspens wear a dramatic display of fall color, unequaled elsewhere in all of southern California's mountains.

Two trails begin at the trailhead. The left fork ascends to the headwaters of Fish Creek; the right fork descends to the aspen grove.

Begin your descent into Fish Creek via the right fork, across manzanita-covered slopes shaded by Jeffrey pine and white fir. After 0.4 mile of descent, enter the aspen grove growing along Fish Creek—a small grove, but pleasant and unique nonetheless.

After enjoying the aspens of Fish Creek, backtrack to the trailhead.

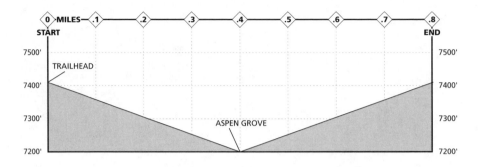

Key points

0.0 Trailhead on FR 1N05.

0.4 Aspen grove.

44 Sugarloaf Mountain

This challenging trip leads to the only subalpine summit in the San Bernardino Mountains outside the San Gorgonio Wilderness; from this mountain, inspiring vistas unfold.

Start: The doubletrack trail begins behind the gate on the west edge of the parking area.

General location: East-central San Bernardino Mountains, San Bernardino National Forest, 6 miles southeast of Big Bear Lake

Distance: 6.5-mile round-trip day hike, part cross-country

Approximate hiking time: 3 hours

Difficulty: Moderate

Trailhead elevation: 8,715 feet

High point: Sugarloaf Mountain, 9,952 feet

Land status: National forest

Best season: Early June through early November

Water availability: None available; bring your own

Maps: USGS Moonridge; San Bernardino National Forest map

Fees and permits: A National Forest Adventure Pass is required to park at the trailhead.

Trail contact: San Bernardino National Forest, Big Bear Ranger District, P.O. Box 290, North Shore Drive, Highway 38, Fawnskin, CA 92333; (909) 866-3437

Finding the trailhead: From California Highway 38, 3.5 miles southeast of Big Bear City, turn west onto signed Forest Road 2N93. You pass the signed Sugarloaf Trail after 1.3 miles—hikers not wishing to negotiate the final segment of this fairly rough dirt road can begin hiking here. Otherwise, continue driving FR 2N93, the Wildhorse Road, to its summit, about 5.75 miles from the highway. Park on the west side of the road, where a gate blocks a northwest-branching dirt road. This parking area lies 0.25 mile north of a cattle guard on FR 2N93.

The trailhead can also be reached from the south by driving 34 miles east from Redlands via CA 38 to the south end of FR 2N93. This junction is hard to locate; it lies 2 miles east of the signed turnoff to Heart Bar State Park. Follow FR 2N93 north for 6 miles to the above-mentioned trailhead.

The Hike

Hikers who are looking for solitude in subalpine surroundings but are tired of encountering the typical hordes of hikers in the San Gorgonio Wilderness will find that Sugarloaf Mountain is just what they have been searching for. The lodgepole- and limber pine–crowned summit provides a comprehensive view of the entire eastern end of the San Bernardino Mountains, a view unrivaled from any other point in the range.

This hike follows the shortest route to the summit and requires a little route finding at the start. The hike begins at a seldom-used trailhead (the highest in the range) and avoids the conventional, longer routes starting at lower elevations.

Looking east along the Sugarloaf Mountain divide in the eastern reaches of the San Bernardino Mountains

From the trailhead, hike west up the faint doubletrack, heading straight up the slope at a right angle to a closed road. Follow this doubletrack to the main ridge, where it fades out near a yellow metal post. Follow the ridge west cross-country through an open forest of Jeffrey pine, large western juniper, and mountain mahogany for 0.25 mile, until you meet another doubletrack. Follow these tracks west along the ridgetop; after hiking 0.8 mile from the trailhead, just after passing through a wire stock gate, reach a trail junction. The northbound trail descends Green Canyon to the previously mentioned trailhead on FR 2N93. The southbound trail descends Wildhorse Canyon to CA 38.

Head west on the signed Sugarloaf Trail. As you climb above 9,400 feet, lodgepole and limber pines become the dominant forest trees. The trail soon climbs up and around Peak 9775, descends to a saddle, then makes a final ascent to the summit of Sugarloaf Mountain, sometimes passing through dense stands of lodgepole pine. Views from the mountain are excellent, especially southward to the San Gorgonio Wilderness, rising above the deep canyon of the Santa Ana River.

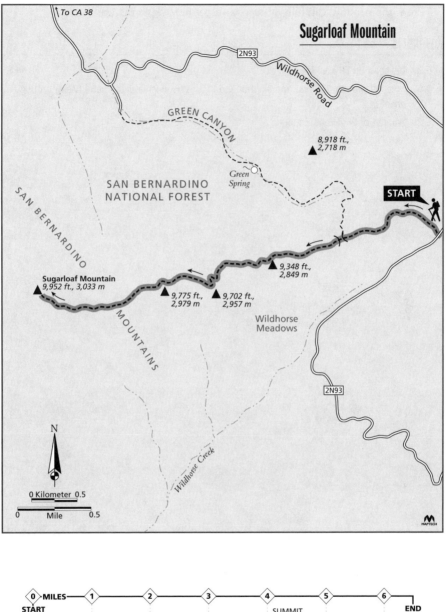

Sugarloaf Mountain

To CA 38

2N93

Wildhorse Road

GREEN CANYON

8,918 ft.,
2,718 m

SAN BERNARDINO
NATIONAL FOREST

Green
Spring

START

SAN BERNARDINO

9,348 ft.,
2,849 m

Sugarloaf Mountain
9,952 ft., 3,033 m

9,775 ft.,
2,979 m

9,702 ft.,
2,957 m

MOUNTAINS

Wildhorse
Meadows

2N93

N

Wildhorse Creek

0 Kilometer 0.5

0   Mile   0.5

MAPTECH

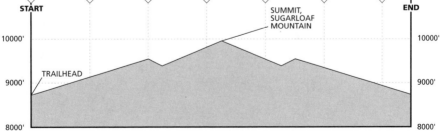

0 MILES 1   2   3   4   5   6

START   END

SUMMIT,
SUGARLOAF
MOUNTAIN

10000'   10000'

TRAILHEAD

9000'   9000'

8000'   8000'

From the summit, carefully retrace your route back to the trailhead.

Key points

0.0 Trailhead on FR 2N93.

0.8 Junction with northbound and southbound trails; continue straight ahead (west) on Sugarloaf Trail.

3.25 Summit of Sugarloaf Mountain.

45 Champion Joshua Tree

Joshua trees, monarchs of the Mojave Desert, reach their grandest proportions on the desert slopes of the San Bernardino Mountains. This easy hike leads to the largest-known Joshua tree in the world and is a rewarding though brief introduction to the "desert side" of these mountains.

Start: The obvious doubletrack trail leads east from the parking area.
General location: Eastern San Bernardino Mountains, San Bernardino National Forest, 10 miles east of Big Bear Lake
Distance: 2.0-mile round-trip day hike
Approximate hiking time: 1 hour
Difficulty: Easy
Trailhead elevation: 6,040 feet
High point: 6,090 feet
Land status: National forest
Best season: Late September through mid-June

Water availability: None available; bring your own
Maps: USGS Rattlesnake Canyon (route not shown on quad); San Bernardino National Forest map
Fees and permits: A National Forest Adventure Pass is required to park at the trailhead.
Trail contact: San Bernardino National Forest, San Gorgonio Ranger District, 34701 Mill Creek Road, Mentone, CA 92359; (909) 794-1123

Finding the trailhead: From California Highway 18, 11 miles south of its junction with California Highway 247 in Lucerne Valley and 6.7 miles northeast of its junction with California Highway 38 at the east end of Big Bear Lake, turn southeast onto signed Forest Road 3N03, directly under a prominent boulder-covered hill. A sign a short distance up this road reads PIONEERTOWN 25. Follow this fair dirt road southeast, avoiding several signed spur roads. The road crosses usually flowing Arrastre Creek 5 miles from the highway, just beyond Smart's Ranch. A quarter mile beyond that crossing is a hard-to-spot junction with an eastbound doubletrack—park here.

The Hike

The Joshua tree is one of many unusual plants found in California's deserts. A member of the agave family, this unique tree is unmistakable with its stiff, narrow, foot-long daggerlike leaves. Its dense flower clusters, from greenish-white to cream in color, appear in April or May. The Joshua tree grows across a wide area—from the Mojave Desert north to the southern Owens Valley and east through southern Nevada to southwestern Utah and western Arizona.

Growing at an elevation of 6,000 feet, the Joshua trees in Arrastre Canyon are near their altitudinal limit. Due to deep well-drained soils and moderate precipitation here, the Joshua trees in this canyon grow to greater dimensions than those anywhere else.

The Joshua trees in Arrastre Canyon, on the north slope of the San Bernardino Mountains, are the largest anywhere. Pictured here is the champion Joshua tree, rising to a height of 32 feet, with a diameter of 15 feet.

This short hike, on doubletrack all the way, passes some of the largest Joshua trees in existence and ends at the impressive champion Joshua tree. The variety of plant life and the open feeling of the piñon woodland combine to make this a thoroughly pleasing, leisurely stroll.

Hikers with energy to burn might consider a cross-country scramble east from the champion to the Granite Peak ridge, which commands a wide view of the eastern end of the San Bernardino Mountains and the Mojave Desert. Granite Peak, at 7,512 feet, is a 1.5-mile jaunt northward along that ridge and offers a satisfying diversion and a fitting complement to the largest Joshua tree anywhere.

The route leads east from FR 3N03, following the doubletrack through an open woodland of piñon, a few scattered Joshua trees, sagebrush, rabbitbrush, some juniper, and bitterbrush. Your destination lies at the foot of Granite Peak ridge, which can be seen on the eastern skyline.

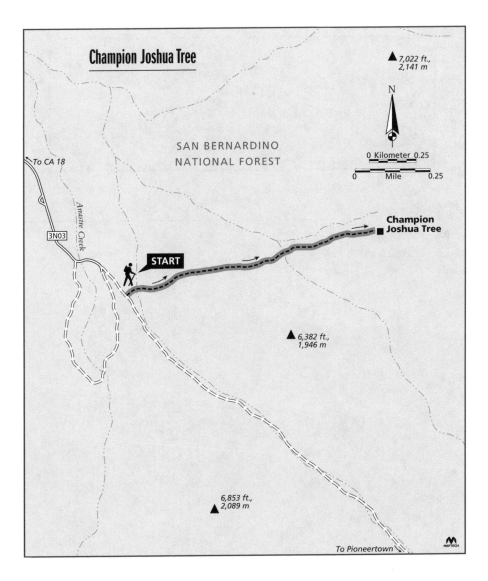

As you approach the east side of wide Arrastre Canyon, large Joshua trees begin to appear, quickly dominating the woodland. After 1.0 mile, just before the double-track fades out, reach the champion Joshua tree. Its huge, rounded multibranched mass obviously outclasses all others in the area and offers a good deal of shade on a hot day.

After enjoying the 32-foot-tall, 15-foot-diameter giant, retrace your route to the trailhead.

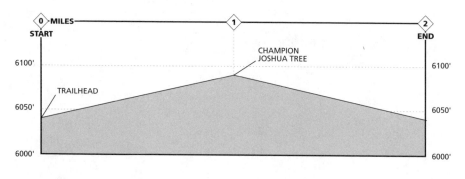

Key points

0.0 Trailhead on FR 3N03.

1.0 Champion Joshua tree.

46 Kitching Peak

This fine day hike leads to a panoramic viewpoint on the edge of the wildest mountain country in southern California.

Start: The trail leads north from the turnaround at the road's end.
General location: Southeast San Bernardino Mountains, San Gorgonio Wilderness (San Bernardino National Forest), 8 miles northeast of Banning
Distance: 9.4-mile round-trip day hike
Approximate hiking time: 4–5 hours
Difficulty: Strenuous
Trailhead elevation: 4,200 feet
High point: Kitching Peak, 6,598 feet
Land status: National forest wilderness (San Gorgonio Wilderness)
Best season: Mid-April through June; mid-September through November

Water availability: Available from East Branch Millard Canyon; treat before drinking, or bring your own
Maps: USGS Cabazon, San Gorgonio Mountain, Catclaw Flat, Whitewater; San Gorgonio Wilderness map; San Bernardino National Forest map
Fees and permits: A Wilderness Permit is required. A National Forest Adventure Pass is required to park at the trailhead.
Trail contact: San Bernardino National Forest, San Gorgonio Ranger District, 34701 Mill Creek Road, Mentone, CA 92359; (909) 794-1123

Finding the trailhead: From Interstate 10 about 4.5 miles east of Banning, take the Fields Road exit. Follow this paved road north, through the Morongo Indian Reservation, for 1.3 miles, then turn right onto Morongo Road; the sign points to Millard Canyon. After 0.5 mile, bear left onto Forest Road 2S05, then bear right after another 0.3 mile; the road turns to dirt 0.2 mile beyond. Your northbound road soon crosses Millard Canyon Creek, about 1.2 miles from the end of the pavement, and continues a northbound course east of the creek. After driving 2.3 miles from the creek crossing, turn right at a well-marked junction where the sign points to Kitching Creek Trail 2E09. Stay left when, after another 0.6 mile, Forest Road 2S03 joins your road on the right. Your road ends after another 1.1 miles, just beyond a creek crossing. Park before crossing the creek.

The Hike

Kitching Peak stands like a great throne overlooking the San Gorgonio Pass country. From its summit, massive San Gorgonio Mountain looms bold in the northwest, and San Jacinto Peak, its majestic northeast escarpment soaring 10,000 feet above the floor of Coachella Valley, seems close enough to touch.

Although Kitching Peak lies at the drier southeast end of the San Bernardino Mountains, it stands high enough to capture adequate moisture from Pacific storms funneling through San Gorgonio Pass. On the upper slopes of the peak, cool stands of white fir offer welcome shade to hikers as well as to the variety of wildlife that inhabits the area.

Dense chaparral and a scattering of white fir mantle the slopes of isolated Kitching Peak.
KEN KUKULKA PHOTO

Kitching Peak lies within the wildest and most remote mountain wilderness within southern California—the headwaters of the Whitewater River. In this mostly trail-less region of the San Bernardino Mountains, hikers can find solitude and a wilderness experience available in few other places in southern California's mountains. Here, in the remote southeastern corner of the San Gorgonio Wilderness, bighorn sheep, mule deer, mountain lion, and black bear thrive. In fact, unusually large black bears inhabit the area, some weighing in excess of 500 pounds. Black bears are not native to southern California; they were introduced in the San Bernardino and San Gabriel Mountains from the southern Sierra Nevada in the 1930s.

Take the unmarked trail north from the turnaround at the end of the road, under the shade of a large big-cone Douglas fir and canyon live oaks. You travel northeast during the first 2.0 miles of your hike while ascending the East Branch Millard Canyon, crossing and recrossing the small creek under the cool shade of canyon live oak, incense-cedar, and big-cone Douglas fir. Then climb up and out of the East Branch and trade the shady forest for chaparral-clad slopes as you negotiate the final

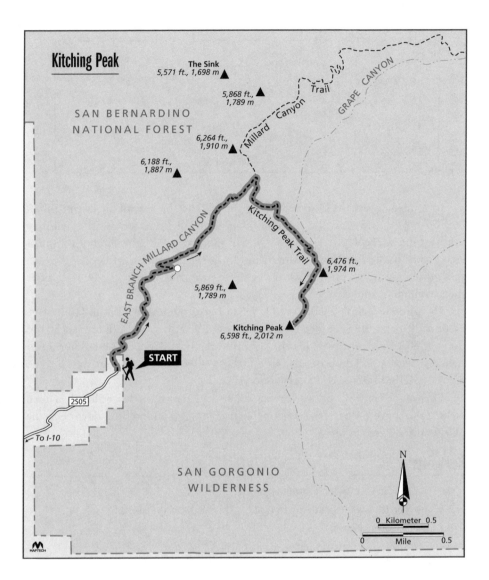

Kitching Peak

The Sink
5,571 ft., 1,698 m ▲

5,868 ft., ▲
1,789 m

SAN BERNARDINO
NATIONAL FOREST

6,264 ft., ▲
1,910 m

Millard Canyon Trail

GRAPE CANYON

6,188 ft., ▲
1,887 m

EAST BRANCH MILLARD CANYON

Kitching Peak Trail

○

5,869 ft., ▲
1,789 m

6,476 ft., ▲
1,974 m

Kitching Peak ▲
6,598 ft., 2,012 m

🚶 **START**

2S05

← To I-10

SAN GORGONIO
WILDERNESS

N

0 Kilometer 0.5
0   Mile   0.5

MAPTECH

switchbacks to surmount a north-south ridge at 3.0 miles, dividing waters flowing west into Millard Canyon from those flowing east into the Whitewater River.

Turn right (south) onto the Kitching Peak Trail at the junction on this 6,000-foot ridge; the sign points to Kitching Peak. The sometimes brushy trail heads south on or near the ridgetop, leading through live oak and chaparral. As you gain elevation, white fir and a few sugar pines begin to cast welcome shade. Just before reaching the summit, the trail fades out in an overgrown patch of deerbrush. You simply bushwhack through the last several yards to reach the summit of Kitching Peak.

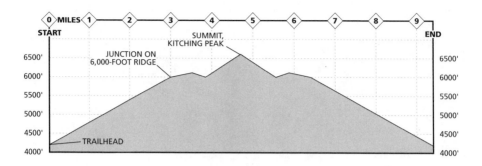

To your southeast, the Coachella Valley sprawls into the haze of the distant Salton Sea. Of special interest is the magnificent upthrust of land that rises immediately south of the exceedingly deep nadir of San Gorgonio Pass, the mighty northeast escarpment of the San Jacinto Mountains. Imagine the immense forces within the earth that shoved that great block of the earth's crust more than 10,000 feet above the surrounding countryside.

The panorama also includes the Little San Bernardino Mountains in Joshua Tree National Park to the east, seen across the huge dry wash of the Whitewater River. To your north and northwest lies the wild landscape of the upper Whitewater River drainage, with a backdrop of 10,000- and 11,000-foot peaks. To your west lies the eastern extension of the San Bernardino Valley.

After absorbing this expansive vista, hikers can return to the trailhead or turn right at the above-mentioned ridgetop junction for a rewarding jaunt down into the Whitewater River country.

Key points

0.0 Trailhead in East Branch Millard Canyon.

3.0 Junction on 6,000-foot ridge; bear right (south) onto Kitching Peak Trail.

4.7 Summit of Kitching Peak.

47 San Jacinto Peak

This rewarding trip surveys some of the best high-mountain country southern California has to offer and ends on a lofty summit that affords perhaps the finest vistas in the region.

Start: The trail begins as paved switchbacks at the exit of Mountain Station.
General location: San Jacinto Mountains, Mount San Jacinto State Park, 5 miles west of Palm Springs
Distance: 10.0-mile round-trip day hike or overnighter
Approximate hiking time: 5 hours
Difficulty: Strenuous as a day hike; moderate as an overnighter
Trailhead elevation: 8,500 feet
High point: San Jacinto Peak, 10,804 feet
Land status: State park wilderness (San Jacinto Wilderness)

Best season: June through mid-November
Water availability: Available from spring in Round Valley at Mile 2.3
Maps: USGS San Jacinto Peak; San Bernardino National Forest map; San Jacinto Wilderness map
Fees and permits: A Wilderness Permit is required. A California Campfire Permit is required for campfires and backpack stoves.
Trail contact: Mount San Jacinto State Park, P.O. Box 308, 25905 State Highway 243, Idyllwild, CA 92349; (951) 659-2607

Finding the trailhead: From California Highway 111 at the north end of Palm Springs, turn west where a large sign indicates the Palm Springs Aerial Tramway. Proceed west along this steep paved road for 4 miles to the parking area at Valley Station.

The tram cars leave Valley Station every half hour, beginning at 10:00 A.M. Monday through Friday and 8:00 A.M. on Saturday, Sunday, and holidays. For more information about the tramway, phone (760) 325-1391.

The Hike

There are two plateaus in the San Jacinto Mountains—the lower and consequently drier plateau containing the Tahquitz Creek drainage, and the higher, more subalpine plateau lying just east of San Jacinto Peak, which boasts two meadows over 9,000 feet in elevation. The Palm Springs Aerial Tramway provides year-round access to this higher plateau, making the ascent to San Jacinto Peak much easier than from any other point in the range.

Due to year-round access and generally good snow conditions, cross-country skiing and snowshoeing are popular winter activities here. Excellent skiing can be found on the upper slopes of the peak, and many visitors spend the night on top to catch the magnificent winter sunrise before enjoying superb runs back to the plateau.

The beauty of an austere, high-mountain landscape is often enhanced by the weathered remains of an ancient tree, such as this limber pine snag in the San Jacinto Mountains.

After the breathtaking tramway ride, step out into Mountain Station, complete with restaurant and tourist facilities. Exit the station and follow the paved switchback trail down into Long Valley. At the bottom the trail bends west, soon passing the Long Valley Ranger Station.

Begin ascending along the course of Long Valley's creek through boulder-dotted terrain, shaded by a canopy of Jeffrey pine and white fir. After hiking 1.5 miles, avoid the southeastbound trail leading to Hidden Lake. Beyond this junction, lodgepole pines increase in frequency among the forest, becoming the dominant tree above Round Valley.

Just before reaching the west end of Round Valley, pass a piped spring immediately south of the trail, which offers the only reliable source of water along the trail. Be sure to tank up here, and filter the springwater before drinking—this is the last water before the peak.

From the junction just ahead, next to the backcountry ranger cabin, bear left and trudge uphill in a westerly direction for 0.8 mile, passing through a heavy lodgepole pine forest, to the trail junction at Wellman Divide, where you turn right. (The

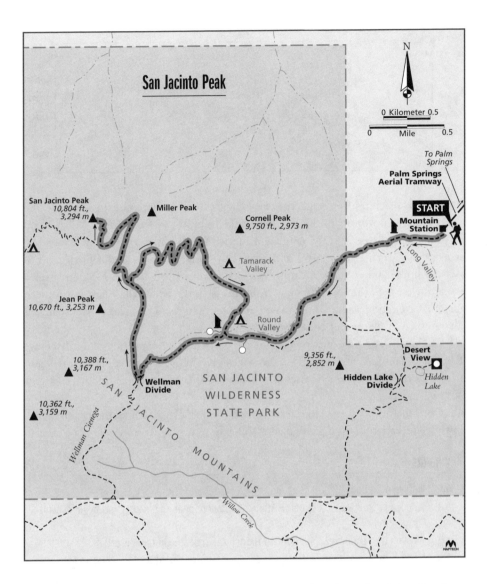

San Jacinto Peak

San Jacinto Peak
10,804 ft.,
3,294 m

Miller Peak

Cornell Peak
9,750 ft., 2,973 m

Tamarack
Valley

Jean Peak
10,670 ft., 3,253 m

10,388 ft.,
3,167 m

Round
Valley

Wellman
Divide

10,362 ft.,
3,159 m

SAN JACINTO
WILDERNESS
STATE PARK

9,356 ft.,
2,852 m

Hidden Lake
Divide

Desert
View

Hidden
Lake

Wellman Cienega

SAN JACINTO MOUNTAINS

Willow Creek

START

Mountain
Station

Palm Springs
Aerial Tramway

To Palm
Springs

Long Valley

N

0 Kilometer 0.5

0 Mile 0.5

northbound trail in Round Valley leads to Tamarack Valley after 0.8 mile, then ascends to the San Jacinto Peak Trail at 2.0 miles, between Jean and Miller Peaks. This trail offers an alternate route back to Round Valley on the return trip.)

The trail contours north along the east slopes of 10,670-foot Jean Peak, where hikers enjoy a good view eastward across the heavily forested plateau. You reach a bench at the 10,000-foot level and the junction with the trail from Tamarack Valley, 0.8 mile from Wellman Divide. Your trail continues first west then generally northward, crossing slopes choked with chinquapin, dotted with granite boulders, and studded by an occasional lodgepole or limber pine. The trail abruptly switchbacks

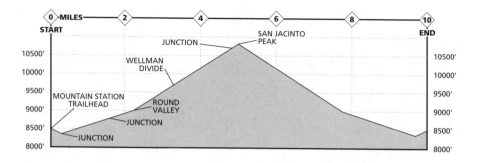

just before reaching the ridgecrest. Peakbaggers will be tempted to scramble the short distance northeast to the boulder-stacked summit of 10,400-foot Miller Peak.

You reach the crest of the range and a junction after hiking 1.5 miles from Wellman Divide. Turn right (north) and ascend the ridge through a subalpine stand of twisted limber pines; hike 0.3 mile to the summit of San Jacinto Peak and pass a stone shelter near the top. The view from this peak is possibly the finest in southern California, encompassing all the major mountain ranges in this part of the state and a large slice of desert and coastal scenery.

The north and east escarpments of the San Jacinto Mountains plummet more than 9,000 feet into surrounding desert valleys, rivaling the great eastern escarpment of the Sierra Nevada, which rises as much as 10,000 feet from the floor of Owens Valley.

From the peak, hikers either retrace their route back to Mountain Station or follow an alternate trail through Tamarack Valley to return to Round Valley (see above).

Key points

0.0 Mountain Station.

0.1 Junction in Long Valley, just below Mountain Station; bear right (west) and begin ascending Long Valley.

1.5 Junction with southeastbound trail to Hidden Lake; bear right (southwest).

2.3 Junction at the west end of Round Valley; bear left (west) and begin ascending toward Wellman Divide.

3.1 Junction at Wellman Divide; turn right (north).

3.9 Junction at 10,000 feet with the trail from Tamarack Valley; bear left (west).

4.7 Junction with northbound spur trail to the summit of San Jacinto Peak; turn right (north).

5.0 San Jacinto Peak.

48 Red Tahquitz

This rewarding trip visits the highlights of the San Jacinto Mountains' rich forests and verdant meadows, one of the most well-watered and scenic mountain regions of southern California.

Start: The signed Devils Slide Trail begins at the east end of the parking area.
General location: San Jacinto Mountains, San Jacinto Wilderness (San Bernardino National Forest), 2 miles northeast of Idyllwild
Distance: 11.7-mile semiloop day hike or overnighter
Approximate hiking time: 5-5.5 hours
Difficulty: Strenuous
Trailhead elevation: 6,300 feet
High point: Red Tahquitz, 8,738 feet
Land status: National forest wilderness (San Jacinto Wilderness)
Best season: June through mid-November
Water availability: Available seasonally from Jolley Spring at Mile 1.1; Middle Spring at

Mile 1.6; Powderbox Spring at Mile 2.6; and in Little Tahquitz Valley at Mile 8.0
Maps: USGS San Jacinto Peak; San Bernardino National Forest map; San Jacinto Wilderness map
Fees and permits: A Wilderness Permit is required. A California Campfire Permit is required for campfires and backpack stoves. A National Forest Adventure Pass is required to park at the trailhead.
Trail contact: San Bernardino National Forest, San Jacinto Ranger District, P.O. Box 518, 54270 Pinecrest, Idyllwild, CA 92349; (951) 659-2117

Finding the trailhead: From the town of Idyllwild, 25 miles south of Banning via California Highway 243 and 22 miles east of Hemet via California Highways 74 and 243. From Idyllwild, turn east onto North Circle Drive, which then becomes South Circle, then Fern Valley Road. Reach Humber Park at the road's end, 2 miles from Idyllwild.

The Hike

The high plateau of the San Jacinto Mountains—with its thick forests of pine and fir, numerous lush meadows, springs and perennial streams, and boulder-dotted landscape—closely resembles the Kern Plateau region of the southern Sierra Nevada. This is one of the most scenic regions in southern California's mountains.

Climbers are attracted to the area near the trailhead by many challenging routes up Suicide Rock and Lily Rock (locally known as Tahquitz Rock). Lily Rock offers some of the most difficult and challenging rock climbing in southern California.

Begin this hike at the east end of the parking area. Ascend slopes alternating between cool, shady stands of pine and fir and open, chaparral-choked slopes. During this ascent, you pass three small springs—Jolley, Middle, and Powderbox—which may dry up as the summer progresses (always check on water availability at the Forest Service's San Jacinto Ranger District office in Idyllwild before your trip). The

Granite crags punctuate the Desert Divide southeast of Red Tahquitz Peak. JOHN REILLY PHOTO

striking, near-vertical walls of either Lily Rock or Suicide Rock are constantly in view during your ascent.

After hiking 2.8 miles from the trailhead, reach 8,100-foot Saddle Junction, where trails lead in five directions. For now, take the extreme right-hand trail, the southbound Pacific Crest Trail (PCT). You will be returning via the southeast-branching trail, where the sign points to Tahquitz Valley.

The PCT leads south for 1.3 miles to the Tahquitz Peak Trail, branching southwest. Continuing eastward along the PCT, reach the northbound trail leading to Little Tahquitz Valley after another 0.6 mile. After climbing Red Tahquitz, you will return to this point and follow that trail back to Saddle Junction.

Continuing eastward on the PCT, the trail soon crosses a small tributary of Tahquitz Creek. During this gentle stretch of trail, you will have occasional forest-framed views down into the Tahquitz Creek plateau, with San Jacinto Peak on the northern horizon. After hiking 1.2 miles from the previous junction, round a minor north-trending spur ridge at the 8,400-foot contour; leave the PCT and proceed southwest on the Red Tahquitz Trail for 0.3 mile to the barren red-rock summit of 8,738-foot Red Tahquitz.

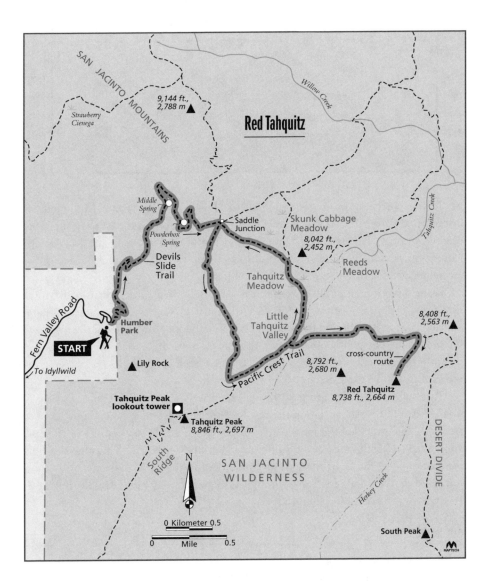

The openness of the peak affords excellent vistas. Southward lies the rugged crest of the range, known as the Desert Divide, capped by craggy summits. To the southwest, Lake Hemet lies at the foot of massive Thomas Mountain, adding contrast to the flat terrain of the Garner Valley. To your southeast lies the deep floor of the Coachella Valley and the Salton Sea, more than 9,000 feet below. That deep trench, partially drowned by the Salton Sea, is known as the Salton Trough. This is the largest dry-land region below sea level in the Western Hemisphere, covering more than 2,000 square miles. With a low point of 273 feet below sea level, the Salton Trough is a mere 9 feet higher than Death Valley.

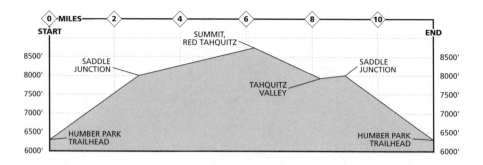

To the northeast are the low hills of the Little San Bernardino Mountains in Joshua Tree National Park, the general dividing point between the Mojave and Colorado (Sonoran) Deserts. To the north stand the highest peaks of the San Jacinto Mountains. All together, the views from Red Tahquitz afford an impressive and interesting perspective of much of southern California.

From this vantage point backtrack for 1.5 miles, then turn right (north), soon skirting the tall grass of the meadow in Little Tahquitz Valley, where water is usually available. Campsites abound from here to Saddle Junction. After leaving the meadow, the trail, shaded by Jeffrey pine and white fir, leads in 0.7 mile to a junction with the northeastbound trail descending along Tahquitz Creek to Caramba Camp, lying on the eastern rim of the plateau.

Turn left (northwest) and pass through the lovely meadow of Tahquitz Valley. A small backcountry ranger station lies just east of the trail, where emergency services are available—provided the ranger isn't out on patrol. As the trail curves northwest, you get a brief glimpse of beautiful Skunk Cabbage Meadow. The meadows on this plateau are ideal locations for spotting mule deer in the early morning or evening hours. After climbing gradually through an open forest, reach Saddle Junction. Retrace your route to the trailhead.

Key points

0.0 Humber Park trailhead.

2.8 Saddle Junction; turn right (south) onto the Pacific Crest Trail (PCT).

4.1 Junction with southwestbound Tahquitz Peak Trail; stay left (east).

4.7 Junction with northbound trail leading to Little Tahquitz Valley; stay right, continuing eastward on the PCT.

5.9 Junction with trail to Red Tahquitz; turn right (southwest) onto the summit trail.

6.2 Summit of Red Tahquitz. From the summit, backtrack to the junction with the trail to Little Tahquitz Valley.

7.7 Junction with the trail to Little Tahquitz Valley; turn right (north) and begin descending.

8.4 Junction with northeastbound trail to Caramba Camp; bear left (northwest).

8.9 Arrive back at Saddle Junction; descend west, backtracking to the trailhead.

11.7 Humber Park trailhead.

49 Arroyo Seco Creek to Agua Tibia Mountain

This rigorous and rewarding all-day trip leads hikers from a deep, brushy canyon to a pine-clad mountain in the southern Peninsular Ranges.

Start: The signed Dripping Springs Trail begins 0.5 mile south of the parking area.
General location: Agua Tibia Range, Agua Tibia Wilderness (Cleveland National Forest), 25 miles northeast of Escondido and 20 miles south of Hemet
Distance: 15.2-mile round-trip day hike or overnighter
Approximate hiking time: 7–8 hours
Difficulty: Strenuous
Trailhead elevation: 1,625 feet
High point: 4,700 feet
Land status: State park
Best season: November through May
Water availability: None available; bring your own

Maps: USGS Vail Lake (lower 6.0 miles of trail not shown on quad); Cleveland National Forest map
Fees and permits: A Wilderness Permit is required only for overnight camping in the Agua Tibia Wilderness (obtain your permit at the Dripping Springs Ranger Station from spring through autumn or at the Palomar District Ranger Station in Ramona). A California Campfire Permit is required for campfires and backpack stoves. A National Forest Adventure Pass is required to park at the trailhead.
Trail contact: Cleveland National Forest, Palomar Ranger District, 1634 Black Canyon Road, Ramona, CA 92065; (951) 788-0250

Finding the trailhead: From Interstate 15, 27 miles north of Escondido and 5 miles south of the Interstate 15/215 junction, take the California Highway 79 South exit, where a sign indicates Indio.

Upon exiting the freeway, turn left (east) where a sign points to Indio and Warner Springs. Follow CA 79 east for 10.7 miles, then turn right (south) where a Forest Service sign points to Dripping Springs Campground and Ranger Station. Follow this paved road south, reaching the ranger station and parking area after 150 feet.

The Hike

Agua Tibia Mountain, the western end of a long hogback ridge known as the Palomar Range or Agua Tibia Range, supports cool forests of Coulter pine on its upper slopes and offers relief to the hikers who slog for miles up the mountain's hot, brush-choked lower slopes.

The Agua Tibia Range is one of many San Diego and Riverside County mountain masses belonging to California's Peninsular Ranges province. Fundamentally, these are southern California's coast ranges, which extend southward from the Los Angeles Basin for the entire length of Baja California.

Coulter pine (or big-cone pine), a conifer indigenous to California and northern Baja California, forms extensive forests along the upper reaches of the Agua

Tibia Range and other relatively high ranges in San Diego County. It inhabits dry rocky slopes between 3,000 and 7,000 feet in elevation, growing in pure stands or mixing with other conifers and oaks. With needles in bundles of three, it resembles the ponderosa and Jeffrey pines. However, its distinguishing characteristic is its large cones. Reaching 10 to 14 inches in length and weighing as much as five pounds, the heavy, clawed cones are the largest of the American pine cones.

During the hot, dry summer of 1989, the Vail Lake Fire consumed 15,600 acres of chaparral in the Agua Tibia region, including nearly 7,000 acres in the Agua Tibia Wilderness. Most of the unusually large shrubs along the Dripping Springs Trail—shrubs that had escaped conflagration for more than one hundred years—were destroyed by that exceedingly hot fire, though regrowth has been vigorous. Fortunately the cool forests of pine and oak atop the crest of Agua Tibia Mountain were, for the most part, spared from destruction.

From the hikers' parking area, follow the paved road south through the campground for 0.5 mile to the Dripping Springs trailhead. Immediately hop across the boulder-strewn bed of seasonal Arroyo Seco Creek, shaded by California sycamore, interior live oak, and Fremont cottonwood. Leaving that creekbed, begin a southwestward ascent along an Arroyo Seco Creek tributary, entering the Agua Tibia Wilderness within a quarter mile of the trailhead.

Soon the route leaves that tributary canyon to surmount a low ridge emanating from Peak 3329, then begins threading its way through a dense blanket of buckwheat, red shank, chamise, scrub oak, and ceanothus. As you gain elevation, the lower reaches of Arroyo Seco Creek come into view, and the shrub cover gradually becomes dominated by chamise, which displays vivid white flower clusters in May and June. Passing above the 2,000-foot contour, red shank joins the chamise to form an impenetrable barrier to off-trail travel.

After 2.5 miles, the trail begins a southeastward course above a precipitous canyon. From here you get your first glimpse of the conifer-clad environs of Agua Tibia Mountain, looming on the skyline ahead. The vegetation at this point consists of black sage, ceanothus, chamise, and buckwheat.

After hiking 4.0 miles from the trailhead, pass a camping area on a ridge at 3,600 feet elevation. Once there were very large specimens of red shank and manzanita here, some reaching 20 feet in height and more than one hundred years in age. Today the blackened root crowns of these once-towering shrubs have vigorously reclaimed the slopes of Agua Tibia Mountain in a vast evergreen thicket of chaparral.

Topping a 3,800-foot ridge beyond the campsites, you are treated to an excellent view of the oak- and Coulter pine–covered northeast slope of Agua Tibia

Although this 20-foot manzanita shrub was reduced to ashes by a brushfire in 1989, the Agua Tibia Wilderness still supports isolated stands of giant shrubs that have escaped fire for more than a hundred years. JOHN REILLY PHOTO

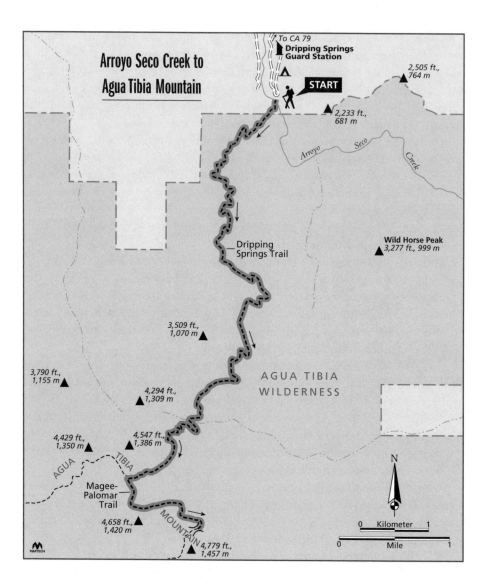

Arroyo Seco Creek to
Agua Tibia Mountain

To CA 79
Dripping Springs
Guard Station

START

2,505 ft.,
764 m

2,233 ft.,
681 m

Arroyo   Seco

Creek

Dripping
Springs Trail

Wild Horse Peak
3,277 ft., 999 m

3,509 ft.,
1,070 m

AGUA TIBIA
WILDERNESS

3,790 ft.,
1,155 m

4,294 ft.,
1,309 m

4,429 ft.,
1,350 m

4,547 ft.,
1,386 m

AGUA   TIBIA

N

Magee-
Palomar
Trail

4,658 ft.,
1,420 m

MOUNTAIN

4,779 ft.,
1,457 m

0   Kilometer   1

0   Mile   1

MAPTECH

Mountain; its shady environs beckon hikers onward. The panoramic views that have accompanied you for several miles reach their breathtaking culmination in this area. Much of southern California is visible—from observatory-crowned Palomar Mountain in the southeast to the Santa Rosa, San Jacinto, San Bernardino, and San Gabriel Ranges. Closer at hand, the Agua Tibia Range plummets into the vicinity of Vail Lake; beyond, the Temecula Valley fades into the distant southern California smog, which often reaches maximum density in the rarely visible Riverside area.

From the ridge, a minor descent ensues, followed by a sequence of sometimes-overgrown switchbacks rising in elevation. Coulter pines begin to appear above

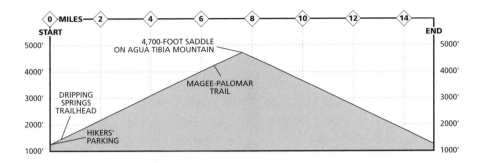

4,000 feet. Above the switchbacks, the trail begins a hillside traverse, first on east-facing and then on south-facing slopes, separated from Agua Tibia Mountain by a shallow gully.

You soon enter the welcome shade of an interior live oak stand and then reach the crest of the range at 6.1 miles and a junction with the Magee-Palomar Trail, where a trail sign points left (south) to Eagle Crag, the apex of the wilderness. The Vail Lake quad shows this ridgetop trail as a road, and indeed it is. However, it has long since been abandoned, and vegetation has encroached to the point that it is hardly recognizable as a road.

Turning left, proceed southeastward then eastward under the shade of live oak and Coulter pine, just below the ridgecrest. The dominant shrubs at this point are silktassel and ceanothus. Blue penstemon decorates some sunny openings in late spring and early summer. After walking 1.0 mile along this abandoned dirt road, reach a saddle at 4,700 feet, shaded by Coulter pine and oak, just north of Peak 4779. The road begins a steady descent, and many hikers go no farther than this point. This saddle has been used as a campsite, and water-packing backpackers will find it a pleasant spot for an overnight stay. Day hikers will find this saddle a fine spot for a lunch break before retracing their panoramic route back to the trailhead.

Key points

0.0 Hikers' parking area; follow paved road south to the trailhead.

0.5 Dripping Springs trailhead.

6.6 Junction with Magee-Palomar Trail; turn left (southeast).

7.6 Reach saddle at 4,700 feet.

50 Borrego Palm Canyon

This hike, part of it cross-country, leads into California's Sonoran Desert via a deep, palm-dotted canyon in the San Ysidro Mountains.

Start: The signed Palm Canyon Trail begins at the west edge of the parking area.
General location: San Ysidro Mountains, Anza-Borrego Desert State Park, 2 miles northwest of Borrego Springs
Distance: 3.0- to 4.0-mile round-trip day hike
Approximate hiking time: 1.5 hours
Difficulty: Easy
Trailhead elevation: 830 feet
High point: 1,600 feet

Land status: State park
Best season: Mid-October through early May
Water availability: None available; bring your own
Maps: USGS Borrego Palm Canyon
Fees and permits: No fees or permits required
Trail contact: Anza-Borrego Desert State Park, Box 299, Borrego Springs, CA 92004; (760) 767-5311

Finding the trailhead: From San Diego County Road S-22, 1.5 miles west of Christmas Circle in downtown Borrego Springs, turn west onto Palm Canyon Road. Borrego Springs is 28 miles west of the junction of S-22 and California Highway 86 in Salton City and 65 miles east of the Interstate 15/California Highway 79 junction at Rancho California.

Turn right after driving 0.1 mile on Palm Canyon Road, where a sign points to campgrounds. The road straight ahead leads 0.3 mile to the state park visitor center, where interpretive displays and slide shows help acquaint visitors with the wonders of the desert.

Proceeding north and then west on Palm Canyon Road, follow signs pointing toward the hiking trail. After 1.8 miles, park in the large parking area at the road's end.

The Hike

Encompassing more than 600,000 acres, Anza-Borrego Desert State Park is the largest state park in the nation. Much of its land is roadless, ranging from remote mountain ranges to low hills and desert plains. The unusual California fan palm, found only in a few canyons and moist areas along the western and northern edge of the Colorado (Sonoran) Desert in California, is well represented in two separate groves in Borrego Palm Canyon.

Experienced and adventurous hikers are urged to explore the rugged forks of the canyon beyond the second palm grove. The Middle Fork leads into the Los Coyotes Indian Reservation, where permission is required for entry. Hikers aren't likely to find campsites in these narrow canyons, which are visited chiefly by day hikers.

The trail leads northwest from the trailhead parking area, where a sign indicates the Palm Canyon Trail. At the trailhead pick up the pamphlet describing the natural history of the canyon. Your trail ascends an alluvial fan northwestward toward the mouth of Borrego Palm Canyon. En route you pass specimens of beavertail cactus,

California fan palms crowd the banks of the small stream in Borrego Palm Canyon, Anza-Borrego Desert State Park.

cholla, indigo bush, catclaw, mesquite, the aromatic desert lavender, creosote bush, brittlebush, ocotillo, chuparosa, and a few desert-willows near the creek. The pamphlet discusses these plants in detail.

The San Ysidro Mountains (also referred to as the Anza Upland) soar skyward to the west, north, and south. In the northwest, the noble crag of 3,960-foot Indianhead pierces the desert sky more than 3,000 feet overhead. To the east, the Borrego Valley sprawls toward the abrupt west face of the Santa Rosa Mountains.

Soon hop south across a small creek and meet an alternate trail leading back to the trailhead via the south side of the creek. From here the first grove of palms is visible, crowding the canyon bottom a short distance ahead. Upon entering the lower palm grove, the trail recrosses the creek to its north side just below a small cascade, then proceeds northwest through a quarter-mile-long grove of fascinating palm trees. California fan palms (*Washingtonia filifera*) were named in honor of George Washington. They are generally found in groves below 3,500 feet, in moist alkaline soil near streams, seeps, and springs. They are the only palms native to the western United States.

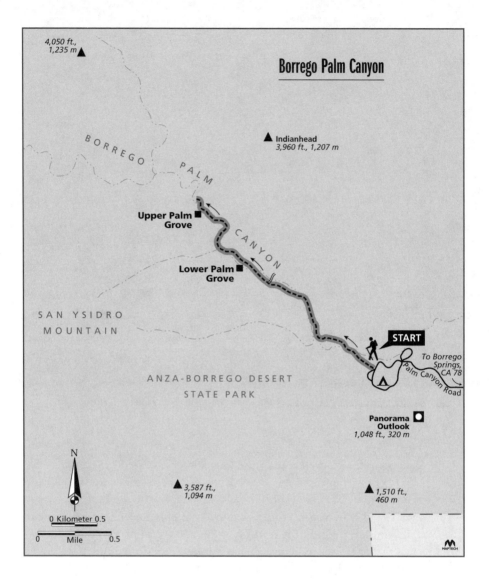

Borrego Palm Canyon

4,050 ft.,
1,235 m

BORREGO

PALM

Indianhead
3,960 ft., 1,207 m

Upper Palm
Grove

CANYON

Lower Palm
Grove

SAN YSIDRO
MOUNTAIN

START

To Borrego
Springs,
CA 78

Palm Canyon Road

ANZA-BORREGO DESERT
STATE PARK

Panorama
Outlook
1,048 ft., 320 m

N

3,587 ft.,
1,094 m

1,510 ft.,
460 m

0 Kilometer 0.5

0   Mile   0.5

MAPTECH

Leaving the palms behind, the trail reaches a point below a cascade where you can proceed no farther along the north bank of the creek. From here, cross back to the south bank and pick up a faint trail leading west up the canyon. Only hikers experienced in cross-country travel should hike beyond the first palm grove.

After passing the last isolated palm, continue up the canyon. Indianhead's ever-present crag looms thousands of feet above to the north. As you climb higher up the rocky, sparsely vegetated canyon, you'll enjoy over-the-shoulder views of the Borrego Valley, often distorted by shimmering heat waves. The sometimes faint path

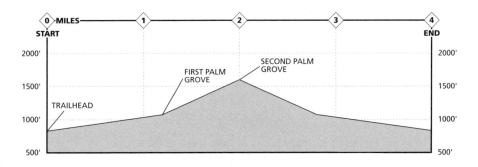

crosses the small creek several times. After hiking 0.5 mile beyond the first palm grove, you reach the second, or upper, grove.

This grove is sparse in comparison with the lower grove, covering less area. However, it is more isolated and sees much less hiking traffic. Thus the area has a more primitive feel to it. From here the trail becomes more difficult to follow upstream and should be used only by experienced hikers, who will find hundreds of palms in the next 2.0 miles.

After exploring this fascinating canyon, you eventually must double back to the trailhead.

Key points

0.0   Borrego Palm Canyon trailhead.

1.2   First palm grove.

2.0   Second palm grove.

51 Elephant Trees Trails

This rewarding desert hike ascends alluvial fans toward the foot of the Vallecito Mountains, where a fascinating array of desert plants and magnificent, austere scenery awaits.

Start: The signed Elephant Trees Discovery Trail begins at the turnaround at the road's end.

General location: East slopes of the Vallecito Mountains, Anza-Borrego Desert State Park, 6 miles south of Ocotillo Wells

Distance: Loop trip (1.5 miles) or round-trip (3.4 miles)

Approximate hiking time: 45 minutes–1.5 hours

Difficulty: Easy

Trailhead elevation: 230 feet

High point: 330 to 450 feet

Land status: National park

Best season: Mid-October through early May

Water availability: None available; bring your own

Maps: USGS Harper Canyon, Borrego Mountain SE (trail and road to trailhead not shown on quads)

Fees and permits: No fees or permits required

Trail contact: Anza-Borrego Desert State Park, Box 299, Borrego Springs, CA 92004; (760) 767-5311

Finding the trailhead: From Ocotillo Wells on California Highway 78, 40 miles west of Brawley and 78 miles east of Escondido, turn south onto the signed Split Mountain Road. Follow this paved road south along the western edge of Lower Borrego Valley. Soon after passing a park ranger station, turn right (west) where a small sign indicates the Elephant Trees Area, just before entering Imperial County. This turnoff is about 5.7 miles south of CA 78.

Follow this dirt road, rough and rocky in places, for 0.8 mile to the turnaround at the signed trailhead.

The Hike

Many persons view California's deserts as a vast wasteland, an area to drive through as quickly as possible on the way to somewhere else. The deserts are vast indeed, but to those who have grown to love them, they are anything but wastelands. This short hike helps dispel that myth, for here on the eastern slopes of the Vallecito Mountains you'll see a broad array of drought-tolerant vegetation, including many rare elephant trees, one of the most unusual plants in the California desert.

This area is at its best in winter and spring, when many plants display brilliantly colorful flowers, providing a dramatic contrast to the stark desert landscape.

At the trailhead, be sure to pick up the Elephant Trees Discovery Trail pamphlet. This pamphlet, keyed to numbered posts along the loop trail, describes flora and natural features representative of this area and should greatly enhance your enjoyment and understanding.

The elephant tree is a rare find in the deserts of southeastern California, but specimens such as this one can be seen near the Mexican border in Anza-Borrego Desert State Park.

From the trailhead proceed westward up a major alluvial fan just north of a range of low hills. Alluvial fans, common near the base of many California mountain ranges, are composed of alluvium: unconsolidated sand, gravel, rocks, and boulders deposited at the base of the mountains by running water. Here this debris has washed out of the Vallecito Mountains to the west during infrequent but often torrential summer thunderstorms. Because there is so little vegetation in this rocky, gravelly country, rain simply washes off the mountains and hillsides. Where the velocity of these flash floods begins to decrease in flatter terrain below the mountains, runoff waters begin to deposit sand, gravel, and rocks carried from higher elevations, forming an alluvial fan.

Among the fascinating variety of plant life encountered are ocotillo, barrel cactus, catclaw, creosote bush (the most widely distributed plant in the California desert), chuparosa, cholla, cheesebush, bursage, and the highly unusual elephant tree. Virtually every shrub and cactus in this area displays very colorful flowers after periods of substantial rainfall, especially in late winter and spring.

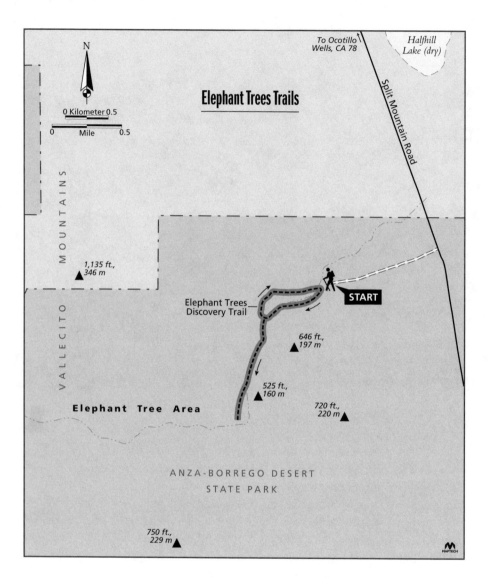

The trail sometimes crosses dry stream courses that meander across the alluvial fan. During flash floods—most common during summer thunderstorms—enormous quantities of water rush out of the Vallecito Mountains on the way to the Salton Sea. This water chooses paths of least resistance and, depending on its velocity and volume, will follow one or more of these numerous stream courses or create new channels through the unconsolidated alluvium.

At Signpost 10, reach the first elephant tree on the hike. This plant, extremely rare in the United States, is found only from the southern Santa Rosa Mountains southward through California's Colorado (Sonoran) Desert and in southwest Arizona. However, it is quite common in northwestern Mexico up to 2,500 feet elevation. This "tree" is a fascinating addition to a typical collection of desert flora. It can reach 16 feet in height, but specimens taller than 10 feet are unlikely to be found in this area. The elephant tree *(Bursera microphylla)* is quite susceptible to frost damage. Because young plants are killed by cold weather, the occurrence of these trees here indicates that frost rarely develops in the area.

This aromatic shrub has a widely spreading crown; thick, sharply tapered, crooked branches; small, pinnately compound, aromatic dull green leaves (*microphylla* means "small leaved"); papery whitish or greenish bark; small white flowers that bloom in early summer; and red to bluish berries. The stout trunk and branches vaguely suggest the legs and trunk of an elephant, hence the name. (A little imagination is required here.)

From the vicinity of Signpost 10, more experienced hikers wishing to extend the hike and see more elephant trees are urged to leave the nature trail here and proceed southwestward up one of the dry stream courses meandering across the alluvial fan. The "trail" is sometimes faint, and the hiking is largely cross-country. Following any one of the dry stream courses, hike toward the massive, stark mountains on the western horizon, just north of a range of low hills. Within 1.0 mile, you should run into a short section of trail that passes a very fine elephant tree. The trail apparently ends a short distance to the south at a sign describing elephant trees.

Adventurous and experienced hikers and backpackers (with a large supply of water) may wish to continue westward up the alluvial fan (labeled ELEPHANT TREES AREA on the quad), where many more specimens are found. From this area you can follow the dry stream course toward a canyon that penetrates westward into the heart of the Vallecito Mountains. Backpackers with adequate water will find a hike up this canyon to be exhilarating and rewarding—a pure desert experience.

From the end of your 1.0-mile side trip, return to the nature trail and resume hiking it, first west, then northeast. The path is occasionally lost in a dry streambed—just watch for the numbered signposts to help guide you. Soon the trail leaves the streambed and loops back to the trailhead.

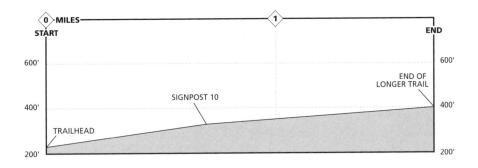

Key points

0.0 Elephant Trees trailhead.

0.7 Signpost 10; continue southwest for the longer round-trip hike, or turn right (west), staying on the nature trail and looping back to the trailhead in 0.8 mile.

1.7 End of longer trail.

Joshua Tree National Park

When most persons think of Joshua Tree National Park, images of stately Joshua trees likely come to mind. Of course there are Joshua trees in the park, and lots of them. But there is so much more to this attractive desert landscape than simply giant yuccas. Here you will also find seven profoundly eroded, nearly barren mountain ranges and broad valleys—some studded with spreading Joshua trees and all of them mantled with coarse desert shrubs and cactus. Vegetation is diverse and includes species from the Great Basin, Mojave, and Colorado (Sonoran) Deserts. In fact, Joshua Tree includes the transition zone between the Mojave and Colorado Deserts. In the park you will find piñon-juniper woodlands and vast stretches of creosote bush and Joshua tree. In the lower and hotter Colorado Desert, there is ocotillo and, surrounding five oases, California fan palm.

The dominant rock in the park is monzogranite, also known as quartz monzonite. Particularly in the western reaches of the park, great mounds and stacks of boulders add to the raw scenic beauty of the landscape and attract rock climbers and boulder scramblers from throughout the world.

Joshua Tree National Park comprises 794,000 acres, of which 630,800 acres were designated wilderness by the California Desert Protection Act of 1994. There are only six maintained hiking trails and ten nature trails in the park, so much of this rugged desert wilderness remains trail-less. However, many user-created singletrack trails and long-closed roads serve as access into the backcountry. The trails in this chapter sample some of the routes described above, plus a few trail-less cross-country routes.

Daytime temperatures in Joshua Tree National Park average 100 degrees or higher from about mid-May through mid-September. Late summer can bring occasional thunderstorms, but the weather at this time of year is typically very hot and dry. The best times to hike in the park are from mid-September through November and from mid-March through mid-May. Winter typically brings occasional cool, windy, showery weather, and snow is not uncommon in higher elevations. Hikers looking for an extended stay have nine campgrounds from which to choose, and only three of those require fees.

52 Black Rock Campground to Peak 5195

This rewarding high-desert hike follows one of the park's westernmost canyons en route to a high peak in the Little San Bernardino Mountains.

Start: The cross-country route begins east of the ranger station and campground, immediately above the dry wash of Black Rock Canyon.
General location: Joshua Tree National Park, 4 miles southeast of Yucca Valley
Distance: 6.0-mile round-trip day hike or overnight trip
Approximate hiking time: 2.5–3 hours
Difficulty: Moderate
Trailhead elevation: 4,000 feet
High point: 5,195 feet
Land status: National park

Best season: Mid-September through mid-May
Water availability: None available; bring your own
Maps: USGS Yucca Valley South (trail not shown on quad); Joshua Tree National Park visitors map
Fees and permits: No fees or permits required
Trail contact: Joshua Tree National Park, 74485 National Park Drive, Twentynine Palms, CA 92277; (760) 367-7511

Finding the trailhead: From California Highway 62 (the Twentynine Palms Highway) in Yucca Valley, turn south onto Joshua Lane and follow signs pointing to Black Rock Campground. After driving 5 miles through residential areas of Yucca Valley, reach the ranger station at the campground; park there.

The Hike

The hike up Black Rock Canyon to the crest of the Little San Bernardino Mountains is an excellent introduction to high-desert hiking. This trip makes a fine midwinter leg-stretcher, and hikers are rewarded with far-flung vistas from Peak 5195.

This trip can be made as an overnighter if you are willing to carry water. Hikers can follow the crest of the Little San Bernardino Mountains for days and see few, if any, other hikers. Backpackers are required to sign in at the backcountry board at the trailhead. Always avoid this and any other desert hike during periods of thunderstorm activity—floods and lightning are real and dangerous possibilities.

From the ranger station, hike due east through the campground for 0.25 mile to the dry wash of Black Rock Canyon. The sandy wash serves as a trail. Proceed westward up the wide alluvial canyon mouth, passing many Joshua trees, some California juniper, and Mojave yucca, which can be easily confused with a small Joshua

The wands of ocotillo often share space with Mojave yuccas in the transition zone between the Mojave and Colorado (Sonoran) Deserts.

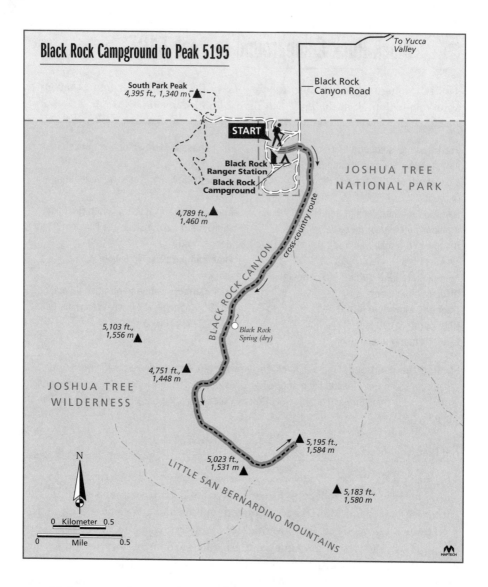

Black Rock Campground to Peak 5195

To Yucca Valley

Black Rock Canyon Road

South Park Peak
4,395 ft., 1,340 m

START

Black Rock
Ranger Station

Black Rock
Campground

JOSHUA TREE
NATIONAL PARK

4,789 ft.,
1,460 m

BLACK ROCK CANYON

cross-country route

5,103 ft.,
1,556 m

Black Rock
Spring (dry)

4,751 ft.,
1,448 m

JOSHUA TREE
WILDERNESS

5,195 ft.,
1,584 m

5,023 ft.,
1,531 m

N

5,183 ft.,
1,580 m

LITTLE SAN BERNARDINO MOUNTAINS

0   Kilometer   0.5

0   Mile   0.5

MAPTECH

tree. Mojave yucca, however, is generally smaller, and its leaves have fibrous, stringy margins. You will also encounter an incredible variety of plant life typical of the Joshua Tree Woodland plant community: clumps of bunchgrass, boxthorn, cholla, some desert willow, Mormon tea, rabbitbrush, and desert almond.

After hiking 1.5 miles, pass sometimes-dry Black Rock Spring—a small, stagnant waterhole frequented by swarms of hornets. At intervals along the way, 4-inch-by-4-inch posts with arrows point in the direction of the trail, making it almost impossible to lose.

Beyond the spring, the canyon narrows and vegetation begins to show signs of more moisture and higher elevation. You are now accompanied by desert scrub oak, piñon-pine, juniper, beavertail cactus, bitterbrush, Mojave yucca, and some birch-leaf mountain mahogany—plants representative of the Piñon-Juniper Woodland vegetation zone.

After hiking 2.75 miles from the trailhead, you top a ridge—the crest of the Little San Bernardino Mountains—where the trail promptly disappears. Turn left (northeast) and hike cross-country along the ridge for 0.25 mile to the stack of weathered rocks that marks the summit of Peak 5195.

The vistas are truly panoramic from here, unlike any others obtained from more popular viewpoints in southern California. To the southwest the Coachella Valley sprawls into the haze of the distant Salton Sea. The San Jacinto Mountains can be seen soaring 10,000 feet above the western margin of that broad valley; with the Santa Rosa Mountains to the south, they form a virtually impenetrable barrier to westward travel.

To the west lies the deep gash of San Gorgonio Pass, with majestic San Gorgonio Mountain also rising 10,000 feet above to the north. The entire eastern end of the San Bernardino Mountains dominates the northwestern horizon, and the Mojave Desert to the north lies vast and flat at your feet. In the southeast, the deeply eroded hills of the Little San Bernardino Mountains dissolve into the desert haze.

There are a few stunted piñons and junipers around the peak in addition to some rabbitbrush, Mormon tea, desert scrub oak, and a few Joshua trees. The sparse vegetation reflects the drier conditions that prevail here on the crest, and ground cover is much less dense than in the sheltered upper reaches of Black Rock Canyon.

From the peak, return the way you came.

Key points

0.0 Trailhead.

0.25 Reach Black Rock Canyon wash; follow wash upcanyon (west).

1.5 Black Rock Spring.

2.75 Top out on crest of Little San Bernardino Mountains.

3.0 Peak 5195.

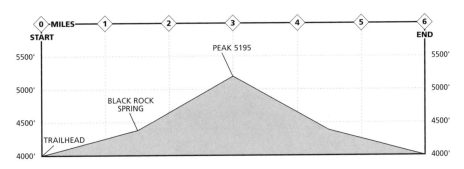

53 Indian Cove Nature Trail

This short loop hike introduces hikers to plants of the creosote bush scrub plant community that dominates much of the park and affords fine views into Joshua Tree's greatest concentration of monzogranite domes—the Wonderland of Rocks.

Start: The signed Indian Cove Nature Trail begins on the west edge of the parking area.
General location: Joshua Tree National Park, 7 miles southwest of Twentynine Palms and 8 miles southeast of Joshua Tree
Distance: 0.75-mile loop nature trail
Approximate hiking time: 20–30 minutes
Difficulty: Easy
Trailhead elevation: 3,334 feet
High point: 3,380 feet
Land status: National park

Best season: October through mid-May
Water availability: None available; bring your own
Maps: USGS Indian Cove (trail not shown on quad); Joshua Tree National Park visitors map
Fees and permits: No fees or permits required
Trail contact: Joshua Tree National Park, 74485 National Park Drive, Twentynine Palms, CA 92277; (760) 367-7511

Finding the trailhead: From the Indian Cove turnoff on California Highway 62 (Twentynine Palms Highway), 14 miles east of Yucca Valley, drive 3 miles south on Indian Cove Road to the campground. Bear right at the junction, where signs point to the nature trail parking area. Turn right and proceed 0.8 mile to the loop at the end of the road. The trail begins at the cluster of signs at the west end of the loop.

The Hike

The nature trails in Joshua Tree National Park are generally short; most are a mile or less. These trails have interpretive signs to help hikers become familiar with the flora, fauna, and natural features of the diverse landscapes found in the park. This particular trail takes you through an interesting collection of plants typical of the creosote bush scrub plant community, such as creosote bush, Mojave yucca, and pencil

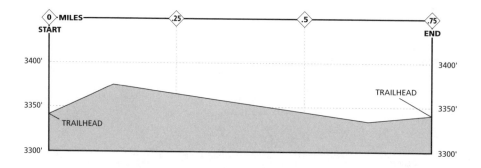

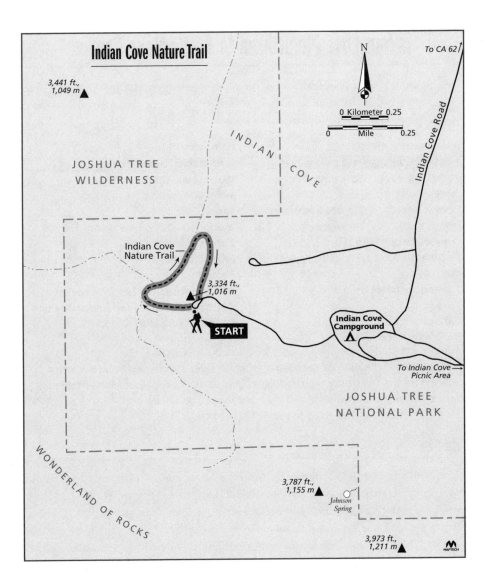

Indian Cove Nature Trail

3,441 ft.,
1,049 m ▲

JOSHUA TREE
WILDERNESS

INDIAN COVE

N

To CA 62

Indian Cove Road

0 Kilometer 0.25
0 Mile 0.25

Indian Cove
Nature Trail

3,334 ft.,
1,016 m

START

Indian Cove
Campground

To Indian Cove
Picnic Area

JOSHUA TREE
NATIONAL PARK

WONDERLAND OF ROCKS

3,787 ft.,
1,155 m ▲
Johnson
Spring

3,973 ft.,
1,211 m ▲

MAPTECH

cholla. These plants are commonly found on the desert floor and in the foothills of desert ranges in southern California, where annual precipitation rarely exceeds 8 inches.

From the end of the road, walk west along the trail, which soon drops into a shallow wash where it all but disappears. Proceed north down the wash, keeping an eye out for the interpretive signs that lead the way. You soon climb out of the wash and loop back to the trailhead, presumably more familiar now with representative species of this plant community and more appreciative of the fascinating California desert.

54 Indian Cove Picnic Area to Rattlesnake Canyon

This rigorous day hike leads to one of the most fascinating landscapes in Joshua Tree National Park—the rockbound monzogranite expanse of the Wonderland of Rocks.

Start: The cross-country route begins on the east side of the picnic site parking area, immediately above the dry wash of Rattlesnake Canyon.
General location: Joshua Tree National Park, 7 miles southwest of Twentynine Palms and 8 miles southeast of Joshua Tree
Distance: Variable; 1.0- to 5.0-mile day hike, cross-country
Approximate hiking time: 30 minutes–2 hours
Difficulty: Moderate to strenuous
Trailhead elevation: 3,017 feet

High point: Variable
Land status: National park
Best season: October through mid-May
Water availability: None available; bring your own
Maps: USGS Indian Cove; Joshua Tree National Park visitors map
Fees and permits: No fees or permits required
Trail contact: Joshua Tree National Park, 74485 National Park Drive, Twentynine Palms, CA 92277; (760) 367-7511

Finding the trailhead: From Yucca Valley follow California Highway 62 (Twentynine Palms Highway) east for 14 miles to the signed Indian Cove Road. Proceed south on this paved road, passing the ranger station after 1 mile, to a Y junction at 3 miles. Turn left, and continue another 1.3 miles to the picnic area at the end of the road and park.

The Hike

The Wonderland of Rocks is exactly what the name implies. To many climbers and boulder scramblers, it is paradise. The Wonderland covers approximately 10 square miles, from Barker Dam in the south to Indian Cove in the north. It is a region of highly eroded boulders and rock formations composed of the granitic rock monzogranite. The area supports little vegetation, and much of what does grow here often grows right out of solid rock. This region is much more arid than the western part of the park, and the vegetation reflects the drier, harsher conditions.

This trip is for more experienced hikers who are well acquainted with cross-country boulder scrambling. There is no true destination other than the Wonderland itself. Having trekked a short distance into Rattlesnake Canyon, hikers are free to explore the boulders and rock formations in any direction.

Hikers are urged, however, to go at least as far as the waterfall area, 0.5 mile upcanyon, where a small seasonal creek falls over solid rock, forming many lovely pools between cascades. Cool rest spots abound where jumbled boulders create small, cavelike rooms.

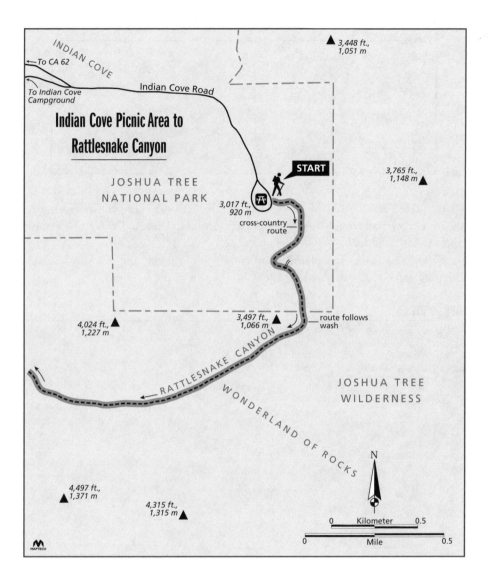

Indian Cove Picnic Area to Rattlesnake Canyon

From the picnic area, walk east into the dry wash of Rattlesnake Canyon through creosote bush, Mojave yucca, and Mormon tea. From the wash, turn right (south) and boulder-hop your way up the canyon, veering to the right where a small tributary canyon branches left.

Once you reach the base of the falls, you can ascend either side of the creek, but it requires some easy scrambling. There is usually water in this area, except during extended dry periods. Above the falls, the canyon is more open.

The relatively smooth slopes of the Queen Mountains, rising east of Rattlesnake Canyon, provide an interesting contrast with the fantastic, often grotesque formations

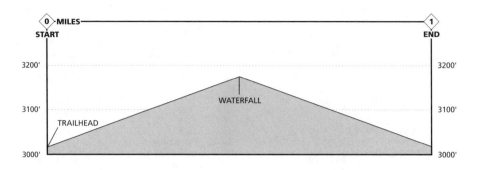

found in the Wonderland of Rocks. The dominant shrubs here are spiny catclaw, desert almond, and jojoba. A few piñons are found here and there, their roots anchored in solid rock.

When you tire of scrambling, climbing, or just enjoying the dramatic scenery, carefully make your way down Rattlesnake Canyon to the trailhead.

Key points

0.0 Trailhead.

0.5 Waterfall.

55 Ryan Mountain

This excellent trail leads to a high, isolated mountain in the west-central area of the park. Expansive vistas open up across much of Joshua Tree and the surrounding desert.

Start: The signed Ryan Mountain Trail begins on the south side of the parking area.
General location: Joshua Tree National Park, 10 miles southwest of Twentynine Palms and 14 miles southeast of Joshua Tree
Distance: 3.2-mile round-trip day hike
Approximate hiking time: 1.5 hours
Difficulty: Moderately strenuous
Trailhead elevation: 4,391 feet
High point: Ryan Mountain, 5,457 feet
Land status: National park

Best season: Mid-September through mid-May
Water availability: None available; bring your own
Maps: USGS Indian Cove, Keys Views; Joshua Tree National Park visitors map
Fees and permits: No fees or permits required
Trail contact: Joshua Tree National Park, 74485 National Park Drive, Twentynine Palms, CA 92277; (760) 367-7511

Finding the trailhead: From California Highway 62 (Twentynine Palms Highway) at the east end of Twentynine Palms, turn south onto Utah Trail, signed for Joshua Tree National Park. After 8.6 miles you reach the Pinto Wye junction; the left fork leads to Cottonwood Visitor Center and Interstate 10, and the right fork leads toward Keys View and the town of Joshua Tree.

Follow the right fork generally westward for 8.1 miles to the signed Ryan Mountain trailhead on the south side of the road.

The Hike

Ryan Mountain, one of the highest peaks in Joshua Tree National Park, is an isolated massif rising between the broad, Joshua tree–covered flats of Lost Horse Valley to the west and Queen Valley to the east. Its open summit and isolated location affords panoramic views of much of the park, including the Queen and Little San Bernardino Mountains and the rockbound landscape of the Wonderland of Rocks. The hike follows one of the best constructed trails in Joshua Tree, though it does rise at a steady, moderate grade. It's an enjoyable hike from autumn through spring, but the mountain is often swept by strong winds. Winter is an ideal time to hike here, when the desert air is clear and vistas stretch to far horizons.

From the trailhead the trail leads you south through a gap in massive outcrops of granite. Desert almond is the dominant shrub, and a scattering of juniper and Mojave yucca cover trailside slopes. Piñons gather at the foot of the large boulders

Lost Horse Valley and the Little San Bernardino Mountains spread out below Ryan Mountain.

nearby. Soon the trail begins rising in earnest, and at 0.2 mile you reach a junction with an eastbound trail leading to Sheep Pass Group Campsite.

Bear right (southwest) and begin a steady, moderate uphill grade with occasional steep but short stretches. Views all along the way are superb, stretching across Lost Horse Valley to the west, its expanse studded with Joshua trees and boulders and mounds of white granite. Beyond the valley are the wooded Little San Bernardino Mountains, and farther still you will see San Gorgonio Mountain and San Jacinto Peak.

At length the trail leads into a shallow draw landscaped with low-growing junipers, just below a 5,200-foot saddle. The trail ahead traverses generally south on the slopes above the draw; the slopes are clothed in blackbrush and studded with Joshua trees.

The trail's grade moderates during the final quarter mile to the summit; you will pass among burned Joshua trees just before reaching the large rock cairn on the 5,457-foot summit of Ryan Mountain.

Vistas are outstanding, stretching across much of the park. Eastward lies sprawling Queen Valley, punctuated by piles of granite and Malapai Hill, a sizable cinder

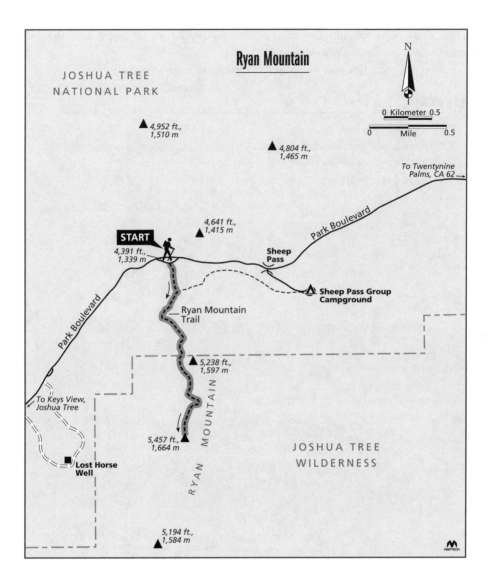

Ryan Mountain

N

JOSHUA TREE
NATIONAL PARK

▲ 4,952 ft.,
1,510 m

▲ 4,804 ft.,
1,465 m

To Twentynine
Palms, CA 62 →

Park Boulevard

▲ 4,641 ft.,
1,415 m

START
4,391 ft.,
1,339 m

**Sheep
Pass**

△ **Sheep Pass Group
Campground**

Ryan Mountain
Trail

Park Boulevard

▲ 5,238 ft.,
1,597 m

To Keys View,
Joshua Tree

R   Y   A   N   M   O   U   N   T   A   I   N

5,457 ft., ▲
1,664 m

■ **Lost Horse
Well**

JOSHUA TREE
WILDERNESS

▲ 5,194 ft.,
1,584 m

0 Kilometer 0.5

0   Mile   0.5

MAPTECH

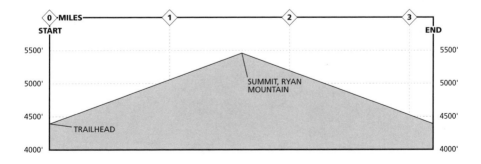

◇ 0 ▷ MILES   ◇ 1 ◇   ◇ 2 ◇   ◇ 3 ◇
START   END

5500'   5500'

SUMMIT, RYAN
MOUNTAIN

5000'   5000'

4500'   4500'
TRAILHEAD

4000'   4000'

cone. Pinto Basin spreads out farther to the east, and in the northwest you enjoy an eagle's-eye view of the Wonderland of Rocks.

After enjoying this fine vista point, retrace your steps to the trailhead.

Key points

0.0 Ryan Mountain trailhead.

0.2 Junction with eastbound trail leading to Sheep Pass Group Campground; bear right (southwest) and continue ascending.

1.6 Summit of Ryan Mountain.

56 Keys View to Inspiration Peak

This short but rewarding hike leads you away from the crowds that gather at Keys View to a quiet peak in the Little San Bernardino Mountains. Inspiring vistas stretch from the Salton Sea in the south, past the San Jacinto and San Bernardino Mountains, and across the vast empty reaches of the Mojave Desert.

Start: The trail begins next to the small HIKER sign at the northwest end of the Keys View parking area.
General location: Joshua Tree National Park, 15 miles southwest of Twentynine Palms and 16 miles southeast of Joshua Tree
Distance: 1.6-mile round-trip day hike
Approximate hiking time: 45 minutes–1 hour
Difficulty: Moderate
Trailhead elevation: 5,160 feet
High point: 5,560 feet

Land status: National park
Best season: October through mid-May
Water availability: None available; bring your own
Maps: USGS Keys View; Joshua Tree National Park visitors map
Fees and permits: No fees or permits required
Trail contact: Joshua Tree National Park, 74485 National Park Drive, Twentynine Palms, CA 92277; (760) 367-7511

Finding the trailhead: From California Highway 62 (Twentynine Palms Highway) at the east end of Twentynine Palms, turn south onto Utah Trail, signed for Joshua Tree National Park. After 8.6 miles, you reach the Pinto Wye junction; the left fork leads to Cottonwood Visitor Center and Interstate 10, and the right fork leads toward Keys View and the town of Joshua Tree.

Follow the right fork generally westward for 10.3 miles to the junction with southbound Keys View Road, and turn left. Hikers approaching from the town of Joshua Tree can reach this junction by following Park Boulevard southeast for 16 miles.

Follow steadily ascending Keys View Road south for 5.5 miles to the spacious parking area at the road's end.

The Hike

Anyone who has ever been to Keys View, on the crest of the Little San Bernardino Mountains, knows how dramatic the aerial-like vista is. If you don't mind doing a little walking, you can enjoy a vista equally as grand from Inspiration Peak, only a short distance northwest of Keys View, and you will likely have the peak to yourself. Choose a clear day for the hike from autumn through spring, since smog often obscures the view. Mornings are best—the smog usually thickens by afternoon.

From the northwest end of the Keys View parking lot, a small HIKER sign marks the beginning of your trail. It is a steady ascent north up the well-worn trail, crossing slopes clothed in blackbrush, buckwheat, ground-hugging junipers, and a scattering of Joshua trees. Views are outstanding from the start, reaching far below to farmland in the Coachella Valley and beyond to the Salton Sea. Across the valley in

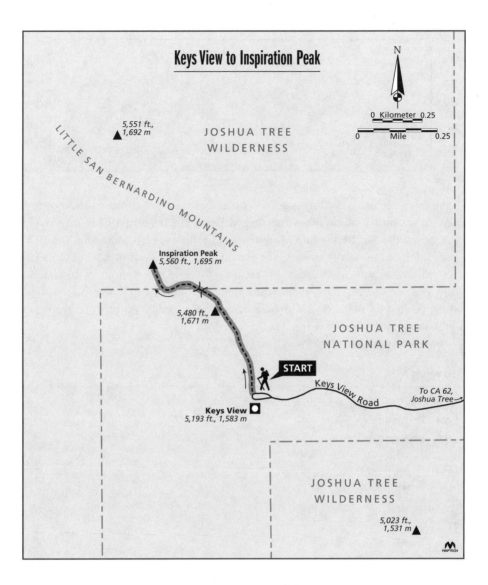

Keys View to Inspiration Peak

N

JOSHUA TREE
WILDERNESS

5,551 ft.,
1,692 m

LITTLE SAN BERNARDINO MOUNTAINS

0   Kilometer 0.25

0   Mile   0.25

Inspiration Peak
5,560 ft., 1,695 m

5,480 ft.,
1,671 m

JOSHUA TREE
NATIONAL PARK

START

Keys View Road

To CA 62,
Joshua Tree

Keys View
5,193 ft., 1,583 m

JOSHUA TREE
WILDERNESS

5,023 ft.,
1,531 m

MAPTECH

the southwest rises the 10,000-foot escarpment of the San Jacinto Mountains. Westward is the deep notch of San Gorgonio Pass and the San Bernardino Mountains.

The trail tops out on the first summit at 5,480 feet after 0.4 mile, its crest capped
by dark slabs of schist. You will have to look for the trail just below (northwest) the
peak and then head west down to a 5,400-foot saddle. Clumps of turbinella oak
appear as you ascend out of the saddle and up to Peak 5558. A cairn crowns the

◄ *The views stretch west from Inspiration Peak across the Little San*
Bernardino Mountains to San Gorgonio Mountain.

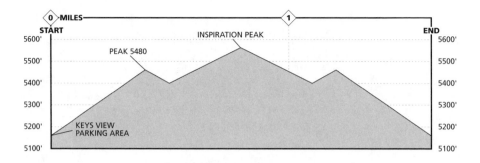

granite summit, and most hikers go no farther. From here, if it is not too smoggy, a view opens up westward across the rugged Little San Bernardino Mountains and stretches to the San Bernardino Mountains and San Gorgonio Mountain.

Fine views across Lost Horse Valley extend north to the Wonderland of Rocks as you make your way north among granite boulders to the summit of Inspiration Peak. You will know you're there when the crest drops sharply away to a saddle, where you'll see a metal shed. The peak marked INSPIRATION on the topo map rises immediately northwest of that saddle.

From the peak, return the way you came.

Key points

0.0   Keys View parking area.

0.4   Top out on Peak 5480.

0.8   Inspiration Peak.

57 Boy Scout Trail to Willow Hole

This trip, nearly level throughout much of its length, leads hikers from Joshua tree–studded flats into the heart of the boulder–stacked landscape of the Wonderland of Rocks.

Start: The signed Boy Scout Trail begins behind the information signboard at the north edge of the parking area.
General location: Joshua Tree National Park, 10 miles southeast of Joshua Tree and 10 miles southwest of Twentynine Palms
Distance: 7.2-mile round-trip day hike
Approximate hiking time: 2.5–3 hours
Difficulty: Moderate
Trailhead elevation: 4,042 feet
High point: 4,150 feet

Land status: National park
Best season: October through mid-May
Water availability: None available; bring your own
Maps: USGS Indian Cove; Joshua Tree National Park visitors map
Fees and permits: No fees or permits required
Trail contact: Joshua Tree National Park, 74485 National Park Drive, Twentynine Palms, CA 92277; (760) 367-7511

Finding the trailhead: From California Highway 62 (Twentynine Palms Highway) at the east end of Twentynine Palms, turn south onto Utah Trail, signed for Joshua Tree National Park. After 8.6 miles, you reach the Pinto Wye junction; the left fork leads to Cottonwood Visitor Center and Interstate 10, and the right fork leads toward Keys View and the town of Joshua Tree.

Follow the right fork generally westward for 10.3 miles to the junction with southbound Keys View Road, and turn right (north) onto Park Boulevard. Pass the Hidden Valley Campground 1.8 miles from the junction; the Boy Scout trailhead parking area and backcountry board are on the north side of Park Boulevard after another 2.3 miles.

Alternately, from CA 62 in Joshua Tree, follow Park Boulevard for 5 miles to the park's west entrance, then another 7 miles to the trailhead.

The Hike

The Wonderland of Rocks is Joshua Tree's largest concentration of monzogranite domes, covering more than 10 square miles between Queen Valley on the southeast and Indian Cove on the northwest. Willow Hole lies near the center of this rock-bound labyrinth, and this very scenic, nearly level hike leads you there, at first across flats studded with picturesque Joshua trees, and then through a winding, dome-embraced canyon in the heart of the Wonderland.

The trail is wide and sandy as you follow it northeast from the trailhead. The grade is nearly level as you stroll through a magnificent "forest" of Joshua trees. Outliers of the Wonderland of Rocks, heaps of granite boulders and slabs, rise west of

The trail to Willow Hole crosses shrub-covered flats studded with Joshua trees en route to the granite-bound landscape of the Wonderland of Rocks.

the trail. After 0.9 mile meet an old southbound road on your right, which is closed for restoration.

The trail heads north from that junction, following the western foot of the Wonderland. Masses of granite studded with piñons rise above to the east. Fine views extend southwest to 5,813-foot Quail Mountain and westward to the San Bernardino Mountains, crowned by 11,499-foot San Gorgonio Mountain.

After 1.3 miles reach a junction where the Scout Trail heads northwest, bound for Indian Cove. Your trail, an old doubletrack, branches northeast and is signed DAY USE ONLY. Soon you enter a small valley that reaches northeast back into the Wonderland and follow it to a minor rise at 4,150 feet. From there you begin a gradual descent into the interior of the granite labyrinth, following a wash fringed with piñons and turbinella oaks. You will follow this wash ahead for more than a mile. Its bed is filled with deep, soft sand and is rocky in places. It is a slow, arduous slog the rest of the way to Willow Hole, but the hike is rewarding. You are surrounded by golden granite cliffs that are jointed, fractured, and sculpted into a tremendous array of shapes and forms.

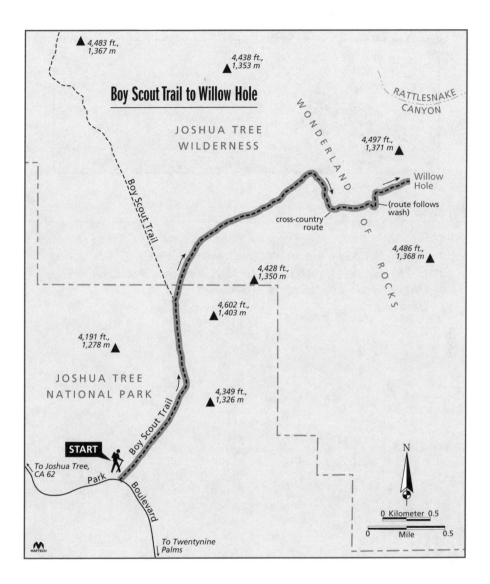

Boy Scout Trail to Willow Hole

JOSHUA TREE
WILDERNESS

JOSHUA TREE
NATIONAL PARK

4,483 ft.,
1,367 m

4,438 ft.,
1,353 m

WONDERLAND

RATTLESNAKE
CANYON

4,497 ft.,
1,371 m

Willow
Hole

(route follows
wash)

cross-country
route

OF

ROCKS

4,486 ft.,
1,368 m

4,428 ft.,
1,350 m

4,602 ft.,
1,403 m

4,191 ft.,
1,278 m

4,349 ft.,
1,326 m

Boy Scout Trail

START

To Joshua Tree,
CA 62

Park

Boulevard

To Twentynine
Palms

N

0   Kilometer 0.5

0   Mile   0.5

MAPTECH

En-route arrow signs point the way at confusing junctions with other washes. At one point, two immense boulders nearly block the wash; just beyond, the wash is briefly narrow until it opens up again 0.25 mile from Willow Hole.

As its name suggests, it is a hole, or depression; the wash ends here, only to reappear a short distance east beyond heads of boulders. Very large willows and a tangle of blowdowns define this small area. A boot-worn trail leads a short distance east, ascending a small draw on its southern margin. This marks the beginning of a challenging cross-country route down Rattlesnake Canyon to the Indian Cove picnic area.

From Willow Hole, retrace your route to the trailhead.

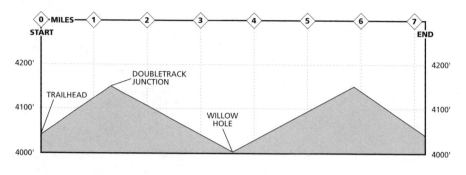

Key points

0.0 Boy Scout trailhead.

0.9 Junction with closed, southbound doubletrack; bear left (north).

1.3 Junction of northeastbound doubletrack and northwestbound Boy Scout Trail. Turn right (northeast) onto the doubletrack signed DAY USE ONLY.

3.6 Willow Hole.

The Cholla Garden Nature Trail loops through a dense ▶
stand of Bigelow cholla that seems to glow in late-after-
noon sunlight.

58 Cholla Garden Nature Trail

This easy stroll in the Mojave Desert/Colorado Desert transition zone of Pinto Basin leads through a dense stand of tall Bigelow cholla cactus.

Start: The signed Cholla Garden Nature Trail begins at the southwest edge of the parking area.
General location: Joshua Tree National Park, 15 miles southeast of Twentynine Palms
Distance: 0.25-mile loop nature trail
Approximate hiking time: 10 minutes
Difficulty: Easy
Trailhead elevation: 2,230 feet
High point: 2,230 feet

Land status: National park
Best season: Late October through April
Water availability: None available; bring your own
Maps: Joshua Tree National Park visitors map
Fees and permits: No fees or permits required
Trail contact: Joshua Tree National Park, 74485 National Park Drive, Twentynine Palms, CA 92277; (760) 367–7511

Finding the trailhead: From California Highway 62 (Twentynine Palms Highway) at the east end of Twentynine Palms, turn south onto Utah Trail, signed JOSHUA TREE NATIONAL PARK. After 8.6 miles, you reach the Pinto Wye junction; the left fork leads to Cottonwood Visitor Center and Interstate 10, and the right fork leads toward Keys View and the town of Joshua Tree. Turn left and drive 9.9 miles to the well-signed trailhead in Pinto Basin.

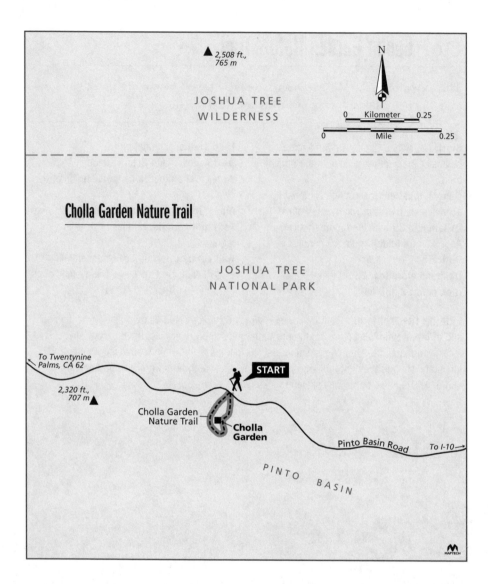

Visitors approaching from I-10 in the south take the Joshua Tree National Park/Cottonwood Canyon exit, 25 miles east of Indio, and follow the paved road 8 miles north to Cottonwood Visitor Center, then continue ahead for another 19.8 miles to the Cholla Garden Nature trailhead.

The Hike

Joshua Tree National Park has a number of excellent self-guiding nature trails, and the Cholla Garden Nature Trail may well be one of the best. It is also the most remote, located on the western margins of lonely Pinto Basin in the center of the park, at the transition zone between the Mojave Desert and the lower—and hotter—Colorado

(Sonoran) Desert. The trail, nearly level all the way, features numbered posts keyed to an interpretive pamphlet available for a small fee from a dispenser at the trailhead. Anyone traveling through this part of the park is urged to stop here. Stretch your legs, and enjoy this unusual stroll through a cactus garden in remote Pinto Basin.

The loop trail leads you in a counterclockwise direction through a dense, almost pure stand of Bigelow, or teddy bear, cholla, one of the most common species in the Colorado Desert. The cholla here, some of them reaching 6 to 8 feet in height, dominate the vegetation, but you will also see a scattering of creosote bush, brittlebush, and jojoba. Wood rat middens, composed primarily of cholla branches, are piled at the base of many creosote bushes.

There are also outstanding vistas reaching north to the Pinto Mountains, the Hexie Mountains stretching from the west to the southeast, the Eagle Mountains on the distant southeast skyline, and the Coxcomb Mountains on the eastern horizon. All of these ranges embrace the sprawling desert valley of Pinto Basin.

59 Lost Palms Oasis

This excellent, view-filled hike in the southeast reaches of the park leads you across the west slopes of the Eagle Mountains to an extensive grove of California fan palms in a rugged, granite-bound canyon.

Start: The paved beginning of the signed trail starts at the east edge of the parking area.
General location: Joshua Tree National Park, 30 miles southeast of Twentynine Palms and 22 miles east of Indio
Distance: 7.6-mile round-trip day hike
Approximate hiking time: 3.5 hours
Difficulty: Moderate
Trailhead elevation: 3,000 feet
High point: 3,450 feet

Land status: National park
Best season: Late October through April
Water availability: None available; bring your own
Maps: Joshua Tree National Park visitors map
Fees and permits: No fees or permits required
Trail contact: Joshua Tree National Park, 74485 National Park Drive, Twentynine Palms, CA 92277; (760) 367-7511

Finding the trailhead: From California Highway 62 (the Twentynine Palms Highway) at the east end of Twentynine Palms, turn south onto Utah Trail, signed JOSHUA TREE NATIONAL PARK. After 8.6 miles, you reach the Pinto Wye junction; the left fork leads to Cottonwood Visitor Center and Interstate 10, and the right fork leads toward Keys View and the town of Joshua Tree.

Turn left and drive 29.7 miles to the Cottonwood Visitor Center. Turn left (east) immediately south of the visitor center, where signs point to Cottonwood Spring, a campground, and a picnic area. After 0.7 mile, ignore the left fork leading to the campground; continue straight ahead for another 0.5 mile to the large parking area just above Cottonwood Spring.

Visitors approaching from I-10 in the south take the Joshua Tree National Park/Cottonwood Canyon exit, 25 miles east of Indio. Follow the paved road 8 miles north to Cottonwood Visitor Center, then follow the directions above to reach the trailhead.

The Hike

In a remote canyon in the southeast corner of Joshua Tree National Park is Lost Palms Oasis. With more than one hundred California fan palms crowding the canyon for 0.5 mile, this is the most extensive oasis in the park. The trail is well marked and easy to follow, but the only shade you will find is in Lost Palms Canyon beneath the palms.

The trail begins as a paved path and leads gradually downhill for several yards to Cottonwood Spring Oasis. Although the grove of tall palms and Fremont cottonwoods is a lovely, welcome sight in this hot desert, these trees are not native to

Lost Palms Oasis is the destination of one of the most rewarding ▶
day hikes in Joshua Tree National Park.

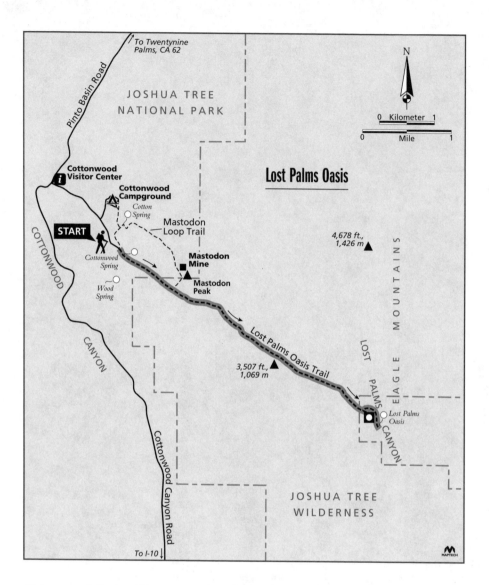

Cottonwood Spring. They were planted here between 1890 and 1910 to shade a way station during the gold mining heyday in the Joshua Tree region.

The trail ahead begins ascending a sandy wash. Climb to a low ridge flanked by granite boulders, then continue across corrugated slopes among a scattering of Mojave yucca; creosote bush; jojoba; pencil, Bigelow, and deerhorn cholla; the tall, thorny wands of ocotillo; and purplebush, an unusual shrub with red leaves and purple blossoms. Soon begin to ascend another sandy wash, where scattered junipers grow in the microclimate of the drainage.

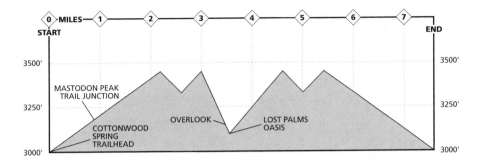

After 0.7 mile, crest a 3,200-foot ridge where the Mastodon Peak Trail (Hike 60) branches left (northeast). Beyond the junction, the trail rises gradually to Milepost 1, where a fine view of the Salton Sea and the Santa Rosa Mountains opens up to the southwest. For the next 1.5 miles, the trail gently undulates, and views of the trailside landscape along the way contrast heaps of rounded granite boulders with the color and texture of the scattered shrubs, yuccas, and cactus.

At Milepost 3, mount a ridge and begin descending among boulder-studded terrain. Vistas stretch to the southeast horizon across miles of open desert and ancient, profoundly eroded mountain ranges.

At length, you top out on a ridge and Lost Palms Canyon opens up before you. Tall palms are massed in the folds of the granite-bound canyon below. Immediately east of the ridge, the trail splits at a signed junction. Here you can continue straight ahead (east) for about 100 yards to a fine overlook of the palm oasis 150 feet below. To truly appreciate the oasis, however, you must walk in the shadow of the palms.

To get there, follow the left-branching trail at the junction, descending its steep, rocky course into the canyon, where old, stately palms share space with younger trees, their trunks matted with skirts of dead fronds. Wander among the palms of the oasis and you'll pass many seeps that provide water to the tall trees, rich grasses, and bighorn sheep that dwell here in the Eagle Mountains. The rugged slopes above, covered in a mantle of granite boulders, are a stark contrast to this rare desert oasis.

After enjoying this beautiful locale, retrace your scenic route to the trailhead. (To allow free access to water for wildlife, no camping is allowed.)

Key points

0.0 Cottonwood Spring trailhead.

0.7 Junction with northeastbound Mastodon Peak Trail; continue straight ahead (southeast).

3.5 Overlook of Lost Palms Oasis. To reach the oasis, follow the trail that descends eastward into Lost Palms Canyon.

3.8 Lost Palms Oasis.

60 Mastodon Peak Loop

This fine short day hike leads past a palm-shaded oasis to the granite-crowned over-look of Mastodon Peak, where broad vistas unfold across the mountains and valleys of southern Joshua Tree National Park. The end of the hike takes you past the historic Mastodon Mine and Winona Mill site.

Start: The paved beginning of the signed trail starts at the east edge of the parking area.
General location: Joshua Tree National Park, 30 miles southeast of Twentynine Palms and 22 miles east of Indio
Distance: 2.7-mile loop day hike
Approximate hiking time: 1.5 hours
Difficulty: Moderate
Trailhead elevation: 3,000 feet
High point: Mastodon Peak, 3,440 feet
Land status: National park

Best season: Late October through April
Water availability: None available; bring your own
Maps: USGS Cottonwood Spring; Joshua Tree National Park visitors map
Fees and permits: No fees or permits required
Trail contact: Joshua Tree National Park, 74485 National Park Drive, Twentynine Palms, CA 92277; (760) 367-7511

Finding the trailhead: From California Highway 62 (the Twentynine Palms Highway) at the east end of Twentynine Palms, turn south onto Utah Trail, signed JOSHUA TREE NATIONAL PARK. After 8.6 miles, you reach the Pinto Wye junction; the left fork leads to Cottonwood Visitor Center and Interstate 10, and the right fork leads toward Keys View and the town of Joshua Tree.

Turn left and drive 29.7 miles to the Cottonwood Visitor Center. Turn left (east) immediately south of the visitor center, where signs point to Cottonwood Spring, a campground, and a picnic area. After 0.7 mile, ignore the left fork leading to the campground; continue straight ahead for another 0.5 mile to the large parking area just above Cottonwood Spring.

Visitors approaching from I-10 in the south take the Joshua Tree National Park/Cottonwood Canyon exit, 25 miles east of Indio. Follow the paved road 8 miles north to Cottonwood Visitor Center, then follow the directions above to reach the trailhead.

The Hike

The Mastodon Peak Loop is an excellent choice for hikers who don't have the time, energy, or inclination to take the longer trail to Lost Palms Oasis. This trip leads you to a commanding vista atop granite-stacked Mastodon Peak. Be sure to bring binoculars; you may spot some of the bighorn sheep that dwell in the Eagle Mountains.

From the trailhead follow the first 0.7 mile of Hike 59, dropping down to Cottonwood Spring and then ascending gradually to the junction with the Mastodon Peak Trail, where you turn left (northeast). This trail rises gradually at first, passing a scattering of creosote bush and Mojave yucca. Soon the grade steepens and the

The crag of Mastodon Peak, rising above the Cottonwood Spring Trailhead, affords panoramic vistas partway along a fine, half-day loop hike.

tread becomes rocky as you rise into the boulder piles that mantle the slopes of Mastodon Peak.

After 0.3 mile, the trail tops out at 3,250 feet, where a spur trail branches right (east), leading 0.1 mile to Mastodon Peak. That trail winds among the monzogranite boulders to a saddle immediately below (southeast of) the summit. The trail turns northwest, but the tread is visible only in sandy areas between boulders. The route leads you on a brief scramble over boulders to the summit, where fine views open up eastward into the heart of the Eagle Mountains and westward to the Hexie Mountains.

From the peak, return to the main trail and turn right (northwest), quickly descending past the site of the Mastodon Mine, which was in operation between 1934 and 1971. As you continue past the mine site, fine views extend northwest across the mountain-encircled expanse of Pinto Basin. Soon you reach a sandy wash and proceed down its sandy course. Bordering the wash are paper bag bush, jojoba, rabbitbrush, and yucca.

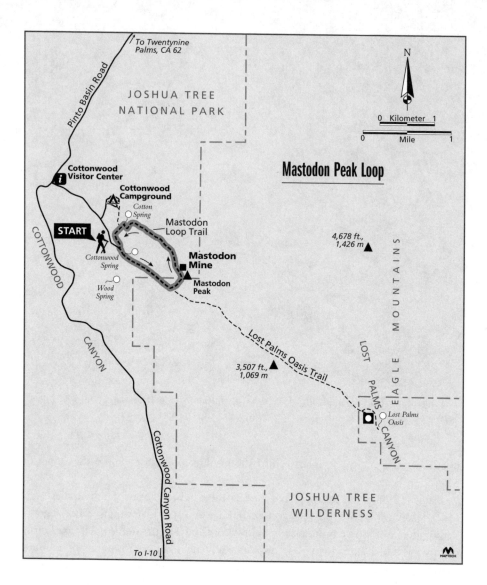

The trail exits the wash where an arrow sign points the way northwest (all entry and exit points of washes on this hike are marked with arrows). After topping a rise, the trail leads you into another broad, sandy wash, over another rise, past the ruins of the Winona Mill, and into the third wash among Fremont cottonwood and introduced eucalyptus trees just below Cotton Spring. A short distance ahead, avoid the right-branching trail leading 0.2 mile to Cottonwood Campground. Your route follows the wash for 0.2 mile to join the paved road, which you follow a short distance to the large trailhead parking area.

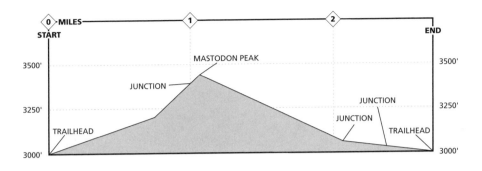

Key points

0.0 Cottonwood Spring trailhead.

0.7 Junction of Lost Palms Oasis and Mastodon Peak Trails; turn left (northeast) onto Mastodon Peak Trail.

1.0 Junction with spur trail to the summit of Mastodon Peak; turn right (northeast).

1.1 Reach the summit of Mastodon Peak.

1.2 After backtracking 0.1 mile, return to the loop trail and turn right (northwest).

2.3 Junction with northbound trail to Cottonwood Campground; bear left, following the wash southeast.

2.6 Reach Cottonwood Spring Road; turn left (southeast), following the road back to the trailhead.

2.7 Cottonwood Spring trailhead.

The Art of Hiking

When standing nose to nose with a mountain lion, you're probably not too concerned with the issue of ethical behavior in the wild. No doubt you're just terrified. But let's be honest. How often are you nose to nose with a mountain lion? For most of us, a hike into the "wild" means loading up the SUV with expensive gear and driving to a toileted trailhead. Sure, you can mourn how civilized we've become—how GPS units have replaced natural instinct and Gore-Tex, true-grit—but the silly gadgets of civilization aside, we have plenty of reason to take pride in how we've matured. With survival now on the back burner, we've begun to reason—and it's about time—that we have a responsibility to protect, no longer just conquer, our wild places: that they, not we, are at risk. So please, do what you can. The following section will help you understand better what it means to "do what you can" while still making the most of your hiking experience. Anyone can take a hike, but hiking safely and well is an art requiring preparation and proper equipment.

Trail Etiquette

Zero impact. Always leave an area just like you found it—if not better than you found it. Avoid camping in fragile, alpine meadows and along the banks of streams and lakes. Use a camp stove versus building a wood fire. Pack up all of your trash and extra food. Bury human waste at least 100 feet from water sources under 6 to 8 inches of topsoil. Don't bathe with soap in a lake or stream—use prepackaged moistened towels to wipe off sweat and dirt, or bathe in the water without soap.

Stay on the trail. It's true, a path anywhere leads nowhere new, but purists will just have to get over it. Paths serve an important purpose; they limit impact on natural areas. Straying from a designated trail may seem innocent but it can cause damage to sensitive areas—damage that may take years to recover, if it can recover at all. Even simple shortcuts can be destructive. So, please, stay on the trail.

Leave no weeds. Noxious weeds tend to overtake other plants, which in turn affects animals and birds that depend on them for food. To minimize the spread of noxious weeds, hikers should regularly clean their boots, tents, packs, and hiking poles of mud and seeds. Also brush your dog to remove any weed seeds before heading off into a new area.

Keep your dog under control. You can buy a flexi-lead that allows your dog to go exploring along the trail, while allowing you the ability to reel him in should another hiker approach or should he decide to chase a rabbit. Always obey leash laws and be sure to bury your dog's waste or pack it in resealable plastic bags.

Respect other trail users. Often you're not the only one on the trail. With the rise in popularity of multiuse trails, you'll have to learn a new kind of respect, beyond the nod and "hello" approach you may be used to. First investigate whether you're on a multiuse trail, and assume the appropriate precautions. When you encounter motorized vehicles (ATVs, motorcycles, and 4WDs), be alert. Though they should always yield to the hiker, often they're going too fast or are too lost in the buzz of their engine to react to your presence. If you hear activity ahead, step off the trail just to be safe. Note that you're not likely to hear a mountain biker coming, so be prepared and know ahead of time whether you share the trail with them. Cyclists should always yield to hikers, but that's little comfort to the hiker. Be aware. When you approach horses or pack animals on the trail, always step quietly off the trail, preferably on the downhill side, and let them pass. If you're wearing a large backpack, it's often a good idea to sit down. To some animals, a hiker wearing a large backpack might appear threatening. Many national forests allow domesticated grazing, usually for sheep and cattle. Make sure your dog doesn't harass these animals, and respect ranchers' rights while you're enjoying yours.

Getting into Shape

Unless you want to be sore—and possibly have to shorten your trip or vacation—be sure to get in shape before a big hike. If you're terribly out of shape, start a walking program early, preferably eight weeks in advance. Start with a fifteen-minute walk during your lunch hour or after work and gradually increase your walking time to an hour. You should also increase your elevation gain. Walking briskly up hills really strengthens your leg muscles and gets your heart rate up. If you work in a storied office building, take the stairs instead of the elevator. If you prefer going to a gym, walk the treadmill or use a stair machine. You can further increase your strength and endurance by walking with a loaded backpack. Stationary exercises you might consider are squats, leg lifts, sit-ups, and push-ups. Other good ways to get in shape include biking, running, aerobics, and, of course, short hikes. Stretching before and after a hike keeps muscles flexible and helps avoid injuries.

Preparedness

It's been said that failing to plan means planning to fail. So do take the necessary time to plan your trip. Whether going on a short day hike or an extended backpack trip, always prepare for the worst. Simply remembering to pack a copy of the U.S. Army Survival Manual is not preparedness. Although it's not a bad idea if you plan on entering truly wild places, it's merely the tourniquet answer to a problem. You need to do your best to prevent the problem from arising in the first place. In order to survive—and to stay reasonably comfortable—you need to concern yourself with the basics: water, food, and shelter. Don't go on a hike without having these bases covered. And don't go on a hike expecting to find these items in the woods.

Water. Even in frigid conditions, you need at least two quarts of water a day to function efficiently. Add heat and taxing terrain and you can bump that figure up to one gallon. That's simply a base to work from—your metabolism and your level of conditioning can raise or lower that amount. Unless you know your level, assume that you need one gallon of water a day. Now, where do you plan on getting the water?

Preferably not from natural water sources. These sources can be loaded with intestinal disturbers, such as bacteria, viruses, and fertilizers. *Giardia lamblia,* the most common of these disturbers, is a protozoan parasite that lives part of its life cycle as a cyst in water sources. The parasite spreads when mammals defecate in water sources. Once ingested, giardia can induce cramping, diarrhea, vomiting, and fatigue within two days to two weeks after ingestion. Giardiasis is treatable with prescription drugs. If you believe you've contracted giardiasis, see a doctor immediately.

Treating water. The best and easiest solution to avoid polluted water is to carry your water with you. Yet, depending on the nature of your hike and the duration, this may not be an option—one gallon of water weighs eight-and-a-half pounds. In that case, you'll need to look into treating water. Regardless of which method you choose, you should always carry some water with you in case of an emergency. Save this reserve until you absolutely need it.

There are three methods of treating water: boiling, chemical treatment, and filtering. If you boil water, it's recommended that you do so for ten to fifteen minutes. This is often impractical because you're forced to exhaust a great deal of your fuel supply. You can opt for chemical treatment, which will kill giardia but will not take care of other chemical pollutants. Another drawback to chemical treatments is the unpleasant taste of the water after it's treated. You can remedy this by adding powdered drink mix to the water. Filters are the preferred method for treating water. Many filters remove giardia, organic and inorganic contaminants, and don't leave an aftertaste. Water filters are far from perfect as they can easily become clogged or leak if a gasket wears out. It's always a good idea to carry a backup supply of chemical treatment tablets in case your filter decides to quit on you.

Food. If we're talking about survival, you can go days without food, as long as you have water. But we're also talking about comfort. Try to avoid foods that are high in sugar and fat like candy bars and potato chips. These food types are harder to digest and are low in nutritional value. Instead, bring along foods that are easy to pack, nutritious, and high in energy (e.g., bagels, nutrition bars, dehydrated fruit, gorp, and jerky). If you are on an overnight trip, easy-to-fix dinners include rice mixes with dehydrated potatoes, corn, pasta with cheese sauce, and soup mixes. For a tasty breakfast, you can fix hot oatmeal with brown sugar and reconstituted milk powder topped off with banana chips. If you like a hot drink in the morning, bring along herbal tea bags or hot chocolate. If you are a coffee junkie, you can purchase coffee that is packaged like tea bags. You can prepackage all of your meals in heavy-duty resealable plastic bags to keep food from spilling in your pack. These bags can be reused to pack out trash.

Shelter. The type of shelter you choose depends less on the conditions than on your tolerance for discomfort. Shelter comes in many forms—tent, tarp, lean-to, bivy sack, cabin, cave, etc. If you're camping in the desert, a bivy sack may suffice, but if you're above the treeline and a storm is approaching, a better choice is a three- or four-season tent. Tents are the logical and most popular choice for most backpackers as they're lightweight and packable—and you can rest assured that you always have shelter from the elements. Before you leave on your trip, anticipate what the weather and terrain will be like and plan for the type of shelter that will work best for your comfort level (see Equipment later in this section).

Finding a campsite. If there are established campsites, stick to those. If not, start looking for a campsite early—around 3:30 or 4:00 P.M. Stop at the first decent site you see. Depending on the area, it could be a long time before you find another suitable location. Pitch your camp in an area that's level. Make sure the area is at least 200 feet from fragile areas like lakeshores, meadows, and stream banks. And try to avoid areas thick in underbrush, as they can harbor insects and provide cover for approaching animals.

If you are camping in stormy, rainy weather, look for a rock outcrop or a shelter in the trees to keep the wind from blowing your tent all night. Be sure that you don't camp under trees with dead limbs that might break off on top of you. Also, try to find an area that has an absorbent surface, such as sandy soil or forest duff. This, in addition to camping on a surface with a slight angle, will provide better drainage. By all means, don't dig trenches to provide drainage around your tent—remember you're practicing zero-impact camping.

If you're in bear country, steer clear of creekbeds or animal paths. If you see any signs of a bear's presence (i.e., scat, footprints), relocate. You'll need to find a campsite near a tall tree where you can hang your food and other items that may attract bears such as deodorant, toothpaste, or soap. Carry a lightweight nylon rope with which to hang your food. As a rule, you should hang your food at least 20 feet from the ground and 5 feet away from the tree trunk. You can put food and other items in a waterproof stuff sack and tie one end of the rope to the stuff sack. To get the other end of the rope over the tree branch, tie a good size rock to it, and gently toss the rock over the tree branch. Pull the stuff sack up until it reaches the top of the branch and tie it off securely. Don't hang your food near your tent! If possible, hang your food at least 100 feet away from your campsite. Alternatives to hanging your food are bear-proof plastic tubes and metal bear boxes.

Lastly, think of comfort. Lie down on the ground where you intend to sleep and see if it's a good fit. For morning warmth (and a nice view to wake up to), have your tent face east.

First Aid

I know you're tough, but get 10 miles into the woods and develop a blister and you'll wish you had carried that first-aid kit. Face it, it's just plain good sense. Many companies produce lightweight, compact first-aid kits. Just make sure yours contains at least the following:

- adhesive bandages
- moleskin or duct tape
- various sterile gauze and dressings
- white surgical tape
- an Ace bandage
- an antihistamine
- aspirin
- Betadine solution
- a first-aid book
- antacid tablets

- tweezers
- scissors
- antibacterial wipes
- triple-antibiotic ointment
- plastic gloves
- sterile cotton tip applicators
- syrup of ipecac (to induce vomiting)
- thermometer
- wire splint

Here are a few tips for dealing with and hopefully preventing certain ailments.

Sunburn. Take along sunscreen or sun block, protective clothing, and a wide-brimmed hat. If you do get a sunburn, treat the area with aloe vera gel, and protect the area from further sun exposure. At higher elevations, the sun's radiation can be particularly damaging to skin. Remember that your eyes are vulnerable to this radiation as well. Sunglasses can be a good way to prevent headaches and permanent eye damage from the sun, especially in places where light-colored rock or patches of snow reflect light up in your face.

Blisters. Be prepared to take care of these hike-spoilers by carrying moleskin (a lightly padded adhesive), gauze and tape, or adhesive bandages. An effective way to apply moleskin is to cut out a circle of moleskin and remove the center—like a doughnut—and place it over the blistered area. Cutting the center out will reduce the pressure applied to the sensitive skin. Other products can help you combat blisters. Some are applied to suspicious hot spots before a blister forms to help decrease friction to that area, while others are applied to the blister after it has popped to help prevent further irritation.

Insect bites and stings. You can treat most insect bites and stings by applying hydrocortisone 1% cream topically and taking a pain medication such as ibuprofen or acetaminophen to reduce swelling. If you forgot to pack these items, a cold compress or a paste of mud and ashes can sometimes assuage the itching and discomfort. Remove any stingers by using tweezers or scraping the area with your fingernail or a knife blade. Don't pinch the area as you'll only spread the venom.

Some hikers are highly sensitive to bites and stings and may have a serious allergic reaction that can be life threatening. Symptoms of a serious allergic reaction can include wheezing, an asthmatic attack, and shock. The treatment for this severe type of reaction is epinephrine. If you know that you are sensitive to bites and stings, carry a pre-packaged kit of epinephrine, which can be obtained only by prescription from your doctor.

Ticks. Ticks can carry diseases such as Rocky Mountain spotted fever and Lyme disease. The best defense is, of course, prevention. If you know you're going to be hiking through an area littered with ticks, wear long pants and a long sleeved shirt. You can apply a permethrin repellent to your clothing and a Deet repellent to exposed skin. At the end of your hike, do a spot check for ticks (and insects in general). If you do find a tick, coat the insect with petroleum jelly or tree sap to cut off its air supply. The tick should release its hold, but if it doesn't, grab the head of the tick firmly—with a pair of tweezers if you have them—and gently pull it away from the skin with a twisting motion. Sometimes the mouth parts linger, embedded in your skin. If this happens, try to remove them with a disinfected needle. Clean the affected area with an antibacterial cleanser and then apply triple antibiotic ointment. Monitor the area for a few days. If irritation persists or a white spot develops, see a doctor for possible infection.

Poison ivy, oak, and sumac. These skin irritants can be found most anywhere in North America and come in the form of a bush or a vine, having leaflets in groups of three, five, seven, or nine. Learn how to spot the plants. The oil they secrete can cause an allergic reaction in the form of blisters, usually about twelve hours after exposure. The itchy rash can last from ten days to several weeks. The best defense against these irritants is to wear clothing that covers the arms, legs and torso. For summer, zip-off cargo pants come in handy. There are also nonprescription lotions you can apply to exposed skin that guard against the effects of poison ivy/oak/sumac and can be washed off with soap and water. If you think you were in contact with the plants, after hiking (or even on the trail during longer hikes) wash with soap and water. Taking a hot shower with soap after you return home from your hike will also help to remove any lingering oil from your skin. Should you contract a rash from any of these plants, use an antihistamine to reduce the itching. If the rash is localized, create a light bleach/water wash to dry up the area. If the rash has spread, either tough it out or see your doctor about getting a dose of cortisone (available both orally and by injection).

Snakebites. Snakebites are rare in North America. Unless startled or provoked, the majority of snakes will not bite. If you are wise to their habitats and keep a careful eye on the trail, you should be just fine. When stepping over logs, first step on the log, making sure you can see what's on the other side before stepping down. Though your chances of being struck are slim, it's wise to know what to do in the event you are.

If a *nonpoisonous* snake bites you, allow the wound to bleed a small amount and then cleanse the wounded area with a Betadine solution (10% povidone iodine).

Rinse the wound with clean water (preferably) or fresh urine (it might sound ugly, but it's sterile). Once the area is clean, cover it with triple antibiotic ointment and a clean bandage. Remember, most residual damage from snakebites, poisonous or otherwise, comes from infection, not the snake's venom. Keep the area as clean as possible and get medical attention immediately.

If you are bitten by a poisonous snake, remove the toxin with a suctioning device, found in a snakebite kit. If you do not have such a device, squeeze the wound—DO NOT use your mouth for suction, as the venom will enter your bloodstream through the vessels under the tongue and head straight for your heart. Then, clean the wound just as you would a nonpoisonous bite. Tie a clean band of cloth snugly around the afflicted appendage, about an inch or so above the bite (or the rim of the swelling). This is NOT a tourniquet—you want to simply slow the blood flow, not cut it off. Loosen the band if numbness ensues. Remove the band for a minute and reapply a little higher every ten minutes.

If it is your friend who's been bitten, treat him or her for shock—make the person comfortable, have him or her lie down, elevate the legs, and keep him or her warm. Avoid applying anything cold to the bite wound. Immobilize the affected area and remove any constricting items such as rings, watches, or restrictive clothing—swelling may occur. Once your friend is stable and relatively calm, hike out to get help. The victim should get treatment within twelve hours, ideally, which usually consists of a tetanus shot, antivenin, and antibiotics.

If you are alone and struck by a poisonous snake, stay calm. Hysteria will only quicken the venom's spread. Follow the procedure above, and do your best to reach help. When hiking out, don't run—you'll only increase the flow of blood throughout your system. Instead, walk calmly.

Dehydration. Have you ever hiked in hot weather and had a roaring headache and felt fatigued after only a few miles? More than likely you were dehydrated. Symptoms of dehydration include fatigue, headache, and decreased coordination and judgment. When you are hiking, your body's rate of fluid loss depends on the outside temperature, humidity, altitude, and your activity level. On average, a hiker walking in warm weather will lose four liters of fluid a day. That fluid loss is easily replaced by normal consumption of liquids and food. However, if a hiker is walking briskly in hot, dry weather and hauling a heavy pack, he or she can lose one to three liters of water an hour. It's important to always carry plenty of water and to stop often and drink fluids regularly, even if you aren't thirsty.

Heat exhaustion is the result of a loss of large amounts of electrolytes and often occurs if a hiker is dehydrated and has been under heavy exertion. Common symptoms of heat exhaustion include cramping, exhaustion, fatigue, lightheadedness, and nausea. You can treat heat exhaustion by getting out of the sun and drinking an electrolyte solution made up of one teaspoon of salt and one tablespoon of sugar dissolved in a liter of water. Drink this solution slowly over a period of one hour.

Drinking plenty of fluids (preferably an electrolyte solution/sports drink) can prevent heat exhaustion. Avoid hiking during the hottest parts of the day, and wear breathable clothing, a wide-brimmed hat, and sunglasses.

Hypothermia is one of the biggest dangers in the backcountry, especially for day hikers in the summertime. That may sound strange, but imagine starting out on a hike in midsummer when it's sunny and 80 degrees out. You're clad in nylon shorts and a cotton T-shirt. About halfway through your hike, the sky begins to cloud up, and in the next hour a light drizzle begins to fall and the wind starts to pick up. Before you know it, you are soaking wet and shivering—the perfect recipe for hypothermia. More advanced signs include decreased coordination, slurred speech, and blurred vision. When a victim's temperature falls below 92 degrees, the blood pressure and pulse plummet, possibly leading to coma and death.

To avoid hypothermia, always bring a windproof/rainproof shell, a fleece jacket, tights made of a breathable, synthetic fiber, gloves, and hat when you are hiking in the mountains. Learn to adjust your clothing layers based on the temperature. If you are climbing uphill at a moderate pace you will stay warm, but when you stop for a break you'll become cold quickly, unless you add more layers of clothing.

If a hiker is showing advanced signs of hypothermia, dress him or her in dry clothes and make sure he or she is wearing a hat and gloves. Place the person in a sleeping bag in a tent or shelter that will protect him or her from the wind and other elements. Give the person warm fluids to drink and keep him awake.

Frostbite. When the mercury dips below 32 degrees, your extremities begin to chill. If a persistent chill attacks a localized area, say, your hands or your toes, the circulatory system reacts by cutting off blood flow to the affected area—the idea being to protect and preserve the body's overall temperature. And so it's death by attrition for the affected area. Ice crystals start to form from the water in the cells of the neglected tissue. Deprived of heat, nourishment, and now water, the tissue literally starves. This is frostbite.

Prevention is your best defense against this situation. Most prone to frostbite are your face, hands, and feet, so protect these areas well. Wool is the material of choice because it provides ample air space for insulation and draws moisture away from the skin. Synthetic fabrics, however, have recently made great strides in the cold weather clothing market. Do your research. A pair of light silk liners under your regular gloves is a good trick for keeping warm. They afford some additional warmth, but more importantly they'll allow you to remove your mitts for tedious work without exposing the skin.

If your feet or hands start to feel cold or numb due to the elements, warm them as quickly as possible. Place cold hands under your armpits or bury them in your crotch. If your feet are cold, change your socks. If there's plenty of room in your boots, add another pair of socks. Do remember, though, that constricting your feet in tight boots can restrict blood flow and actually make your feet colder more quickly. Your socks need to have breathing room if they're going to be effective.

Dead air provides insulation. If your face is cold, place your warm hands over your face, or simply wear a head stocking.

Should your skin go numb and start to appear white and waxy, chances are you've got or are developing frostbite. Don't try to thaw the area unless you can maintain the warmth. In other words, don't stop to warm up your frostbitten feet only to head back on the trail. You'll do more damage than good. Tests have shown that hikers who walked on thawed feet did more harm, and endured more pain, than hikers who left the affected areas alone. Do your best to get out of the cold entirely and seek medical attention—which usually consists of performing a rapid rewarming in water for twenty to thirty minutes.

The overall objective in preventing both hypothermia and frostbite is to keep the body's core warm. Protect key areas where heat escapes, like the top of the head, and maintain the proper nutrition level. Foods that are high in calories aid the body in producing heat. Never smoke or drink when you're in situations where the cold is threatening. By affecting blood flow, these activities ultimately cool the body's core temperature.

Altitude sickness (AMS). High lofty peaks, clear alpine lakes, and vast mountain views beckon hikers to the high country. But those who like to venture high may become victims of altitude sickness (also known as Acute Mountain Sickness—AMS). Altitude sickness is your body's reaction to insufficient oxygen in the blood due to decreased barometric pressure. While some hikers may feel lightheaded, nauseous, and experience shortness of breath at 7,000 feet, others may not experience these symptoms until they reach 10,000 feet or higher.

Slowing your ascent to high places and giving your body a chance to acclimatize to the higher elevations can prevent altitude sickness. For example, if you live at sea level and are planning a weeklong backpacking trip to elevations between 7,000 and 12,000 feet, start by staying below 7,000 feet for one night, then move to between 7,000 and 10,000 feet for another night or two. Avoid strenuous exertion and alcohol to give your body a chance to adjust to the new altitude. It's also important to eat light food and drink plenty of nonalcoholic fluids, preferably water. Loss of appetite at altitude is common, but you must eat!

Most hikers who experience mild to moderate AMS develop a headache and/or nausea, grow lethargic, and have problems sleeping. The treatment for AMS is simple: stop heading uphill. Keep eating and drinking water and take meds for the headache. You actually need to take more breaths at altitude than at sea level, so breathe a little faster without hyperventilating. If symptoms don't improve over twenty-four to forty-eight hours, descend. Once a victim descends about 2,000 to 3,000 feet, his signs will usually begin to diminish.

Severe AMS comes in two forms: High Altitude Pulmonary Edema (HAPE) and High Altitude Cerebral Edema (HACE). HAPE, an accumulation of fluid in the lungs, can occur above 8,000 feet. Symptoms include rapid heart rate, shortness of breath at rest, AMS symptoms, dry cough developing into a wet cough, gurgling sounds, flu-like or bronchitis symptoms, and lack of muscle coordination. HAPE is life threatening so descend immediately, at least 2,000 to 4,000 feet. HACE usually occurs above 12,000 feet but sometimes occurs above 10,000 feet. Symptoms are similar to HAPE but also include seizures, hallucinations, paralysis, and vision disturbances. Descend immediately—HACE is also life threatening.

Hantavirus Pulmonary Syndrome (HPS). Deer mice spread the virus that causes HPS, and humans contract it from breathing it in, usually when they've disturbed an area with dust and mice feces from nests or surfaces with mice droppings or urine. Exposure to large numbers of rodents and their feces or urine presents the greatest risk. As hikers, we sometimes enter old buildings, and often deer mice live in these places. We may not be around long enough to be exposed, but do be aware of this disease. About half the people who develop HPS die. Symptoms are flu-like and appear about two to three weeks after exposure. After initial symptoms, a dry cough and shortness of breath follow. Breathing is difficult. If you even think you might have HPS, see a doctor immediately!

Natural Hazards

Besides tripping over a rock or tree root on the trail, there are some real hazards to be aware of while hiking. Even if where you're hiking doesn't have the plethora of poisonous snakes and plants, insects, and grizzly bears found in other parts of the United States, there are a few weather conditions and predators you may need to take into account.

Lightning. Thunderstorms build over the mountains almost every day during the summer. Lightning is generated by thunderheads and can strike without warning, even several miles away from the nearest overhead cloud. The best rule of thumb is to start leaving exposed peaks, ridges, and canyon rims by about noon. This time can vary a little depending on storm buildup. Keep an eye on cloud formation and don't underestimate how fast a storm can build. The bigger they get, the more likely a thunderstorm will happen. Lightning takes the path of least resistance, so if you're the high point, it might choose you. Ducking under a rock overhang is dangerous as you form the shortest path between the rock and ground. If you dash below treeline, avoid standing under the only or the tallest tree. If you are caught above treeline, stay away from anything metal you might be carrying, Move down off the ridge slightly to a low, treeless point and squat until the storm passes. If you have an insulating pad, squat on it. Avoid having both your hands and feet touching the ground at once and never lay flat. If you hear a buzzing sound or feel your hair standing on end, move quickly as an electrical charge is building up.

Flash floods. On July 31, 1976, a torrential downpour unleashed by a thunderstorm dumped tons of water into the Big Thompson watershed near Estes Park. Within hours, a wall of water moved down the narrow canyon killing 139 people and causing more than $30 million in property damage. The spooky thing about flash floods, especially in western canyons, is that they can appear out of nowhere from a storm many miles away. While hiking or driving in canyons, keep an eye on the weather. Always climb to safety if danger threatens. Flash floods usually subside quickly, so be patient and don't cross a swollen stream.

Bears. Most of the United States (outside of the Pacific Northwest and parts of the Northern Rockies) does not have a grizzly bear population, although some rumors exist about sightings where there should be none. Black bears are plentiful, however. Here are some tips in case you and a bear scare each other. Most of all, avoid scaring a bear. Watch for bear tracks (five toes) and droppings (sizable with leaves, partly digested berries, seeds, and/or animal fur). Talk or sing where visibility or hearing are limited. Keep a clean camp, hang food, and don't sleep in the clothes you wore while cooking. Be especially careful in spring to avoid getting between a mother and her cubs. In late summer and fall bears are busy eating berries and acorns to fatten up for winter, so be extra careful around berry bushes and oakbrush. If you do encounter a bear, move away slowly while facing the bear, talk softly, and avoid direct eye contact. Give the bear room to escape. Since bears are very curious, it might stand upright to get a better whiff of you, and it may even charge you to try to intimidate you. Try to stay calm. If a bear does attack you, fight back with anything you have handy. Unleashed dogs have been known to come running back to their owners with a bear close behind. Keep your dog on a leash or leave it at home.

Mountain lions. Mountain lions appear to be getting more comfortable around humans as long as deer (their favorite prey) are in an area with adequate cover. Usually elusive and quiet, lions rarely attack people. If you meet a lion, give it a chance to escape. Stay calm and talk firmly to it. Back away slowly while facing the lion. If you run, you'll only encourage the curious cat to chase you. Make yourself look large by opening a jacket, if you have one, or waving your hiking poles. If the lion behaves aggressively throw stones, sticks, or whatever you can while remaining tall. If a lion does attack, fight for your life with anything you can grab.

Moose. Because moose have very few natural predators, they don't fear humans like other animals. You might find moose in sagebrush and wetter areas of willow, aspen, and pine, or in beaver habitats. Mothers with calves, as well as bulls during mating season, can be particularly aggressive. If a moose threatens you, back away slowly and talk calmly to it. Keep your pets away from moose.

Other considerations. Hunting is a popular sport in the United States, especially during rifle season in October and November. Hiking is still enjoyable in those months in many areas, so just take a few precautions. First, learn when the different hunting seasons start and end in the area in which you'll be hiking. During this time frame, be sure to wear at least a blaze orange hat, and possibly put an orange vest over your pack. Don't be surprised to see hunters in camo outfits carrying bows or muzzleloading rifles around during their season. If you would feel more comfortable without hunters around, hike in national parks and monuments or state and local parks where hunting is not allowed.

Navigation

Whether you are going on a short hike in a familiar area or planning a weeklong backpack trip, you should always be equipped with the proper navigational equipment—at the very least a detailed map and a sturdy compass.

Maps. There are many different types of maps available to help you find your way on the trail. Easiest to find are Forest Service maps and BLM (Bureau of Land Management) maps. These maps tend to cover large areas, so be sure they are detailed enough for your particular trip. You can also obtain National Park maps as well as high quality maps from private companies and trail groups. These maps can be obtained either from outdoor stores or ranger stations.

U.S. Geological Survey topographic maps are particularly popular with hikers—especially serious backcountry hikers. These maps contain the standard map symbols such as roads, lakes, and rivers, as well as contour lines that show the details of the trail terrain like ridges, valleys, passes, and mountain peaks. The 7.5-minute series (1 inch on the map equals approximately ⅖ mile on the ground) provides the closest inspection available. USGS maps are available by mail (U.S. Geological Survey, Map Distribution Branch, P.O. Box 25286, Denver, CO 80225), or at mapping.usgs.gov/esic/to_order.html.

If you want to check out the high-tech world of maps, you can purchase topographic maps on CD-ROM. These software-mapping programs let you select a route on your computer, print it out, then take it with you on the trail. Some software mapping programs let you insert symbols and labels, download waypoints from a GPS unit, and export the maps to other software programs.

The art of map reading is a skill that you can develop by first practicing in an area you are familiar with. To begin, orient the map so the map is lined up in the correct direction (i.e. north on the map is lined up with true north). Next, familiarize yourself with the map symbols and try and match them up with terrain features around you such as a high ridge, mountain peak, river, or lake. If you are practicing with a USGS map, notice the contour lines. On gentler terrain these contour lines are spaced further apart, and on steeper terrain they are closer together. Pick a short loop trail, and stop frequently to check your position on the map. As you practice map reading, you'll learn how to anticipate a steep section on the trail or a good place to take a rest break, and so on.

Compasses. First off, the sun is not a substitute for a compass. So, what kind of compass should you have? Here are some characteristics you should look for: a rectangular base with detailed scales, a liquid-filled housing, protective housing, a sighting line on the mirror, luminous alignment and back-bearing arrows, a luminous north-seeking arrow, and a well-defined bezel ring.

You can learn compass basics by reading the detailed instructions included with your compass. If you want to fine-tune your compass skills, sign up for an orienteering class or purchase a book on compass reading. Once you've learned the basic skills of using a compass, remember to practice these skills before you head into the backcountry.

If you are a klutz at using a compass, you may be interested in checking out the technical wizardry of the GPS (Global Positioning System) device. The GPS was developed by the Pentagon and works off twenty-four NAVSTAR satellites, which were designed to guide missiles to their targets. A GPS device is a handheld unit that calculates your latitude and longitude with the easy press of a button. The Department of Defense used to scramble the satellite signals a bit to prevent civilians (and spies!) from getting extremely accurate readings, but that practice was discontinued in May 2000, and GPS units now provide nearly pinpoint accuracy (within 30 to 60 feet).

There are many different types of GPS units available and they range in price from $100 to $400. In general, all GPS units have a display screen and keypad where you input information. In addition to acting as a compass, the unit allows you to plot your route, easily retrace your path, track your travelling speed, find the mileage between waypoints, and calculate the total mileage of your route.

Before you purchase a GPS unit, keep in mind that these devices don't pick up signals indoors, in heavily wooded areas, on mountain peaks, or in deep valleys.

Pedometers. A pedometer is a small, clip-on unit with a digital display that calculates your hiking distance in miles or kilometers based on your walking stride. Some units also calculate the calories you burn and your total hiking time. Pedometers are available at most large outdoor stores and range in price from $20 to $40.

Trip Planning

Planning your hiking adventure begins with letting a friend or relative know your trip itinerary so they can call for help if you don't return at your scheduled time. Your next task is to make sure you are outfitted to experience the risks and rewards of the trail. This section highlights gear and clothing you may want to take with you to get the most out of your hike.

Day Hikes
- camera/film
- compass/GPS unit
- pedometer
- daypack
- first-aid kit
- food
- guidebook
- headlamp/flashlight with extra batteries and bulbs
- hat
- insect repellent
- knife/multipurpose tool
- map
- matches in waterproof container and fire starter
- fleece jacket
- rain gear
- space blanket
- sunglasses
- sunscreen
- swimsuit
- watch
- water
- water bottles/water hydration system

Overnight Trip

- backpack and waterproof rain cover
- backpacker's trowel
- bandanna
- bear repellent spray
- bear bell
- biodegradable soap
- pot scrubber
- collapsible water container (2–3 gallon capacity)
- clothing—extra wool socks, shirt and shorts
- cook set/utensils
- ditty bags to store gear
- extra plastic resealable bags
- gaiters
- garbage bag
- ground cloth
- journal/pen
- nylon rope to hang food
- long underwear
- permit (if required)
- rain jacket and pants
- sandals to wear around camp and to ford streams
- sleeping bag
- waterproof stuff sack
- sleeping pad
- small bath towel
- stove and fuel
- tent
- toiletry items
- water filter
- whistle

Equipment

With the outdoor market currently flooded with products, many of which are pure gimmickry, it seems impossible to both differentiate and choose. Do I really need a tropical-fish-lined collapsible shower? (No, you don't.) The only defense against the maddening quantity of items thrust in your face is to think practically—and to do so before you go shopping. The worst buys are impulsive buys. Since most name brands will differ only slightly in quality, it's best to know what you're looking for in terms of function. Buy only what you need. You will, don't forget, be carrying what you've bought on your back. Here are some things to keep in mind before you go shopping.

Clothes. Clothing is your armor against Mother Nature's little surprises. Hikers should be prepared for any possibility, especially when hiking in mountainous areas. Adequate rain protection and extra layers of clothing are a good idea. In summer, a wide-brimmed hat can help keep the sun at bay. In the winter months the first layer you'll want to wear is a "wicking" layer of long underwear that keeps perspiration away from your skin. Wear long underwear made from synthetic fibers that wick moisture away from the skin and draw it toward the next layer of clothing, where it then evaporates. Avoid wearing long underwear made of cotton as it is slow to dry and keeps moisture next to your skin.

The second layer you'll wear is the "insulating" layer. Aside from keeping you warm, this layer needs to "breathe" so you stay dry while hiking. A fabric that provides insulation and dries quickly is fleece. It's interesting to note that this one-of-a-kind fabric is made out of recycled plastic. Purchasing a zip-up jacket made of this material is highly recommended.

The last line of layering defense is the "shell" layer. You'll need some type of waterproof, windproof, breathable jacket that will fit over all of your other layers. It should have a large hood that fits over a hat. You'll also need a good pair of rain pants made from a similar waterproof, breathable fabric. Some Gore-Tex jackets cost as much as $500, but you should know that there are more affordable fabrics out there that work just as well.

Now that you've learned the basics of layering, you can't forget to protect your hands and face. In cold, windy, or rainy weather you'll need a hat made of wool or fleece and insulated, waterproof gloves that will keep your hands warm and toasty. As mentioned earlier, buying an additional pair of light silk liners to wear under your regular gloves is a good idea.

Footwear. If you have any extra money to spend on your trip, put that money into boots or trail shoes. Poor shoes will bring a hike to a halt faster than anything else. To avoid this annoyance, buy shoes that provide support and are lightweight and flexible. A lightweight hiking boot is better than a heavy, leather mountaineering boot for most day hikes and backpacking. Trail running shoes provide a little extra cushion and are made in a high-top style that many people wear for hiking. These running shoes are lighter, more flexible, and more breathable than hiking boots. If you know you'll be hiking in wet weather often, purchase boots or shoes with a Gore-Tex liner, which will help keep your feet dry.

When buying your boots, be sure to wear the same type of socks you'll be wearing on the trail. If the boots you're buying are for cold weather hiking, try the boots on while wearing two pairs of socks. Speaking of socks, a good cold weather sock combination is to wear a thinner sock made of wool or polypropylene covered by a heavier outer sock made of wool. The inner sock protects the foot from the rubbing effects of the outer sock and prevents blisters. Many outdoor stores have some type of ramp to simulate hiking uphill and downhill. Be sure to take advantage of this test, as toe-jamming boot fronts can be very painful and debilitating on the downhill trek.

Once you've purchased your footwear, be sure to break them in before you hit the trail. New footwear is often stiff and needs to be stretched and molded to your foot.

Hiking poles. Hiking poles help with balance, and more importantly take pressure off your knees. The ones with shock absorbers are easier on your elbows and knees. Some poles even come with a camera attachment to be used as a monopod. And heaven forbid you meet a mountain lion, bear, or unfriendly dog, the poles can make you look a lot bigger.

Backpacks. No matter what type of hiking you do you'll need a pack of some sort to carry the basic trail essentials. There are a variety of backpacks on the market, but let's first discuss what you intend to use it for. Day hikes or overnight trips?

If you plan on doing a day hike, a daypack should have some of the following characteristics: a padded hip belt that's at least 2 inches in diameter (avoid packs with only a small nylon piece of webbing for a hip belt); a chest strap (the chest strap helps stabilize the pack against your body); external pockets to carry water and other items that you want easy access to; an internal pocket to hold keys, a knife, a wallet, and other miscellaneous items; an external lashing system to hold a jacket; and a hydration pocket for carrying a hydration system (which consists of a water bladder with an attachable drinking hose).

For short hikes, some hikers like to use a fanny pack to store just a camera, food, a compass, a map, and other trail essentials. Most fanny packs have pockets for two water bottles and a padded hip belt.

If you intend to do an extended, overnight trip, there are multiple considerations. First off, you need to decide what kind of framed pack you want. There are two backpack types for backpacking: the internal frame and the external frame. An internal frame pack rests closer to your body, making it more stable and easier to balance when hiking over rough terrain. An external frame pack is just that, an aluminum frame attached to the exterior of the pack. An external frame pack is better for long backpack trips because it distributes the pack weight better and you can carry heavier loads. It's easier to pack, and your gear is more accessible. It also offers better back ventilation in hot weather.

The most critical measurement for fitting a pack is torso length. The pack needs to rest evenly on your hips without sagging. A good pack will come in two or three sizes and have straps and hip belts that are adjustable according to your body size and characteristics.

When you purchase a backpack, go to an outdoor store with salespeople who are knowledgeable in how to properly fit a pack. Once the pack is fitted for you, load the pack with the amount of weight you plan on taking on the trail. The weight of the pack should be distributed evenly and you should be able to swing your arms and walk briskly without feeling out of balance. Another good technique for evaluating a pack is to walk up and down stairs and make quick turns to the right and to the left to be sure the pack doesn't feel out of balance. Other features that are nice to have on a backpack include a removable day pack or fanny pack, external pockets for extra water, and extra lash points to attach a jacket or other items.

Sleeping bags and pads. Sleeping bags are rated by temperature. You can purchase a bag made of synthetic fiber, or you can buy a goose down bag. Goose down bags are more expensive, but they have a higher insulating capacity by weight and will keep their loft longer. You'll want to purchase a bag with a temperature rating that fits the time of year and conditions you are most likely to camp in. One caveat: The techno-standard for temperature ratings is far from perfect. Ratings vary from manufacturer to manufacturer, so to protect yourself you should purchase a bag rated 10 to 15 degrees below the temperature you expect to be camping in. Synthetic bags are more resistant to water than down bags, but many down bags are now made with a Gore-Tex shell that helps to repel water. Down bags are also more compressible than synthetic bags and take up less room in your pack, which is an important consideration if you are planning a multiday backpack trip. Features to look for in a sleeping bag include a mummy style bag, a hood you can cinch down around your head in cold weather, and draft tubes along the zippers that help keep heat in and drafts out.

You'll also want a sleeping pad to provide insulation and padding from the cold ground. There are different types of sleeping pads available, from the more expensive self-inflating air mattresses to the less expensive closed-cell foam pads. Self-inflating air mattresses are usually heavier than closed-cell foam mattresses and are prone to punctures.

Tents. The tent is your home away from home while on the trail. It provides protection from wind, snow, rain, and insects. A three-season tent is a good choice for backpacking and can range in price from $100 to $500. These lightweight and versatile tents provide protection in all types of weather, except heavy snowstorms or high winds, and range in weight from four to eight pounds. Look for a tent that's easy to set up and will easily fit two people with gear. Dome type tents usually offer more headroom and places to store gear. Other tent designs include a vestibule where you can store wet boots and backpacks. Some nice-to-have items in a tent include interior pockets to store small items and lashing points to hang a clothesline. Most three-season tents also come with stakes so you can secure the tent in high winds. Before you purchase a tent, set it up and take it down a few times to be sure it is easy to handle. Also, sit inside the tent and make sure it has enough room for you and your gear.

Cell phones. Many hikers are carrying their cell phones into the backcountry these days in case of emergency. That's fine and good, but please know that cell phone coverage is often poor to nonexistent in valleys, canyons, and thick forest. More importantly people have started to call for help because they're tired or lost. Let's go back to being prepared. You are responsible for yourself in the backcountry. Use your brain to avoid problems, and if you do encounter one, first use your brain to try to correct the situation. Only use your cell phone, if it works, in true emergencies.

Hiking with Children

Hiking with children isn't a matter of how many miles you can cover or how much elevation gain you make in a day; it's about seeing and experiencing nature through their eyes.

Kids like to explore and have fun. They like to stop and point out bugs and plants, look under rocks, jump in puddles, and throw sticks. If you're taking a toddler or young child on a hike, start with a trail that you're familiar with. Trails that have interesting things for kids, like piles of leaves to play in or a small stream to wade through during the summer, will make the hike much more enjoyable for them and will keep them from getting bored.

You can keep your child's attention if you have a strategy before starting on the trail. Using games is not only an effective way to keep a child's attention, it's also a great way to teach him or her about nature. Play hide and seek, where your child is the mouse and you are the hawk. Quiz children on the names of plants and animals. If your children are old enough, let them carry their own daypack filled with snacks and water. So that you are sure to go at their pace and not yours, let them lead the way. Playing follow the leader works particularly well when you have a group of children. Have each child take a turn at being the leader.

With children, a lot of clothing is key. The only thing predictable about weather is that it will change. Especially in mountainous areas, weather can change dramatically in a very short time. Always bring extra clothing for children, regardless of the season. In the winter, have your children wear wool socks, and warm layers such as long underwear, a fleece jacket and hat, wool mittens, and good rain gear. It's not a bad idea to have these along in late fall and early spring as well. Good footwear is also important. A sturdy pair of high top tennis shoes or lightweight hiking boots are the best bet for little ones. If you're hiking in the summer near a lake or stream, bring along a pair of old sneakers that your child can put on when he wants to go exploring in the water. Remember when you're near any type of water, always watch your child at all times. Also, keep a close eye on teething toddlers who may decide a rock or leaf of poison oak is an interesting item to put in their mouth.

From spring through fall, you'll want your kids to wear a wide-brimmed hat to keep their face, head, and ears protected from the hot sun. Also, make sure your children wear sunscreen at all times. Choose a brand without Paba—children have sensitive skin and may have an allergic reaction to sunscreen that contains Paba. If you are hiking with a child younger than six months, don't use sunscreen or insect repellent. Instead, be sure that their head, face, neck, and ears are protected from the sun with a wide-brimmed hat, and that all other skin exposed to the sun is protected with the appropriate clothing.

Remember that food is fun. Kids like snacks so it's important to bring a lot of munchies for the trail. Stopping often for snack breaks is a fun way to keep the trail interesting. Raisins, apples, granola bars, crackers and cheese, cereal, and trail mix all make great snacks. If your child is old enough to carry her own backpack, fill it with treats before you leave. If your kids don't like drinking water, you can bring boxes of fruit juice.

Avoid poorly designed child-carrying packs—you don't want to break your back carrying your child. Most child-carrying backpacks designed to hold a forty-pound child will contain a large carrying pocket to hold diapers and other items. Some have an optional rain/sun hood.

Hiking with Your Dog

Bringing your furry friend with you is always more fun than leaving him behind. Our canine pals make great trail buddies because they never complain and always make good company. Hiking with your dog can be a rewarding experience, especially if you plan ahead.

Getting your dog in shape. Before you plan outdoor adventures with your dog, make sure he's in shape for the trail. Getting your dog into shape takes the same discipline as getting yourself into shape, but luckily, your dog can get in shape with you. Take your dog with you on your daily runs or walks. If there is a park near your house, hit a tennis ball or play Frisbee with your dog.

Swimming is also an excellent way to get your dog into shape. If there is a lake or river near where you live and your dog likes the water, have him retrieve a tennis ball or stick. Gradually build your dog's stamina up over a two- to three-month period. A good rule of thumb is to assume that your dog will travel twice as far as you will on the trail. If you plan on doing a 5-mile hike, be sure your dog is in shape for a 10-mile hike.

Training your dog for the trail. Before you go on your first hiking adventure with your dog, be sure he has a firm grasp on the basics of canine etiquette and behavior. Make sure he can sit, lie down, stay, and come. One of the most important commands you can teach your canine pal is to "come" under any situation. It's easy for your friend's nose to lead him astray or possibly get lost. Another helpful command is the "get behind" command. When you're on a hiking trail that's narrow, you can have your dog follow behind you when other trail users approach. Nothing is more bothersome than an enthusiastic dog that runs back and forth on the trail and disrupts the peace of the trail for others. When you see other trail users approaching you on the trail, give them the right of way by quietly stepping off the trail and making your dog lie down and stay until they pass.

Equipment. The most critical pieces of equipment you can invest in for your dog are proper identification and a sturdy leash. Flexi-leads work well for hiking because they give your dog more freedom to explore but still leave you in control. Make sure your dog has identification that includes your name and address and a number for your veterinarian. Other forms of identification for your dog include a tattoo or a microchip. You should consult your veterinarian for more information on these last two options.

The next piece of equipment you'll want to consider is a pack for your dog. By no means should you hold all of your dog's essentials in your pack—let him carry his own gear! Dogs that are in good shape can carry 30 to 40 percent of their own weight.

Most packs are fitted by a dog's weight and girth measurement. Companies that make dog packs generally include guidelines to help you pick out the size that's right for your dog. Some characteristics to look for when purchasing a pack for your dog include a harness that contains two padded girth straps, a padded chest strap, leash attachments, removable saddle bags, internal water bladders, and external gear cords.

You can introduce your dog to the pack by first placing the empty pack on his back and letting him wear it around the yard. Keep an eye on him during this first introduction. He may decide to chew through the straps if you aren't watching him closely. Once he learns to treat the pack as an object of fun and not a foreign enemy, fill the pack evenly on both sides with a few ounces of dog food in resealable plastic bags. Have your dog wear his pack on your daily walks for a period of two to three weeks. Each week add a little more weight to the pack until your dog will accept carrying the maximum amount of weight he can carry.

You can also purchase collapsible water and dog food bowls for your dog. These bowls are lightweight and can easily be stashed into your pack or your dog's. If you are hiking on rocky terrain or in the snow, you can purchase footwear for your dog that will protect his feet from cuts and bruises.

Always carry plastic bags to remove feces from the trail. It is a courtesy to other trail users and helps protect local wildlife.

The following is a list of items to bring when you take your dog hiking: collapsible water bowls, a comb, a collar and a leash, dog food, plastic bags for feces, a dog pack, flea/tick powder, paw protection, water, and a first-aid kit that contains eye ointment, tweezers, scissors, stretchy foot wrap, gauze, antibacterial wash, sterile cotton tip applicators, antibiotic ointment, and cotton wrap.

First aid for your dog. Your dog is just as prone—if not more prone—to getting in trouble on the trail as you are, so be prepared. Here's a rundown of the more likely misfortunes that might befall your little friend.

Bees and wasps. If a bee or wasp stings your dog, remove the stinger with a pair of tweezers and place a mudpack or a cloth dipped in cold water over the affected area.

Porcupines. One good reason to keep your dog on a leash is to prevent it from getting a nose full of porcupine quills. You may be able to remove the quills with pliers, but a veterinarian is the best person to do this nasty job because most dogs need to be sedated.

Heat stroke. Avoid hiking with your dog in really hot weather. Dogs with heat stroke will pant excessively, lie down and refuse to get up, and become lethargic and disoriented. If your dog shows any of these signs on the trail, have him lie down in the shade. If you are near a stream, pour cool water over your dog's entire body to help bring his body temperature back to normal.

Heartworm. Dogs get heartworms from mosquitoes which carry the disease in the prime mosquito months of July and August. Giving your dog a monthly pill prescribed by your veterinarian easily prevents this condition.

Plant pitfalls. One of the biggest plant hazards for dogs on the trail are foxtails. Foxtails are pointed grass seed heads that bury themselves in your friend's fur, between his toes, and even get in his ear canal. If left unattended, these nasty seeds can work their way under the skin and cause abscesses and other problems. If you have a long-haired dog, consider trimming the hair between his toes and giving him a summer haircut to help prevent foxtails from attaching to his fur. After every hike, always look over your dog for these seeds—especially between his toes and his ears.

Other plant hazards include burrs, thorns, thistles, and poison oak. If you find any burrs or thistles on your dog, remove them as soon as possible before they become an unmanageable mat. Thorns can pierce a dog's foot and cause a great deal of pain. If you see that your dog is lame, stop and check his feet for thorns. Dogs are immune to poison oak but they can pick up the sticky, oily substance from the plant and transfer it to you.

Protect those paws. Be sure to keep your dog's nails trimmed so he avoids getting soft tissue or joint injuries. If your dog slows and refuses to go on, check to see that his paws aren't torn or worn. You can protect your dog's paws from trail hazards such as sharp gravel, foxtails, lava scree, and thorns by purchasing dog boots.

Sunburn. If your dog has light skin he is an easy target for sunburn on his nose and other exposed skin areas. You can apply a nontoxic sunscreen to exposed skin areas that will help protect him from overexposure to the sun.

Ticks and fleas. Ticks can easily give your dog Lyme disease, as well as other diseases. Before you hit the trail, treat your dog with a flea and tick spray or powder. You can also ask your veterinarian about a once-a-month pour-on treatment that repels fleas and ticks.

Mosquitoes and deer flies. These little flying machines can do a job on your dog's snout and ears. Best bet is to spray your dog with fly repellent for horses to discourage both pests.

Giardia. Dogs can get giardia, which results in diarrhea. It is usually not debilitating, but it's definitely messy. A vaccine against giardia is available.

Mushrooms. Make sure your dog doesn't sample mushrooms along the trail. They could be poisonous to him, but he doesn't know that.

When you are finally ready to hit the trail with your dog, keep in mind that national parks and many wilderness areas do not allow dogs on trails. Your best bet is to hike in national forests, BLM lands, and state parks. Always call ahead to see what the restrictions are.

About the Author

Ron Adkison, a dedicated naturalist and explorer of wild country, began his outdoor explorations in southern California at the age of six. After more than thirty-five years of hiking, scrambling, snowshoeing, and cross-country skiing, he has logged more than 10,000 trail miles in ten western states (California, Oregon, Washington, Idaho, Montana, Wyoming, Nevada, Colorado, Arizona, and Utah). He has walked every trail in this guide multiple times. Ron shares his enthusiasm for wild places in *Hiking Southern California*.

Other guidebooks by Ron Adkison:
—*Hiking Northern California*
—*Hiking Washington*
—*Exploring Beyond Yellowstone*
—*Hiking Wyoming's Wind River Range*
—*Hiking Grand Canyon National Park*
—*Best Easy Day Hikes Grand Canyon*
—*Hiking Grand Staircase–Escalante and the Glen Canyon Region*
—*Best Easy Day Hikes Grand Staircase–Escalante and the Glen Canyon Region*
—*Best Easy Day Hikes Northern Sierra*
—*Wild Northern California*
—*Best Easy Day Hikes Southern Sierra*